LONDON BUS HANDBOOK

David Stewart
& Colin Lloyd

Capital Transport

Twenty-first edition 2000

ISBN 185414 227 5

Published by Capital Transport Publishing
38 Long Elmes, Harrow Weald, Middlesex

Printed by CS Graphics, Singapore

Front cover In the period since the last Handbook, a very large quantity of low floor double deckers has entered service with many of the large, and some not so large, bus operators in London. Those bearing the Alexander ALX400 bodywork have become the most prolific, with Arriva, Metroline and Stagecoach taking substantial numbers, and with London Central, London United and Connex Bus following suit early in 2000. Metroline has Dennis Tridents with both Alexander and Plaxton bodywork, and the first examples of the former breed commenced work in summer 1999 on route 16 from Cricklewood garage. TA 74 pauses at the southern end of the Edgware Road in August 1999. *Mark Lyons*

Back cover One of the main events within the industry in London during 1999 was the passing of Metrobus Ltd, the largest 'independent' in London, into the Go Ahead Group on 3rd September. Had it passed into one of the other large groups, no doubt within days a change to the image would have occurred, but thus far there has been no outward indication of group ownership. No.855, one of the East Lancs Pyoneer bodied Volvo Olympians bought for route 119, traverses High Street, Croydon. *Mark Lyons*

The photographs overleaf are by Colin Stannard and Geoff Rixon

Contents

INTRODUCTION 4
AIRLINKS 10
ARMCHAIR 11
ARRIVA 13
BLUE TRIANGLE 26
CONNEX BUS 27
CRYSTALS 28
EPSOM BUSES 29
FIRST CAPITAL 30
FIRST CENTREWEST 38
FIRST LONDON BUSLINES 45
HARRIS BUS 46
HACKNEY COMMUNITY TRANSPORT 48
LIMEBOURNE 49
LONDON CENTRAL 50
LONDON GENERAL 55
LONDON TRAVELLER 60
LONDON UNITED 61
METROBUS 68
METROLINE 70
MITCHAM BELLE 79
NOSTALGIABUS 80
SOVEREIGN 81
STAGECOACH 84
TELLINGS-GOLDEN MILLER 90
THORPE'S 94
TRAVEL LONDON 95
WING'S 96
TYPE TOTALS 97
FLEET LISTS 98

Two limited-stop routes (M1 and M2) were introduced by London Central on 1st January 2000 to carry visitors to the Millennium Dome who arrive by train at Charlton and Greenwich Stations. Three of the batch of seventeen DAF SB220s with East Lancs bodies – christened the Myllennium – are LPG-powered and MD 10 at North Greenwich shows off its roof-mounted gas tanks. They are high-specification vehicles with double-glazing and air-conditioning, but what will happen to them after the 'Year of The Dome' has elapsed? *Colin Stannard*

INTRODUCTION

This book gives details at February 2000 of buses that operate London Transport Buses (LTB) contract services. We acknowledge the assistance given by some of the operating companies. The fleet information is extracted principally from the records of the London Omnibus Traction Society (LOTS) and readers needing regular updated information are recommended to membership of LOTS or the PSV Circle.

Since the 1999 edition of this book, changes in the industry have seen Metrobus Ltd, formerly the largest independent in the London area, passing into the Go Ahead Group in September, although there has been no obvious outward alteration and the familiar blue and yellow buses in south-east London continued as before under their own management. In the west, Capital Logistics began 1999 still in trouble on route 60, with assorted hired buses plying the route. Although their new DAF low floor double deckers duly arrived from March – six months after they were needed – projected losses on the service were a factor in the sell-off of the whole company to Tellings-Golden Miller on 1st June 1999. Soon afterwards, it became known that a new national grouping of small companies was evolving. Called the Status Bus & Coach Group, both Capital Logistics and T-GM were two of the founder companies. They remained separate operationally until 8th January 2000, when all the bus services were consolidated under the T-GM banner.

Most of the services depicted in this book and run by the vehicles listed herein are run under London Transport auspices. LT's publicity, whether maps or timetables, is well-known and instantly recognised as of generally good quality and to a high standard. There are several travel offices around London, with many opened in recent years at new bus stations, but to supplement these the Travel Information Service has RCL 2221 converted as a mobile office-cum-shop. It visits many sites throughout London, as well as special events, promoting the system. *Colin Brown*

The big groups continued to consolidate, and the distinctions between constituent operating companies were increasingly blurred. At Arriva, after the Edmonton depot of the former County Bus was placed under Arriva London North in October 1998, the Beddington depot of Arriva Surrey & West Sussex came under Arriva London South from 30th October 1999. Most of the buses at the latter depot were still in London & Country colour schemes and a repaint programme into red commenced within days of the takeover. Conversely, at Edmonton there were still one or two buses in 'County Bus' dark green and cream at the start of 2000. Arriva London North East, the former Grey-Green, continued to have its buses repainted to red through 1999, so much so that only ten Darts remained in grey and green at the start of 2000. Stamford Hill garage was due to have closed by the time this book is published, following the extension and refurbishment of the nearby Tottenham garage of A-LN, and then the A-LNE fleet was to be formally absorbed into Arriva London North's stock. The 'country' Arriva companies still operate some outer London LTB routes, and enter Greater London on commercial services, but "Arriva serving London" has really become the dominant force on the group's LTB services, with the largest proportion (about 21%) of the London bus market of any one company.

Arriva's corporate livery has advanced rapidly since the last edition of this book, with the London operations retaining red, with the rather curious so-called 'cow-horns' swish of corporate cream (officially 'stone'). It was adopted because the intended full-front cream area fell foul of LT Buses' 80%-red edict. This rule applies to buses operating within the Central London Zone 1, but Arriva, after painting some buses with full cream fronts and some with cow-horns, depending on where they were meant to be used, settled on cow-horns for all the fleet. The Routemaster fleet however, has so far not been so adapted although they do bear cream relief. Nevertheless, buses painted with full cream fronts stayed in that condition without change into 2000. The 'country' Arriva companies did not have such a problem, and the national livery of turquoise (officially 'aquamarine') and full cream front was almost universally adopted. This gives the strange anomaly of turquoise buses operating as close to central London as Greenwich because they are owned by Arriva Kent Thameside, but others can be in red and cow horns when running from Croydon to Caterham. Also anomalous is the application of red and full cream front livery to 'country' buses allocated to routes 310 and 402, which only enter London (at Enfield and Bromley respectively) at the outer edges. Indeed, what was meant to have been a national corporate image, actually has several different variations!

LT Buses' 80%-red rule now reigns supreme in Zone 1, with all operators using a red-based livery, albeit mostly with another relief colour, and with Sovereign's RMLs still in their orange-red scheme. The last non-red buses were those still in Grey-Green colours in summer 1999, and nowadays just about the only incursion would be with the rare occasional visit of one of First Capital's yellow buses to one of their Central London routes. One now has to go to the suburbs to see the yellow of First Capital and London Buslines, the orange of Armchair, and the variations of blue of Crystals, Metrobus, Sovereign, Tellings-Golden Miller and of course the 'country' Arriva operations. FirstGroup did introduce a national corporate livery, but none in that condition operate in London. The only application of group identity is the *f* symbol on the vehicles of the four First companies, and of some yellow and off-white wavy-line stripes on the red sides of a few (but by no means all) new buses delivered since the summer of 1999.

LT Buses has always maintained that it wants more competition in the tendered route arena, and indeed five operators new to LT tendering did take up routes during 1999. These were Blue Triangle (route 474), Hackney Community Transport (mobility routes in north-east London), London Traveller (187,487), Mitcham Belle (127) and Wing's Buses (U7). Strictly speaking, London Traveller was not totally new as they had already been running some school buses, but these were their first all-day services. Even so, only about three dozen buses were needed for all these new operations. A more high profile operation came in February 2000 with the entry of Connex Bus, part of the same French-owned group running trains in the South East. Routes 3 and N3 were taken over from London Central, and route 322 from Arriva was due to follow a couple of months later. Another French-owned operator London United, quietly and gradually dropped the separate Westlink name on its vehicles. After its unsteady entry into 1999, Limebourne remained independent throughout the year, though Travel London was facing an uncertain future because of problems over its operating base. By November 1999 it was made known that both Armchair and Harris Bus were available for sale, and the first to fall was Harris Bus when it was put into receivership on 15th December. Capital's route 60 has already been mentioned as a loss-maker, and some other LTB contract agreements seemed to be verging on the marginal in financial terms.

Staff shortages became endemic as 1999 wore on, and the situation shows little sign of improvement. Limebourne helped out Arriva with its staff shortage from August 1999, when it took on route G1, together with some of Arriva's Darts. LT Buses has continued to increase frequencies and extend periods of operation with great gusto and, while this is undoubtedly good for passengers in theory, more and more cases of service cuts due to staff shortages have been evident Arriva Surrey & West Sussex (the trading name for the former London & Country group of companies) seemed to suffer more than some, and was also affected by revenue shortfalls. In four stages during 1999, one operating base (Leatherhead) was closed, another two were transferred to other operators, and all of the company's LTB services passed elsewhere, with Tellings-Golden Miller, London United and Arriva London South being the beneficiaries. Low profitability at Surrey & West Sussex also saw Arriva embarking on a programme of fleet replacement. Instead of new buses, over forty redundant Arriva London Metrobuses were refurbished to replace almost all other double deckers, thus increasing its age profile considerably.

A rare excuse to depict a picture of a Leyland National comes with the somewhat extravagant provision of several of them, together with Lynxes from Blue Triangle, to give an emergency coverage for whenever the Jubilee Line breaks down. Thorpe's have the contract for the service from the Millennium Dome to Canning Town, using former London United 'urban bus' National conversions, like LS 96 largely unaltered since its busier days at Hounslow. *Geoff Rixon*

However in Greater London itself, new buses flooded into stock, with 1999 seeing the highest intake for several years. Around 1300 buses have entered the London fleets since the last edition of this book, with 27 of the operating companies taking various numbers. Around 600 were double deckers, all of which were low floor except the twenty 'dealer stock' standard-floor Olympians bought by First CentreWest for route 83 in spring 1999. The latter must surely be the last such new vehicles to enter service in London. The Dennis Trident and DAF DB250LF were initially supreme, with the first long-awaited Volvo B7L finally arriving in London with London Central in December 1999. This type was set to become more prolific as production finally got under way. On the single deck front, the intake was dominated almost entirely by various lengths and body styles of the Dennis Dart SLF. A minor indent was made by the new Volvo B6BLE when, in the autumn of 1999, London Traveller took fifteen and Arriva the Shires three, for routes 187/487 and H18 respectively. Otherwise, just a mere handful of minibuses arrived, some for mobility bus work. The DAF SB220 has been around for some years, but the latest low floor model has been used as the basis for East Lancs' futuristic design, the Myllennium. London Central took seventeen of these to a high internal specification, for use on special services to the Millennium Dome at North Greenwich from New Year's Day 2000. Although in use outside London, a new type to London bus services, in both chassis and body terms, is the Volvo B10BLE with Alexander ALX300 bodywork, due for Tellings-Golden Miller's route 726 from March 2000.

Most of the new low floor double deck buses in London have used blue – in various shades – for much of their interior decor,usually coupled with yellow handrails. Arriva started it off, and Metroline, London Central and Connex are recent additions, although Stagecoach favour shades of red, even extending to flooring and handrails. In these views of a Metroline TA (above) and Arriva DLA (below) note the high backed seats at the rear, which restrict visibility and daylight, and also the big steps up to the rear seats, rendering the low floor concept somewhat meaningless to many passengers.
Capital Transport

With around 2000 low floor buses now in service in Greater London, the needs of passengers are being ever more embraced by London Transport and the operators. The three low floor double deck body designs, the Alexander ALX400, Plaxton President and East Lancs Lolyne were all represented. Since their introduction, many modifications have been made. Initially, LT had specified that such vehicles should have separate entrance and exit, with the staircase opposite the exit door – itself positioned further back on the body than hitherto. The low floor configuration precluded seats over the forward wheel arches, wasting space and resulting in much criticism over the relatively small number of seats in the low floor area. The early production examples had no rear lower deck window, but with the fairly cramped area at the rear, especially with some seats perched atop the rear wheel arches, this led to more complaints. Gradually, these concerns are being addressed – at least most such buses now have rear windows. Stagecoach's Tridents have had forward mounted staircases from the start, and now Arriva has followed suit, the wheelchair position having been generally moved to a point opposite the centre door. In turn, the wheelchair ramp is now usually fitted to the centre door and, although being slightly more difficult to access from the kerb, at least avoids the damage that was being incurred to ramps fitted to the forward doors. Nevertheless, deliveries of buses in the first part of 2000 and which were ordered many months earlier continue to have central staircases and reduced lower deck seating capacity.

A consequence of the enormous intake of new buses during 1999 was the disposal of older vehicles and, since our 1999 book, it is the Metrobus that has borne the brunt of fleet disposals. Many went for scrap or re-sale, although Arriva London 'cascaded' many of theirs to Surrey & West Sussex, East Herts & Essex and to several other provincial Arriva companies. CentreWest was able to pass some of its Metrobuses to fellow group member First Capital, initially to assist their take-up of routes W8, 1 and 25 until Tridents could be delivered. Some of them were then used again, to replace other time-expired Metrobuses from the Capital fleet. After a few years of Titan disposals, Stagecoach has sold their ex-London Buses L-class Olympians, leaving Arriva London South as the sole operator of this breed. Moreover, a plan was announced in 1999 to refurbish the latter buses for continued use on routes such as the 2 and 249. Lots of older – and not so old – Darts have been sold off, as newer and generally larger and more accessible versions have arrived with many companies. Midibuses are very much in the minority in London, though the newer types such as the Optare Solo, Mercedes-Benz Vario and the small 8.8-metre Dart SLF can be found in small numbers. Isolated examples of older types such as the MetroRider and StarRider still survive, often because of some physical route restriction. One type that has totally gone is one of the newest – the ill-fated and unloved Marshall Minibus. During 1999, both London General and CentreWest exchanged them for new Marshall bodied Dart SLFs.

Not everything in London's bus world can possibly be contained in this one volume, and we have only covered buses and companies engaged on local bus work in Greater London, almost all of it under various types of contract to London Transport Buses. Several of the companies herein, notably Blue Triangle, First Capital, Metroline and Nostalgiabus, engage part of their fleet on contract, school routes or rail replacement work, and this is supplemented by large numbers of buses from private operators from within and outside London as is required. Millennium Year 2000 has already seen a new bus type on services to the Dome, improvements to existing types continue to be made, another new operator (Connex Bus) has entered into the scene, and more and more new buses are ordered to service LT Buses contracts. Rail-based developments, the Jubilee Line and DLR Extensions have seen much change to bus services in east and south-east London. The Croydon Tramlink – after several delays – was due to open in spring 2000, and yet more new buses came into stock for dedicated feeder services This book represents the fleet situation at early February 2000, together with details of buses known to be on order.

February 2000 David Stewart and Colin Lloyd

The former Speedlink company, re-named to AirLinks during 1999, provides many services surrounding London's airports, but is also responsible for just one LTB contract route, the H30. This is free, as it operates totally within the Heathrow free-fare zone, and is mainly financed by the BAA. Dart SLF T74WWV departs from Hatton Cross, via the long way round to the Central area, oddly without 'Free' signing on the front. *Colin Brown*

AIRLINKS (formerly Speedlink)

AirLinks the Airport Coach Company Ltd, 682 Armadale Road, Feltham, Middx, TW14 0LW

A large operator of coach and contract services at all the London airports, together with inter-airport services, mostly branded as Speedlink, Jetlink, Airlink and Cambridge Coach Services. There is just a brief mention here of the operation of six buses on an LT and British Airways joint contract route H30 at Heathrow Airport. The company is within the National Express Group, and the six dedicated buses for the H30 are operated from the Armadale Road, North Feltham coach base.

London United's Airbus services between Heathrow Airport and central London were upgraded in 1995/96 with Alexander Royale bodied Olympians with coach seating. In 1999, a fares promotion meant that accompanied children could travel free, but the service gradually declined and the A1 variation to Victoria has been withdrawn. From 5th February 2000 the Airbus services were sold on to the National Express group and included with AirLinks. N128YRW is one of the Olympians transferred to the new owners. *Colin Brown*

Armchair's double deck fleet is composed entirely of Olympians, in three batches with three different bodywork styles, and used on routes 65 and 237. The G-registered Alexander-bodied examples are the oldest, originally bought for when the company ran route 260. G365YUR sets down at Cromwell Road, near to the final Kingston terminus of route 65 in September 1999. *Stephen Madden*

ARMCHAIR

Armchair Passenger Transport Co. Ltd, Commerce Way, Brentford, TW8 8LZ

After adventures in Surrey and Berkshire, Armchair has been quite successful with LT tendering, although their first route, the 260, has since been lost. The bus fleet is now concentrated on LT work, routes operated being all fairly local to their base; indeed two of them (E2 and E8) actually terminate there. The three batches of Olympians are mixed on routes 65 and 237, standard Darts on the 117 and 190, Plaxton Dart SLFs on routes E2 and E8 and the Alexander Dart SLFs on route 209. The SLFs carry a revised livery with a white roof and black window surrounds and skirts. LT routes operated are 65, 117, 190, 209, 237, E2, E8 and school journeys on 371 and 609. The fleet carries orange and white livery, and is housed at Commerce Way, Brentford. There is also a large coach fleet.

Seven Northern Counties Palatine II bodied Olympians were added to the fleet over the winter of 1997/98, and have been useful to upgrade the services, mainly on route 65. Richmond town centre in May 1999 sees R781SOY. *Gerald Mead*

In May 1997, the 'Ealing E-route network' that initially had been developed by CentreWest was tendered by LTB. Two main services, the E2 and E8, were won by Armchair, and a batch of twenty-five Dart SLFs was purchased for them. The routes were extended in Brentford to terminate at the handy and nearby company depot. P678RWU traverses Haven Green at Ealing Broadway in June 1999. *David Stewart*

A further tender success came in 1999 when Armchair won route 209, which was specified for larger (and heavier) buses. Unfortunately the weight restricted Hammersmith Bridge was on the 209 and the buses had to be re-deployed for five months by means of a route switch with London United for that period. At the end of October, this batch of Alexander ALX200 Dart SLFs finally came to route 209, and T152AUA passes down Castelnau in Barnes on 31st October 1999. *Colin Stannard*

ARRIVA

Arriva London North Ltd, 16 Watsons Road, Wood Green, London, N22 7TZ
Arriva London North East Ltd, 16 Watsons Road, Wood Green, London, N22 7TZ
Arriva London South Ltd, Bus Garage, Brighton Road, Croydon, CR2 6EL
Arriva the Shires Ltd, Castle Street, Luton, Bedfordshire, LU1 3AJ
Arriva East Herts & Essex Ltd, Fourth Avenue, Harlow, Essex, CM20 1DU
Arriva Southern Counties (Kent Thameside and Kent & Sussex), Invicta House, Armstrong Road, Maidstone, Kent, ME15 6TY
Arriva Surrey & West Sussex, PO Box 473, Crawley, West Sussex, RH10 2FH

This large group has eight of its subsidiaries running local bus routes within Greater London, and as far as London is concerned, is organised into three groups of operating companies for management purposes. *Arriva serving London* is controlled from Wood Green, and comprises London North (formerly Leaside), Leaside Travel, London North-East (formerly Grey-Green) and London South (formerly South London Transport). Apart from Leaside Travel, it is fast progressing toward a London red livery with cream relief, although a handful of buses in former County Bus, Grey-Green and London & Country liveries were still holding on early in 2000. Garages are at Battersea, Barking, Beddington Farm, Brixton, Clapton, Croydon, Edmonton, Enfield, Norwood, Palmers Green, Thornton Heath, Tottenham and Wood Green. The Beddington Farm garage was assumed from its 'country cousins' from 30th October 1999 and the Arriva blue and cream or London & Country style liveries on its vehicles are being altered to standard Arriva London red condition.

In late February 2000, it was made known that route 60, together with its sixteen DAF double deckers were to be transferred from Tellings-Golden Miller and Capital Logistics ownership to Arriva London South from March, to be based at their Beddington Farm garage.

Vehicles of the 'country' operations are now mostly repainted to the national version of Arriva livery of turquoise and cream (officially called aquamarine and light stone), with appropriate fleetnames (officially known as strap-lines). *Arriva serving the Shires* is controlled from Luton and includes the buses of the Shires based at Watford and High Wycombe garages in this book, running into Greater London on routes 142, 340, 350, H18 and U9. Luton also controls the former County Bus fleets (some still with Townlink, Lea Valley and Thameside names) now trading as *Arriva serving East Herts and Essex,* operating from bases at Debden, Grays, Harlow and Ware. Only the buses in this fleet normally used on routes 256, 310, 311, 327, 346, 363, 370, 373, 517, W13, W14, which are those operated under various LTB contracts, are listed in this book.

Arriva Southern Counties at Maidstone controls the fleets of Kent Thameside and Kent & Sussex, and the former London & Country fleet which is divided into three operating companies, Arriva Croydon & North Surrey, Guildford & West Surrey, West Sussex. LT Buses contracts run by the Kent fleets are routes 126, 286, 402, 428, B11, B13, R5, R8 and school buses on 132 and 601. Three Leyland Nationals are used on Mobility Bus services in south London, but were to be withdrawn in April 2000. Garages of the group running buses into London are Dartford, Northfleet and Tunbridge Wells. The three former London & Country companies all trade as *Arriva serving Surrey & West Sussex,* and operate into London from garages at Crawley, Guildford, Merstham and Woking. Recent cut-backs and transfers of operations mean that the company's buses now only operate into Greater London on longer routes (e.g. 405, 406, 409, 415, 420, 479) to places such as Croydon, Sutton and Kingston. The whole operation is now outside the formal LT contract system, hence the non-appearance of their fleet in this publication.

Left Arriva London North operate two frequent Routemaster services (38 and 73). However, frequency increases and the finite number of RMLs have caused some standard RMs to be restored to service to maintain full coverage, and these are all to be seen on the 38. The striking but somewhat garish branding applied to these buses can be seen on RM 1725 at Victoria in July 1999. *Stephen Madden*

Below Unlike Routemasters on route 38, those on the 73 have cream, orange and yellow relief to indicate their Arriva ownership. In common with some other routes in the area, buses on route 73 carry slogans to advertise Sadler's Wells Theatre in Rosebery Avenue, which is not actually on the 73 route! RML 2611 prepares to turn right at the Angel, Islington in June 1999. *Tony Wilson*

The DBS class of DAF DB250s with Palatine II bodywork came to Leaside Buses in 1995, specifically for route 263, and it is fairly rare for any to be found on any other service. DBS 3 is one which has had all reference to former Leaside and Cowie ownership removed, but still has the Cowie stripes. Even in early 2000, DBSs without Arriva identity were more numerous than those with. *Geoff Rixon*

Arriva was the first operator in London to introduce low floor double deckers, and adopted several new features specified by LT Buses. One such feature was a central straight staircase, which caused much wasted space in the forward low floor area. The large blank offside panelling is very evident in this view of DLA 90 at Wood Green, but this bus is an example of the second batch of deliveries, which at least did have some minor internal improvements. *Laurie Rufus*

The former Grey-Green operation, re-christened Arriva London North East, retained its separate identity, albeit with standard Arriva London red colours. However a small element of individuality survived with the use of 'Grey-Green' fleet numbers as a 'shadow system' to the official DLA coding. Here No.301 (DLA 101) serves Euston Station on route 188, and displays the much neater nearside arrangement of the class, as well as showing glimpses of the pale blue interior décor. *Laurie Rufus*

Arriva's DLA deliveries from October 1999, the batch numbered from DLA 126 onwards, have had their staircases positioned forward and, even though they are shorter than earlier examples, have an almost identical seating capacity. This batch has rear windows, and is also a little higher, giving better headroom, and the re-design has made a better product for both passenger and operator. So far, all of these later DLAs have gone to London South, and Norwood garage's DLA 133 pauses at the familiar Waterloo Bridge stop. *Geoff Rixon*

As pretty as the back of a bus! Well, perhaps. Passenger protests caused Arriva to have a re-think over the provision of rear lower deck windows on their new buses, although even now some operators have failed to realise that passengers do prefer, and indeed need them. At Enfield Garage, a handy chance saw DLA 116 and DLP 7 displaying their slightly different rear end treatment, but the larger window of the elderly Metrobus in between still puts them both to shame. *Colin Brown*

Still on a DAF DB250LF chassis, but one of twenty with Plaxton President bodywork, is DLP 6. They are all allocated to Enfield garage for route 279, and this example calls at Edmonton Green bus station on 11th September 1999, shortly after first entry into service of the class. Otherwise standard body designs do exhibit certain differences, so compare the window design with other Presidents illustrated in this Handbook. *Colin Brown*

Once all in Grey-Green colours, the high floor Volvo B10Ms with Alexander bodywork are mainly to be found on routes 24, 125 and 275. On Sundays the allocation on route 19, otherwise worked by London South's RMLs on weekdays, is run by these buses from London North East. No.146 serves Hyde Park Corner on its cross-London journey in April 1999. *Colin Brown*

The 1986/87 delivery of ECW-bodied Leyland Olympians was a substantial investment by the then London Buses. Latterly, most had lost their sparkle, and those that finished up with Stagecoach and London Central were all withdrawn and most were sold. Conversely, Arriva London South, who had the majority, has repainted most of them and indeed are to refurbish many during 2000 to comply with LTB tender conditions on routes 2 and 249. L 185 picks up passengers opposite the closed Streatham bus garage in March 1999. *Colin Brown*

Forty Alexander RH-bodied Leyland Olympians came to Leaside Buses in 1992 and, ever since, have been the mainstay of busy inner suburban route 253 which, even today, needs forty-eight buses on a weekday to run its full schedule. L 346, one of those treated to Arriva's London livery, was photographed at Aldgate in June 1999. *Stephen Madden*

The central London operations of Kentish Bus were progressively transferred to other group companies. The forty-three Northern Counties bodied Olympians bought when Kentish Bus was jointly owned with Northumbria – note the Newcastle registrations – moved over to Arriva, both North and South. Many run from Norwood garage, like L 546 on the 417 at Clapham Common, this route being another that had been arbitrarily renumbered (from 137A) to suit the latest LT principle. *Colin Stannard*

Just nine Scania double deckers with Northern Counties Palatine I bodywork were inherited from the Grey-Green fleet, and all are invariably to be found on route 24. They can be distinguished at a distance from other Palatines by the rather higher body styling on the Scania N113 chassis. In spite of the road markings pointing to Camden Town (which is behind the bus), No.161 heads south through Mornington Crescent. *Geoff Rixon*

Arriva remains a major operator of the Metrobus, although more and more are being 'cascaded' on to other Arriva companies around the country as they are replaced in London service. Even now, many remain in plain red or with yellow stripes inherited from Cowie Group days, but at least half of them have been treated to Arriva's 'cow horns' livery variation, though the positioning of the adverts renders this livery somewhat irrelevant. M 1154 poses outside the familiar Prudential building in Holborn. *Geoff Rixon*

Many Metrobuses with Arriva North and South still carry the rear yellow striping dating from the brief Cowie era, even after two years of Arriva ownership. They haven't displayed any fleetnames either, after the Cowie names were summarily ripped off, and present a rather old-fashioned image now. M 1098 is in Norwood on route 468, which was in the process of conversion to DLA in early months of 2000. *Colin Brown*

When Arriva unveiled its new national livery of turquoise and stone (i.e. a light cream), buses in London were to adopt the style but with red replacing the turquoise. However, LT Buses intervened and insisted that the area of cream was too large and breached the 80%-red rule for Central London operations. The result was the 'cow horns' variation, but not before a number of Darts were treated to the original full-fronted version. Such examples work only in the suburbs, and are exemplified by LDR 36 running on route 166 which gets right to (and just beyond) the London boundary at Chipstead Valley. *Colin Brown*

Later repaints were treated to 'cow horns' and on Darts the cream area was swept much further back on the bodywork than on double deckers, in consequence presenting a more prominent livery variation. After LDR 36 right down in the south, LDR 41 is about as far north as one can go in Greater London, seen in Barnet on Enfield garage's route 307. *Colin Brown*

This view sees a refugee from the large contingent of Northern Counties Paladin bodied Dennis Darts which were delivered to Kentish Bus in 1994. One of KB's routes, the 225, was worked for a short while by Grey-Green, but after they in turn surrendered it (to Selkent), the five Darts used thereon gravitated to Arriva London North, by then under common management. Hence the rather unlikely appearance of DRN 117 at Enfield garage for use on route 192. *Colin Brown*

Grey-Green had seventeen Dart SLFs with the then new Alexander ALX200 bodywork delivered in 1997 for routes 20 and 167. The majority have since been repainted to Arriva red, and their heritage is only maintained by the old Grey-Green fleet number. No.966 in Debden shows the slightly hooded nature of the blind boxes on this type of bodywork which makes it almost impossible to see the blinds properly in any photograph taken in the sun! *Keith Wood*

The Arriva Croydon & North Surrey depot at Beddington Farm Road, once a major base for London & Country, passed to Arriva London South ownership on 30th October 1999. Within a few weeks, the various Dart types on route 407 were replaced by a batch of fifteen long Dart SLFs with Alexander ALX200 bodywork, an unusual combination in this part of London. ADL 15 has just arrived at the Sutton terminus on 7th January. *Geoff Rixon*

The former County Bus operations from Edmonton depot passed to Arriva London North ownership in October 1998. Gradually, red livery has supplanted the green and cream on the Edmonton based vehicles, including the batch of Mercedes-Benz 811D used on route W15. This route was due to get new Plaxton-bodied Dart SLFs in spring 2000, with the 811Ds re-deployed elsewhere in the group. MD 609 departs from Walthamstow Central. *Colin Lloyd*

Every bus of Arriva Kent Thameside that works into Greater London is in Arriva livery, the company being among the first in the Group to complete its repaint programme, admittedly aided by many new buses in 1998/99. The company had surrendered most of its LTB services by early 1999, although a handful of routes do remain. One is the 126, worked by Northern Counties Paladin bodied Darts, and No.3128 arrives at its Bromley South terminus in October 1999. *Colin Brown*

Still with Arriva Kent Thameside, a batch of Dart SLF/ Plaxton Pointers provides the service on route 286. No.3271 is standing at the terminus at Queen Mary's Hospital, Sidcup, after travelling from Greenwich. Recently, the route has been re-tendered and has been won by the company for a further five-year term, ensuring that this batch of Darts continues to be needed. *Laurie Rufus*

A mere handful of the original LCBS LR-class Olympians remain in service with Arriva's 'London Country' companies. One such example is the Shires' No.5077 (formerly LR 73) newly repainted into corporate colours, entering Edgware bus station on LTB route 142. This route is now into its third tender renewal period, and the buses used thereon are into their third livery as well. *Colin Brown*

An odd occurrence, and one rather difficult to comprehend, was the decision to paint the five Olympians used on route 402 (Tunbridge Wells & Bromley) into Arriva national style but in red and cream, whereas everything else on a similar service would have been into turquoise and cream. Notwithstanding, they at least stand out, and Arriva Kent & Sussex (formerly Maidstone & District) No.5902 picks up at Bromley South on a journey which will finish at a school in Tonbridge, taking 'London red' deep into Kent. *Colin Brown*

To the north of London, another Arriva 'country' service utilises red and cream buses, this being more historical, as red had been originally used for a marketing exercise between two companies (the then County Bus and MTL London Northern) along the Lea Valley corridor. Gradually during 1999, ex-London Metrobuses had been passed on, after refurbishment, to Arriva East Herts & Essex, for route 310 (Enfield & Hertford). M 612, now numbered 5252, stops at Waltham Cross. *Stephen Madden*

Arriva East Herts & Essex seemed initially very reluctant to adopt Arriva corporate livery and, until recently, repaints were few with new buses delivered in 1997/98 even coming in County Bus's dark green and cream. Some commercial routes with LT agreement operate in outer north London, one such being route 363 which runs as far into London as Tottenham Hale. It is usually worked by Mercedes-Benz Varios, an example of which is No.2371 at Picketts Lock. *Colin Brown*

From 4th September 1999, Arriva the Shires won Harrow local route H18. An unusual purchase was a batch of three Volvo B6BLEs with Wright Crusader bodywork, both types being exceedingly rare so far in the London area. It was not until November that they finally entered service, and No.3260 is seen on its first day, 18th November, in Kenton Lane, Belmont. *David Stewart*

Blue Triangle vehicles have been a common sight in and around London for several years, mostly because of their predilection for vintage buses, as well as their frequency of operation on sightseeing work (now ceased) and rail replacements. On 1st May 1999, their first LTB route began, the 474 (Canning Town & East Beckton) and, after some months of Metrobus operation, new Dennis Tridents eventually appeared from October. Compare the window treatment of bonded glazing on this East Lancs example, DL 905, with nominally similar buses of Metrobus. *Colin Stannard*

BLUE TRIANGLE

Blue Triangle Buses Ltd, Unit 3C, Denver Trading Estate, Ferry Lane, Rainham, Essex, RM13 9BU

The company has been around for over fifteen years working on contract, rail replacement and certain bus routes in Essex, and during 1999 on emergency coverage on LT routes 1, 60 and 127 when other operators were unable to fully cover all the services. It was only on 1st May 1999 that it began its first LT Buses contract route, the 474 (Canning Town & East Beckton). Initially worked by Metrobuses, the reported order for Volvo B7Ls was superseded by one for nine Dennis Tridents, which were delivered in the autumn. The Metrobuses continue to be extensively used on London Underground replacement services all over London, and a small vintage bus fleet has been used on special occasions. A number of Leyland Lynx buses are on contract to LUL for emergency coverage of the Jubilee Line and are stationed at the Millennium Dome.

The first new bus operator in London of the year 2000 was Connex Bus, an offshoot of the railway operator familiar in south London. Their first route was the 3 taken up from 5th February and a batch of Alexander ALX400 bodied Tridents with central staircases was bought to operate thereon. Outwardly a normal red London bus, but the colours used on Connex trains are evident with the narrow yellow stripe and blue skirt. TA 18 is seen on Lambeth Bridge on its first day in service.
Geoff Rixon

CONNEX BUS

Connex Bus UK Ltd, Selhurst Traincare depot, Selhurst Road, London, SE25 6LJ

The major surprise in the LT tendered route arena in 1999 was the award of routes 3 and N3 to Connex Bus, for take up from 5th February 2000. The company had never operated buses in Britain before, although members of its parent group do operate in continental Europe. Dennis Tridents were ordered for the 3/N3 and an operating base set up at Beddington Cross, as well as a parent base at the Selhurst rail depot. Second-hand Metrobuses have been obtained, and are intended for use when Connex's rail services need replacing. Then Connex Bus won route 322 for commencement from late April 2000, and Dart SLFs are on order for this service.

Crystals have been well-known for their fleet of accessible minibuses, several of which are used on LT Buses Mobility Bus networks in various parts of south London. However, they do operate a handful of outer London LTB bus routes, all with midibuses. Beginning on 30th January 1999, Bexleyheath and Sidcup local service B14 replaced an earlier commercial venture (494, formerly 492A) that had been worked by Kentish Bus, and before them Transcity Coaches. Vario S107HGX shows off the unusual colour scheme used on the LTB bus routes at Queen Mary's Hospital, Sidcup. *Laurie Rufus*

CRYSTALS

J.Springham, 127 Dartford Road, Dartford, Kent, DA1 3EN

Starting life as a taxi firm in 1970, Crystals bought their first minibus in 1972. The company was one of the first operators of LT tendered routes when route 146 was taken over in August 1985, although the contract was lost in 1993. The company has since gained two minibus routes (R2, R7) at Orpington and another (B14) at Bexleyheath, together with a range of LT Mobility Bus routes right across south London from Putney to Bexleyheath and from Southwark to Croydon. Vehicles on the bus routes carry a livery of turquoise, whilst those on Mobility Bus routes are in red with yellow relief. Vehicles are now all kept at the 127 Dartford Road address.

The 'Quality Line' branding on Epsom Buses began with the delivery of Mercedes-Benz Varios, mostly to upgrade commercial routes K9 and K10 between Epsom and Kingston, and followed a period of financial crisis over support for the routes. Both UVG and Plaxton bodied vehicles arrived, and an exceedingly smart example of the latter marque, S452LGN, stands in Kingston in July 1999. *Colin Brown*

Epsom Buses was the first operator in Greater London of the 'MPD', the so-called Mini Pointer Dart. A batch was introduced on routes S1 and 413 at the beginning of 1999, the S1 being one of the few LT routes that cross the boundary into Surrey. The type remains fairly rare in London but was starting to gain favour in 2000. S465LGN is one of eleven similar buses, and is pictured in Lower Morden on the 413. *Colin Stannard*

EPSOM BUSES

R.Richmond Ltd, Blenheim Road, Longmead Estate, Epsom, Surrey, KT19 9AF

Epsom Buses is the trading name for the local bus work undertaken by Epsom Coaches, founded in 1920 by Mr H.R. Richmond. Bus work started in 1986 with one minibus route, but blossomed with several former London Country routes assumed at deregulation in October 1986. Subsequently, there have been several adjustments to the network, with a mix of commercial and Surrey County Council routes operated. LT work began when routes 413 and S1 were taken over from London General during the autumn of 1997, and routes 166 (worked jointly with Arriva), 404, 463, S4 and S5 have followed. Other routes in the Epsom and Kingston area are E3, E5, E9, K9, K10, 518, 562. The fleet livery for buses is cream with maroon relief, applied in different proportions, and all are based at the Blenheim Road address. There is also an extensive coach operation, which is not included in this publication.

From summer 1998 Capital Citybus, as it was then, took a number of former London General Metrobuses, and followed this up over the next year with many more from CentreWest. They were used to service newly-won LTB routes until Tridents could be delivered, and more recently have provided the allocation on several Walthamstow area routes. No.338 (formerly M 488) provides a substitute on route 25 at Stratford in July 1999. *Colin Lloyd*

FIRST CAPITAL

Capital Citybus Ltd, Chequers Lane, Dagenham, Essex, RM9 6QD

The origin of this large fleet came when Ensignbus of Purfleet gained LT route 145 from 21st June 1986, and a blue and silver livery was used. Many more routes and vehicles followed until the business was sold to the CNT group of Hong Kong on 29th December 1990. By now the Capital Citybus name was used, and a new yellow livery was introduced, initially featuring Chinese characters in the fleetname. The company was bought back by a management-led team on 21st December 1995, and a revised fleetname style started to appear on vehicles following the breaking of ties with its former owner. With a remarkable twist, Ensignbus re-emerged in 1999 with a short-lived bus operation, again using the blue and silver colours. Its routes were those formerly worked commercially by none other than Capital Citybus, but have since been sold on to another Essex operator, Town & Country Buses.

Considerable success with LT tendering followed, more and more routes were won, and by 1997 three depots were being used, at Dagenham (Chequers Lane), Northumberland Park (Marsh Lane) and Hackney (Waterden Road). The company was sold to the FirstGroup on 8th July 1998, and buses soon acquired the group's logo and the 'First Capital' trading name started to be used, even though the formal Capital Citybus company title was kept. Over one hundred of the fleet still carries the older livery of yellow with red relief, though about 70% now have the new red fleet livery with yellow relief. During the late summer of 1998, most of Thamesway's LT routes and their buses were swiftly assimilated, together with the Ponders End (Morson Road) depot. A programme of repaints into Capital's red and yellow livery soon began, but about twenty buses remained in Thamesway's yellow and mauve colours early in 2000.

Several changes of plan regarding the numbering of the First Capital and CentreWest fleets resulted in the Dennis Tridents being in a common sequence, using Capital's numbers and CentreWest's letter prefixes. Capital received the majority of the eighty-seven TNs delivered in 1999, and here TN 804 operates route 1, indeed really a 'First' in London route terms, won on tender in 1999. The bus is heading for its new Canada Water terminus, connecting with the Jubilee Line Extension, opened in stages during the year. *Colin Brown*

The 80%-red livery was first developed by Capital Citybus for buses on routes that ran into the Central London fare zone 1. The colour scheme has been subsequently adopted for the whole fleet – even though a number of yellow buses remain in service in 2000. A batch of Alexander (Belfast) bodied Olympians was bought in 1997 for route 91, but here No.224 is on route 67 at Wood Green. *Laurie Rufus*

Northern Counties bodied Olympians came in 1996 for route 67, and were all in the then standard yellow livery. These are now being repainted to red, and in contrast to the last view of a 'route 91' bus on route 67, here is a 'route 67' bus on the 91. No.247 circuits the war memorial at Euston Bus Station in July 1999. *Stephen Madden*

The first buses to arrive under FirstGroup ownership in 1998 were more Northern Counties bodied Volvo Olympians, and have always carried First titling. They operate on route 341, one of several routes won in that year from other London operators, and most carry Sadler's Wells lettering, similar to many Arriva buses serving Islington. No.208 is at Holborn Circus. *Geoff Rixon*

Long wheelbase Dennis Arrows with East Lancs Pyoneer bodywork are the main fare on route 369, and were the first of their body styling to appear on Capital's routes in 1997. As with many batches of yellow buses, these are currently going through a repaint programme into red, No.417 being the first of its batch to do so. *Colin Brown*

Capital Citybus had always been known for favouring the Dennis Dominator, and both new and second hand examples with several varieties of bodywork have entered the fleet. One of the Northern Counties bodied buses is No.270, here at Chingford. *Keith Wood*

Several batches of second hand East Lancs Dominators were acquired during the 1990s from cities such as Southampton and Leicester, coincidentally places now also within the First domain and now receiving surplus buses from First Capital. No.342, one from Leicester, is seen at Bethnal Green on route D6, although since conversion of the busy route to Dart, they are now mostly to be found on school bus services from Hackney depot. *Gerald Mead*

Right Still in full pre-FirstGroup yellow garb one year after the take-over, No.151 is one of the twenty-three Leyland bodied Olympians that arrived in 1991. One of their mainstays is the long route 123 between Wood Green and Ilford, and this example bowls along Bruce Grove in Tottenham, served exclusively by trolleybuses forty years earlier. *David Stewart*

Below Typifying the common group ownership, the majority of Thamesway's London operations came under the control of First Capital in stages, culminating on 26th September 1998 when the buses and routes at Ponders End depot were assumed. Even now, a number of buses still display the Thamesway fleet livery of yellow and mauve, although more and more have succumbed to red colours. No.781 is near Edmonton Green. *Laurie Rufus*

In summer 1998, seven former DW class Darts were transferred from First CentreWest. Their main weekday home is on routes W6 and W10, where they replaced smaller midibuses. No.639 serves Edmonton when on such a duty. *Colin Brown*

Route S2 is a short but very busy service in east London, passing under several low bridges. Single deck buses are thus essential, and thirteen Dart SLFs were delivered in February 1998 with the first examples of the East Lancs Spryte body to be seen on LTB services. Buses display yellow blinds towards Stratford and most of the batch has side route branding for the route. However, No.715 in Clapton does not have this latter feature. *Colin Brown*

Optare Excels are scheduled to work route 396 between Ilford and Goodmayes but rarely more than a couple are actually used each day. However, No.703 is found on its correct service, being the only route actually to set down at Ilford Broadway, not on any map but locally regarded as the junction of High Road and Ilford Lane. *Colin Stannard*

The link with CentreWest, who had patronised Marshall bodywork for some years, resulted in Capital taking several batches, with more to come in 2000. The latest deliveries are to both short and long designs, and carry the red livery with First's London style of side striping. Since conversion, route D7 has suffered from a lack of capacity and double-deck buses seem likely to make a return to this Isle of Dogs lifeline service. DML 307 turns through the bus-only road outside Limehouse Police Station. *Colin Stannard*

The Optare MetroRider is now a fairly rare type in Greater London, but Capital do have a batch of ten, mostly working alongside the "DW" Darts on route W6 as well as on route 299, and the whole class now has been repainted red. No.630 is seen in Muswell Hill at the southern end of the short 299. *Colin Lloyd*

Marshall bodywork graces the small batch of nine narrow-bodied Mercedes-Benz Varios that arrived with Thamesway in 1998. They were bought especially for routes 362 and 462, the latter service passing through a width restriction in Barkingside. Thamesway's No.416 (alias Capital's No.576) returns to Ilford at Fulwell Cross. *Colin Stannard*

Limited-stop route 607 between Uxbridge and Shepherd's Bush has gone from strength to strength, and is quite a flagship service for CentreWest. Enhanced seating features on the batch of fifteen Volvo Olympians dedicated to the service. V 43 calls outside the RAF station at Uxbridge in November 1999, and already has a healthy load aboard. *Colin Brown*

FIRST CENTREWEST

First CentreWest London Buses Ltd, Macmillan House, Paddington, London W2 1TY

CentreWest was purchased from London Buses by a management-led team on 2nd September 1994, the fleet already including a large proportion of midibuses. In December 1995 CentreWest branched out across London when they won some LT contract routes in the Orpington area. In March 1996, the holding company of CentreWest purchased the Bee Line and London Buslines companies, and some interchange of vehicles has since taken place between the fleets.

On 26th March 1997 the CentreWest group was sold to FirstBus (renamed to FirstGroup in November 1997). The group's *f* logo and First names now precede the local marketing names which are used by buses based at Acton Tram Depot and Uxbridge (Uxbridge Buses), Alperton (Challenger), Greenford (Ealing Buses), Orpington (Orpington Buses) and Westbourne Park (Gold Arrow). Traditional London red livery continued to be carried by most of the fleet, although most buses have now been adapted with yellow relief and fleetnames, and have lost the grey skirt.

Substantial patronage of Marshall bodywork has been evident in recent years, and many Darts so bodied have been used to oust earlier and smaller midibuses, many of the latter being cascaded to Beeline. During 1999, First CentreWest's fleet numbering sequence was integrated with that of First Capital, but the concept was a compromise between the two systems and so far has only been adopted in respect of new vehicles, with Dart and Trident fleet numbers intermixed between the two fleets. The application of First-style stripes on vehicle sides has not been adopted as widely as with Capital. The company is also involved with Croydon Tramlink operations in a management sense, and is to operate two of the dedicated feeder services (T31, T32) to trams in New Addington, Darts used thereon being in a red and white livery to match the trams.

Something of a surprise in spring 1999 was the purchase of twenty (of the 22) stock-built Volvo Olympians for route 83, doubtless destined to be the last new standard-floor double deckers for London. Suffering something of an identity crisis, fleet numbers VN 888–907 were allocated to follow on from Capital and CentreWest Tridents TN 801–887, but were later altered to VN 88–107. Seen here before physical renumbering, VN 89 travels through West Ealing. *Colin Brown*

Legends extolling the benefits of route 23 adorn the sides of RML 2717 at Marble Arch. In common with route 11, the 23 is one of the best routes to ride to see the central London sights. Note the large driver's duty number in the cab window – these have replaced traditional London running numbers with CentreWest. *Geoff Rixon*

The Metrobus is a dying breed in CentreWest territory, with trunk routes 18 and 83 having lost all but two or three reserve vehicles in 1999. The main service left is the 207, and that is due to receive new Tridents in spring 2000. School buses and substitutions are destined to be their last refuge, and an example of the latter is with M 358, covering for a low floor Dennis Lance on route 222 on the Bath Road at Heathrow North in September 1999. *Geoff Rixon*

Once the two companies were in common ownership, the double deck buses of London Buslines were gradually absorbed into the CentreWest fleet, and the Buslines routes went over to all-Dart operation. Many have since moved on to Capital and Eastern Counties, but the five highbridge Alexander bodied Olympians stayed as the main allocation on route E1. LA 26 begins its short run to Ealing when pictured in Greenford in September 1999. *Colin Brown*

The section of Harrow Road between Sudbury and Wembley can look quite sylvan at times, as seen in this view of Dennis Trident/ Plaxton President TN 843 on route 18 in August 1999. Full First London wavy-line striping on the outside is coupled with First interior décor of mainly purple and turquoise. *Colin Brown*

Several Metrobuses act as driver trainers with former London Buses companies in north, south and west London. CentreWest paint theirs in a striking yellow and red livery, so that everyone can see a learner coming! The instructor on M 1338 discusses some points with his pupil while out for the day in Greenford. *Colin Brown*

In spite of First London striping appearing elsewhere, most of the new Marshall bodied Darts delivered during 1998/99 have carried traditional red with yellow relief. They have come in short, standard or long lengths, some have single-door and some dual-door bodywork, though all are essentially similar in appearance. DML 247 is at Wembley Triangle on route 92. *Gerald Mead*

Above One of the shortest Marshall bodied Darts is DMS 259, this example being one of those supplied by Marshall as replacements for the ill-fated home-grown Minibus, all of which have now departed. The purple and turquoise First interior can be seen in this view on Ealing Common, on a section of route opened up to buses as recently as May 1997. *Colin Brown*

Left Several hundred buses in London carry rear advertisements, though most are on double deck buses to make a greater impact. There are a few single deckers so treated, and most of these advertise businesses local to the routes they are likely to be seen upon, rather than the generally national-based adverts on the double deckers. Darts on routes 28, 31 and 328 are never going to wander far, so the Kensington and Chelsea College will get its message across locally. *Capital Transport*

Medium length Dart SLFs took over the 28, 31 and 328 by the summer of 1999 from the smaller DW class, which in turn had replaced the even smaller MA a few years earlier. The routes are still very busy and need seventy buses for the full weekday service. A packed DM 301 calls at a busy stop in Kensington High Street. *Geoff Rixon*

Stockley Park provides support for route U1, which connects the high-tech. Business Park with Hayes, Uxbridge and Ruislip. Prominent side branding on DML 194 in Uxbridge shows off the connection. *Colin Lloyd*

Some of CentreWest's buses were just smartened up a little with the addition of yellow relief. One such is DW 163, still carrying the LBL-style of grey skirt, at Golders Green on route 226. This was a route won from Metroline, and still travels close to three of Metroline's garages while being remote from its own home base of Alperton. *Laurie Rufus*

'Heathrow Fast' is a livery designed by *Best Impressions* on a route supported by the British Airports Authority and Stockley Park. The striking style is carried on Dart L 4 at the RAF station at Uxbridge heading for Heathrow, which it should reach in just twenty minutes. *Stephen Madden*

Quite a rare vehicle unless you know where to look for it is LLW 31, a low floor Dennis Lance transferred into CentreWest in 1999 for the Buckinghamshire contract route 335 between Slough and Chalfont. The bus had previously been around First companies in Yorkshire and the South-West. This picture shows the vehicle taking a short layover outside Slough bus station. *Colin Brown*

Top The link between London Buslines and its parent CentreWest has drawn ever closer, with the transfer of route 258 – with ten Darts – to work from CentreWest's Alperton garage. In spite of this, one year after the transfer the ten retained London Buslines names and fleet numbers into 2000. No.601 (alias D 601 with CentreWest) stops in Harrow Weald in September 1999. *Geoff Rixon*

Bottom Usually, the Dart SLFs of Buslines can be found on routes 105 and 490, and most are branded for these services. Heathrow supports the 105, and the 'Heathrow Freeflow' symbol and side flash are prominent on DML 642 on the Bath Road at Heathrow North. Even though allocated, both London Buslines and its sister Beeline company do not display fleet letter prefixes. *Colin Brown*

FIRST LONDON BUSLINES

First Beeline Buses Ltd (t/a London Buslines), Middlesex Business Centre, Bridge Road, Southall, Middlesex, UB2 4AB

In the very first round of LT tendering, Len Wright gained LT route 81 (Hounslow and Slough) from 13th July 1985, and a yellow and brown livery was adopted with London Buslines names. In later years various routes and vehicles came and went under Mr Wright's Q-Drive group ownership. On 20th March 1996, the Q Drive bus operations, which included the Beeline and London Buslines fleets, was purchased by CentreWest, leaving Q-Drive with its other interests, mainly in coaching. In 1997 a swap of some routes took place with CentreWest, resulting in the fleet becoming all-Dart except for three Renault minibuses used on Mobility Bus routes 981–994. LT routes are 105, 203, 285, 490, and the Darts also appear on Sundays on Surrey County Council services 441, 446, 456, 461 and 481. The fleet bears a livery of yellow with red relief, and is kept at the Bridge Road, Southall base. Route 258 is now controlled by parent CentreWest and operates from Alperton, even though the vehicles used retain yellow London Buslines colours and fleet numbers.

HARRIS BUS

Harris Bus Company Ltd, Manor Road, West Thurrock, Essex, RM20 4EH

Harris Bus was set up as a separate company from the associated Frank Harris (Coaches) in September 1986 in preparation for bus work following deregulation, and developed a network centred on the Lakeside shopping centre. The company decided to branch into LT tendered work, and gained LT route 108 from 19th April 1997, following this with 128, 129, 150 later in 1997 and 132 and 180 in 1998. Vehicles carry a most unusual livery of blue and green and several carry appropriate branding for the various routes. Buses for the 128,129,150 are based at West Thurrock, with the 108,132,180 at Crabtree Manor Way North, Belvedere, south of the River.

After a period when the bus operations were said to be up for sale, the company went into receivership on 15th December 1999. In February 2000 LT Buses took a hand in the day-to-day running of the operation, following the failure to sell the company. In a dramatic move, a new Operators Licence in the name of London Buses Ltd was applied for, the intention being to re-open Ash Grove garage to work four of the routes, while retaining the 132 and 180 at Belvedere. In was anticipated that, although the Harris Bus fleetname was likely to be removed, the existing vehicles would continue to operate the routes for the foreseeable future.

Facing page Thirty-five Volvo Olympians with East Lancs Pyoneer bodies provide – with eight DB250s – the main service on route 180 south of the River, as well as the 128, 129 and 150 in Ilford. No.352 in Ilford shows how the early dayglo yellow blinds fade after constant exposure to the light, almost returning to the old style of white on black! *Laurie Rufus*

Above Optare Excels provide the service on routes 132 and 108, being essential on the latter route due to height restrictions in the Blackwall Tunnel. Route 108 was the first service to be rerouted to North Greenwich, in fact operating since 21st November 1998, and of course several more have followed. This 8th January 2000 view, though, shows No.320 after the Millennium Dome had opened to the public. *Geoff Rixon*

HACKNEY COMMUNITY TRANSPORT

Hackney Community Transport, 2 Hertford Road, Dalston, London N1 5SH

The large group of Mobility Bus services in north and east London, and formerly worked by Arriva, were taken over from 26th June 1999. A fleet of four Fiat Ducato tri-axle minibuses operates the routes, undoubtedly the most unusual vehicles on any LT Buses service.

Possibly a candidate for the most unusual shape of vehicle to work on an LTB service is the Fiat Ducato tri-axle with bodywork by Rohill of Andover. Four of these operate on a large range of Mobility Bus services in north and east London and can be found on certain days as far apart as Enfield and the Isle of Dogs, Romford and Brent Cross. At the latter location is T248FLJ on the Monday-only route 924. *Colin Brown*

Opposite top When the last book in this series was published, Limebourne had just had all its buses repossessed, and was looking for replacements. Eleven eight-year-old DT-class Darts from Metroline were the first to come to the rescue, and now provide the main service on routes C3 and C10. All are named after 'Halls' in Great Western Railway tradition, and 'Barton Hall' rounds the Elephant & Castle on 6th July 1999. *Stephen Madden*

Opposite lower Otherwise, Limebourne re-equipped during 1999 with thirty-four Dart SLFs with the new Caetano Compass body built in Hampshire. Names are only carried on the nearside, so we cannot see that T417LGP is 'Kirby Muxloe Castle'. These buses are bigger than the DTs, Castles are bigger than Halls, hence the rationale for the naming! Will the Metrobuses become Palaces? *Geoff Rixon*

LIMEBOURNE

Independent Way Ltd, t/a Limebourne, Silverthorne Road, Battersea, London, SW8 3HE

After London Buslines and Berks Bucks Bus Company were sold to CentreWest on 20th March 1996, Q-Drive retained its London coach business. One LT route (C10) had been won and thus a small bus operation was set up at the Battersea base from May 1996. The livery used was the first by a contract operator to utilise the 80% red scheme as was then being laid down by LT for buses operating contracts within Central London Fare Zone 1. The company later assumed routes 42 and 156, and the C3 followed in October 1997. However, the Q-Drive group was put into receivership in October 1998, and on 20th November the local management staged a buy-out of the bus business in the name of Independent Way Ltd. All the existing buses were re-possessed by finance companies, and the new management had to hire replacement buses from several operators. Before very long, the new company obtained its own Operator's Licence, another LT route (344) was won, and thirty-four new Caetano bodied Dart SLFs came into the fleet. Since August 1999 Limebourne has been running Arriva's route G1, together with some of Arriva's Darts on their behalf, to assist with their driver shortages.

Recalling pre-war practice, this quite beautiful livery adorns three of the London Central 'private hire and special event' fleet. Often to be found on the rather unglamorous Bingo Bus shuttle from Surrey Quays, T 172 shows off its colours in summer 1999. *Malc McDonald*

LONDON CENTRAL

London Central Bus Co Ltd, 25 Raleigh Gardens, Mitcham, Surrey, CR4 3NS

London Central was purchased by the Go Ahead Group on 18th October 1994. The basic bus livery has remained traditional London red with white relief, accompanied by a stylised fleet logo based on a Thames clipper ship. The purchase by the Go Ahead group of London General resulted in London Central's administrative functions gradually moving from the Camberwell head office to the Mitcham offices of London General between 1997 and 1999. The livery has also been modified with a thin yellow band above the grey skirt, this being a London General influence.

In recent years, new bus deliveries consisted of Olympians and Darts, but late in 1999 the company received the first examples of two exciting new types. Seventeen DAF single deckers branded for special services to the Millennium Dome began service on 1st January 2000, and some are to operate on a new guided busway system right up to the Dome. The company became the first in London to receive the new Volvo B7L low floor double decker, Alexander bodied examples arriving for routes 45 and 63. Unlike low floor double deckers with other companies, they are painted in the company's traditional style livery of red with a grey skirt. Others with Plaxton President bodywork will come later in 2000 for routes at Bexleyheath, and will see the withdrawal of all but a handful of the Titans, for so long a feature of the company's area. The fleet operates from garages at Bexleyheath, Camberwell, New Cross and Peckham.

The opening of the Bluewater shopping complex in Kent in March 1999 was the impetus for many new services. One such is the 710 Express from much of south-east London to the complex. It is worked by the 'private hire' fleet at New Cross, and thus NV 7, also treated to the pre-war style of livery, can be found thereon most days. *Colin Brown*

The first three of the VC class of Volvo Citybuses are fitted with coach style seating and, as such, have operated variously with the 'private hire and special event' fleets of both London Central and General. During 1999, VC 3 acquired London Central fleetnames and was used frequently on the the service to Bluewater, where it is seen arriving. *Colin Brown*

Wearing its yellow ribbon branding well, RML 2482 passes the garish pink edifice of the Elephant & Castle shopping centre. Although curtailed at both ends in recent years, route 12 remains one of the longer and most frequent crew-operated services in London, needing thirty-eight buses on a weekday. *Malc McDonald*

Looking somewhat care-worn, RM 436 departs from the familiar Terminus Place at Victoria. As with route 12, yellow ribbon branding is carried. Late in 1999, this route was re-awarded to London Central for another term, but conditions were set regarding the refurbishment of some of the vehicles used on the service. *Stephen Madden*

Two standard RMs (9 and 202) are kept in a more traditional London red with cream relief and, although RM 9 has gold London Transport fleetnames, RM 202 is unique in carrying small company names on the traditional scheme. In spite of the dent in the bodywork, it looks fine in this Hyde Park Corner view. *Geoff Rixon*

The Titan still forms a substantial part of the London Central fleet, although by the end of 2000 very few are likely to be left in stock, once the Volvo B7L takes over most of their routes. Woolwich town centre is the setting for T 1051 on one such route, the 422 which was extended to make the Jubilee Line connection in 1999. *Colin Brown*

The small class of nine Alexander Royale bodied Olympians have always worked route P11 – renumbered to 381 in October 1999. AV 7 on the Rotherhithe peninsula has had its blind adapted by the new number stuck over the old – which does not show up at night! This class of buses, new in 1995, was starting to gain first repaints early in 2000.
Gerald Mead

Until 1999, the Northern Counties Palatine bodied Volvo Olympian could perhaps be regarded as the standard modern double decker for both of Go Ahead's red London fleets. Its dominance will be eclipsed by the Volvo B7L during 2000. Looking very like a traditional London bus in its almost-LBL styling, NV 53 travels down the Walworth Road.
Malc McDonald

The first London operator of the Volvo B7L low floor double decker was London Central, who took their first batch of forty-six early in 2000 for routes 45 and 63. This modern-day advance on the Volvo Olympian has been a long time coming, the Trident having had nearly two years head-start. A darker-grey skirt is carried on these. *Geoff Rixon*

Several DW-class Wright Handybus bodied Darts transferred within the group from London General to London Central, and they provide the service on route P5 and part of the 484, both somewhat obscure back-street routes in inner south London. Coming out onto the open road at the Elephant & Castle is DW 44 in July 1999. *Stephen Madden*

The Go Ahead group bought fifteen short and twenty-nine long Marshall bodied Dart SLFs in 1999, and all but five (which are with London General at Putney) went to Bexleyheath to service five routes (244,469,B12,B15,B16) won on tender from January 1999. DML 21 picks up in Woolwich in July 1999. *Colin Brown*

London Pride, Big Bus Company and Arriva may run the 'official' London tourist services, but London General runs the cheapest. For one pound most of the main tourist sights can be seen from a number 11, passing as it does through Westminster, Trafalgar Square, St Paul's and The City. Among the branded RMLs on the route, just one standard RM can be found, this being RM 994 seen at Victoria. *Laurie Rufus*

LONDON GENERAL

London General Transport Services Ltd, 25 Raleigh Gardens, Mitcham, Surrey, CR4 3NS

London General was purchased by a management-led team on 2nd November 1994, and at a total of 636 vehicles, was the largest fleet of any of the privatised London Buses companies. In May 1996, the company was in turn purchased by the Go-Ahead Group, and rationalisation with London Central has since taken place at the management level. Traditional London livery of red with white relief has been retained, but is accompanied by a white and orange fleetname incorporating a vertical orange stripe and a thin yellow band. Although the original privatisation logo, a B-type bus from the General of the First World War era, has now been largely abandoned, a small handful of buses carries a traditional pre-war style of livery and retains this emblem. As with London Central, many new low floor double deckers are on order for delivery in 2000, and will replace the majority of the large fleet of Metrobuses. The fleet operates from garages at Merton, Putney, Stockwell, Sutton and Waterloo.

As with London Central, several 'specials' exist in the London General fleet. One such is RML 2732 at Victoria, treated to gold relief but with somewhat over-sized gold GENERAL fleetnames in an approximation of LGOC style. *Stephen Madden*

London General is still one of the largest operators of the Metrobus, although that is set to change in 2000 as Volvo B7Ls and Dennis Tridents arrive to supplant them. M 260 at Clapham Junction shows off the traditional white relief and grey skirt, only enhanced by a thin yellow band. This variation was introduced in London General's early days of private ownership, and later spread to London Central once the two companies were joined under common ownership. *Colin Brown*

Many of London General's Volvo Citybuses have been re-registered so as to keep the potentially lucrative former RM marks 'in the family'. These high-floor buses with their underfloor engines are the mainstay of route 133, and VC 39 pauses on the approach to London Bridge. *Geoff Rixon*

Many of London General's NV class of Olympians can be found on most of Sutton's double deck routes, and NV 117 in Wimbledon travels south on the very old-established 93. Other large groups might have imposed corporate identity upon their vehicles, but Go-Ahead choose to keep the company liveries with just a modest group name on the side.
Geoff Rixon

Late in 1997, a batch of twenty-seven Olympians with Northern Counties Palatine II bodywork with coach type seating came into the fleet to provide a somewhat unexpected touch of luxury for passengers on route 74. NV 168 at Hyde Park Corner shows the side route branding which is limited enough to be also relevant when these buses are used on route 14 during evenings and Sundays.
Geoff Rixon

Inspired by the treatment given to Go Ahead's buses in its native North-East, livery variations are often applied to driver training buses that would not be tolerated in London Transport's rule book. Certainly devised to attract attention, we see M 1389 out on Epsom Downs, teaching another recruit.
Geoff Rixon

Just five of the 1999 delivery to Go-Ahead of Marshall bodied Dart SLFs came to London General, and they are usually inter-mixed with older Dart types on routes 239 and 265, taking them to points as far apart as Victoria and Tolworth. At the latter terminal of route 265, DMS 3 takes its layover in May 1999. *Geoff Rixon*

Leyland Nationals dating from 1981 received the 'Greenway' treatment in 1992/3/4 for further service on the Red Arrow network in central London, and they were still operational early in 2000. The routes are mainly for the benefit of railway commuters to and from main stations, and have a large standing capacity. They are only scheduled for Monday to Friday service. *Stephen Madden*

The standard Pointer Dart is still around London in considerable numbers, but tends to get rather sidelined nowadays with all the new low-floor examples coming into service. Most operate in the suburbs, but DRL 63 at Terminus Place, Victoria exemplifies its breed. *Laurie Rufus*

Low floor buses of many companies carry some form of individual identification. In London Central and General, the LDP class of Plaxton Pointer bodied Dart SLFs have a thick white band on the sides of the roof to distinguish them at a distance. One of the latest deliveries was a batch for route 219, and LDP 121 is seen in Wimbledon in July 1999. *Geoff Rixon*

The first LDPs in London General came at the end of 1996 and in two lengths. They were used in a major scheme to upgrade routes in the Sutton and Morden areas, a far cry from the cheap-rate 'Suttonbus' operation of a few years earlier which mostly employed DMS Fleetlines. Route 163 covers most of what was once one of the early LT 'flat fare' routes (the M1) on its course through Raynes Park to Morden. LDP 17 leaves Wimbledon in July 1999. *Colin Brown*

Traditional red and white pre-war livery is carried by two of the three open-top Metrobuses in the fleet, all handily converted after a series of low bridge accidents! OM 241 carries the original General privatisation logo, the B-type bus, on the front panel. The buses can be seen on the various special services worked during the summer, such as to the Chelsea Flower Show, Wimbledon Tennis, etc, and here it is in July 1999 going to the Hampton Court flower show. *Geoff Rixon*

London Traveller won route 187 from September 1999, after working only school and contract services before that date. The 187 was split into 187 and 487, and V505EFR turns into South Harrow Station on the western variation. After a good start at applying the full livery of stripes and fleetnames, enthusiasm soon waned and six months on only one third of the batch carries the full scheme. *Colin Brown*

LONDON TRAVELLER

Metropolitan Omnibus Co (London) Ltd, Unit 2 Goodhall Street, Harlesden, NW10 6AE

This company has had a short but varied existence, with different names and operating bases in use until August 1999. A new Operator's Licence in the name of Metropolitan, but keeping the London Traveller trading identity, was set up from that date. A separate operation in Hertfordshire, initially part of London Traveller, was devolved to a new company Watford & District at the same time, even though some buses continue to be loaned back and forth. London Traveller won their first daily LT routes (187 and 487) from 4th September 1999 and obtained new Volvo B6BLE low floor buses to operate them. The company had already been operating school journeys on LT routes 143, 302, 626, 643 and has added the H12 school runs to this portfolio. Metrobuses originating from the West Midlands fleet have been supplemented by more from Metrobus Ltd, and most of the latter remain in that company's blue and yellow colours.

The London United fleet contains Darts of several different marques, and unusual in London is the batch of just eight Wright Crusader bodied variants that arrived in 1996 for route H25 at Hounslow. They can often be found substituting for other types, and here CD 1 is at Bell Corner, Hounslow on one such duty on the H98. *Colin Stannard*

LONDON UNITED

London United Busways Ltd, Wellington Road, Fulwell, Middlesex, TW2 5NX

London United was purchased by a management-led team on 5th November 1994, and the traditional London red livery was soon adapted to a new style with silver grey roof, grey upper-deck window-surrounds, and a thin white band above the grey skirt. Routemasters received grey (instead of white) relief, with yellow used for external transfers such as fleet numbers and garage codes. In September 1995, the holding company of London United purchased Stanwell Bus, better known as Westlink, from the National Express Group. Then in the summer of 1997 Transdev, a French-based holding company purchased the London United group. Gradually, Westlink's own livery was eliminated with the Westlink name no longer used to market the services. However, a handful of buses, mostly those used on routes 57 and 371, continue to display the Westlink name until they are next repainted.

London United has adopted route branding in some measure, although an earlier use of a 'Harrier' logo on many Darts has been abandoned as buses are repainted. Stronger branding is with all-blue Darts on routes 555/6/7 and a red, blue and orange livery on yet more Darts for express services between Feltham Station and Heathrow terminals. Rather different styling is with side slogans and various designs on buses on routes 57, 216, 371 and R68. The company does not operate only in London, but also has several routes in north-west Surrey, mostly on contract to that county.

The former Westlink bases at Kingston and Hounslow Heath remain in use, while the main LU fleet is kept at garages at Fulwell, Hounslow and Shepherd's Bush, with some of the latter's buses outstationed at Stamford Brook. This latter garage had been kept 'in reserve' for some years, and also houses the company's driver training buses and maintenance facilities as well as being used to store delicensed vehicles.

The Airbus services, based at an open site at Heathrow North's West Ramp, running between Heathrow Airport and Central London, were much scaled-down during 1999. The Airbus service was sold to National Express from 5th February 2000, together with control of the West Ramp base.

Yellow fleet numbers and garage codes, plus a flake grey relief band, distinguish the main Routemaster fleet with London United. RML 2704 heads west to Hammersmith on the Number Nine. The route was curtailed from its traditional terminus at Mortlake due to a weight restriction being imposed on Hammersmith Bridge. *Stephen Madden*

Some weeks after London Central had put London's first Volvo B7Ls into service, London United followed suit. Theirs also have Alexander ALX400 bodywork, becoming the sixth London operator of the type, but so far the only one to have any form of branding to advertise the low floor facility. The first vehicle to work on route 220 was V176 OOE, seen here in Putney Bridge Road on 22nd February 2000. *Geoff Rixon*

One of many Arriva Croydon & North Surrey routes to be passed over to other operators in 1999 due to garage closures and staff shortages was the 85 between Kingston and Putney Bridge. Thus from 4th September twelve (of their thirteen) DAF DB250s were transferred to London United with the route. Although most remained in blue Arriva national colours, DN 9, needing a repaint after some damage, received London United's current colours. *Geoff Rixon*

When London United lost route 140 in the September 1999 re-tendering exercise, most of the ECW bodied Olympians were sold. However, nine were kept and are normally used on routes 81 and 116, as well as some routes just into north west Surrey in the Ashford area. L 302 at Hampton Court is on one such service, the infrequent 416 that links Stanwell with Kingston. *Geoff Rixon*

After none had been dealt with for some time, several of the Metrobuses still in old London Buses livery and getting increasingly shabby, were treated to company colours in autumn 1999. Some of Kingston garage's small allocation were repainted, and M 881 is just 'ex works' on route 411 in East Molesey on 14th October 1999. *Geoff Rixon*

With delivery of fifty-three during 1996/7/8, the Volvo Olympian and Alexander bodywork combination became London United's standard double decker. They are now the mainstay of routes 57, 131 and 281 in the Kingston area. Those on the 281 carry side slogans enticing students, shoppers and commuters to avail themselves of the route for their different purposes. VA 36 is looking for commuters. *Stephen Madden*

London United invested heavily in the Plaxton Pointer 2 bodied Dart SLF during 1999, with 104 coming into stock. Many of them, though not all, carry the Easy Access logo and designs on the sides. One delivery ousted the Leyland Nationals from route H37 during the summer of 1999, and DP 45 shows the new order on this busy route while turning into Richmond bus station. *Geoff Rixon*

Eleven of the DP-class Darts (23–33) carry all-over blue livery, and carry various sorts of branding for the group of routes (555/6/7) that connect Heathrow with the Sunbury and Walton area. The roof sides carry lettering for the cross-airport facility that these buses also provide, with support from the BAA to give free travel on this section. DP 30 is in Sunbury. *Geoff Rixon*

Another eleven DPs (12–22) combine the familiar three colours of Stagecoach (operators of the SWT rail link to Feltham) with the red front to make it more like a London bus. Two non-stop services operate from Feltham Station to Heathrow's Central Terminals and to Terminal Four, but although running since March 1999 have never carried many passengers. From 5th February 2000 an extra stop at Hatton Cross was added. *Geoff Rixon*

The R68 route between Richmond and Hampton Court was treated to a route branding exercise in 1999 and DR 3 shows London United's almost unlimited inventiveness in this regard. Three different designs with Hampton Court Palace connections are spread over just seven buses. The Maze and Henry VIII are pictured on the other members of the batch. *Colin Brown*

The Duple/Carlyle bodied 8.5-metre DT class was once very numerous, and nowhere more so than with London United. Very few now remain, and DT 160 on route 33 represents the swan-song of the type which is due for imminent withdrawal. *Stephen Madden*

Route 216 between Kingston and Staines is a very old-established service, once home to the RF class for many years. It still runs, but now mostly with Wright-bodied Darts. Six of the longer DWL variant (7–12) have this odd 'balloon' style of route branding. DWL 7 passes through Sunbury Village in March 1999. *Geoff Rixon*

Below The LLW class of Dennis Lances dating from 1993/4 show how long low floor buses have been around. Route 120 was one of the first low floor routes but the service requirement outstripped the vehicle allocation some years ago, and Metrobuses have to support the service each day, although new low-floor double-deckers are due later in 2000. *Malc McDonald*

The six London United Lynxes have been off and on route 81 more than once during the years they have spent in the Hounslow area. They were back again in 1999, and LX 8 leaves the town for the long straight run out to Slough. Note the yellow fleet number on the black front grille. *Stephen Madden*

Eight MAN-Optare Vectas and six Optare Excels are the allocation for route 371 between Kingston and Richmond via the back roads of Ham and Richmond Hill, and both types are unique in the fleet and, moreover are both rare in the whole of London. Some of these buses still carried the Westlink fleetname in 1999, as seen on MV 5 in Richmond. *Geoff Rixon*

Optare Excel XL 7 calls at Richmond Station for its next trip back to Kingston. All the Vectas and Excels carry slogans on the sides, and they are even different on each side. The caption writers of London United had to devise 28 different slogans about features along the route – some were a but contrived, although many were quite inspired. *Geoff Rixon*

The first London operator of the East Lancs Lolyne bodywork, here on a Dennis Trident chassis, was Metrobus who introduced fifteen onto route 161 in the late summer of 1999. The family resemblance with the earlier Pyoneer body design is evident. No.414 departs from the Chislehurst War Memorial terminus on the service, which was one of those extended to North Greenwich during 1999, several months in advance of the opening date of the Millennium Dome. *Geoff Rixon*

METROBUS

Metrobus Ltd, Oak Farm, Farnborough Hill, Green Street Green, Orpington BR6 6DA

Following the collapse of the Orpington & District Bus Company in February 1981, operations were taken over by the Tillingbourne Bus Company from 2nd March 1981 and a local company was formed, Tillingbourne (Metropolitan) Ltd. Public confidence was soon restored and new routes were developed in the area between Orpington and Croydon on roads never before served by London Transport services. Metrobus Ltd was born in a management-led buy-out on 24th September 1983. Further commercial routes were developed in the Bromley and Beckenham areas, more LT contracts were won and routes were taken on when other operators surrendered them. During 1997, the buses and routes of East Surrey Buses of South Godstone were acquired, and further expansion took the company to Brighton and Newhaven with another base at Lewes.

On 3rd September 1999, the company passed into the Go Ahead Group, but with the existing management, fleet, bases and livery being retained unaltered. Both before and after this date, considerable investment in new buses has been evident, supplemented by purchases of relatively modern second-hand Darts. Bus routes operated on LT contract or with LT agreement are 64, 119, 138, 146, 161, 181, 233, 246, 261, 284, 320, 351, 352, 353, 358, 359, 361, 464, 494, 630, 654, 693, T33. The fleet is in blue and yellow livery, and those for LT work are kept at Green Street Green, although those on routes 146, 246, 464 come from the South Godstone base. The fleet list in this book covers only the buses normally used on these services.

Left Two batches of Olympians with East Lancs Pyoneer bodywork have been taken into stock, the 1997 intake of fifteen being for route 64 and thirteen 1998 deliveries for the 119. One of the former is No.836 seen in South Croydon. *Malc McDonald*

Right The familiar Northern Counties Palatine I bodywork was perhaps the last of what could be termed the standard double deck design of the 1990s. Metrobus took eleven in 1996 for route 261 and another eight in 1998 for route 320. The company became the third operator on the Bromley – Biggin Hill corridor in a short space of time, and devolved the 'out-county' section to Westerham to a new commercial service 246. No.860 travels down Bromley High Street. *David Stewart*

Seen in Bromley is Optare Excel No.509, one of ten that are dedicated to the long route 358 between Orpington and Crystal Palace. The service has proved very popular and has been increased in frequency several times in its short life. It is one of several routes that the innovative company has developed in the south-eastern suburbs outside the auspices of London Transport – even though revenue agreement has been reached over the acceptance of LT tickets. *David Stewart*

Formerly one of Kentish Bus's many LT services in south-east London, route 181 was one taken over by Metrobus when KB fell into difficulties with some of them. During 1998 route 181 was enhanced with a frequency increase and new standard low-floor Dart SLFs. No.743 is one of those normally to be found on the 181, seen here approaching its Lewisham terminus. *Colin Lloyd*

The Alexander bodied Volvo Olympian was acquired too late to ever become a standard vehicle with Metroline, and just thirty-eight eventually came into stock. The first batch was to replace acquired Titans on route 52, and AV 8 turns into Ladbroke Grove, closely followed by a Metrobus on the 302, a service that has been cut back short of this point since this picture was taken. Indeed, the 302 still covers what was in earlier times the northern half of a much longer 52. *Malc McDonald*

METROLINE

Metroline Holdings plc (Metroline Travel and Metroline London Northern),
118–122 College Road, Harrow, Middlesex, HA1 1DB

Metroline Travel was purchased by a management-led team on 7th October 1994. Very soon afterwards, on 28th November 1994, Atlas Bus was acquired from the Pullmans Group, together with route 52 and its 26 Leyland Titans, these soon moving to nearby Willesden garage. In June 1997, Metroline Holdings plc was floated on the Stock Exchange.

London Northern was purchased by MTL Trust Holdings of Liverpool on 26th October 1994. MTL then took over R&I Tours in October 1995, whilst by 1996 London Suburban Bus had come into MTL ownership by virtue of the takeover of its parent company Liverbus in Liverpool. By June 1996 both sets of acquired buses were absorbed into the MTL London fleet, and MTL's allover unrelieved red livery was soon adopted. The enlarged London Northern business was purchased by Metroline Holdings on 2nd July 1998, being ratified by 17th August. Within a matter of a couple of months, the Highgate offices were closed and the whole combined operations were run from Harrow.

Metroline's livery is red with a blue skirt but, although repainting of the former MTL fleet started soon after the take-over in 1998, even in early 2000 around 150 buses were still in unrelieved all-over red without fleetnames. The fleet operates from garages at Cricklewood, Edgware, Harrow Weald, Holloway, North Acton, North Wembley, Potters Bar and Willesden. Vehicles of the Contract Services fleet are based at Cricklewood, and the former Atlas Bus base at Harlesden is retained in reserve, whilst being used as a site to store withdrawn vehicles. Around two-dozen vehicles from Potters Bar garage are operated on a mix of commercial and county council contracted routes in southern Hertfordshire.

London Northern had a large stock of Metrobuses, although many were replaced during 1999. Nevertheless, plenty remain and the long trunk route 82 between Victoria and North Finchley is a stronghold of the type, worked by Potters Bar garage, about seven miles even further north of its outer terminus. M 1158 reaches journey's end at Victoria in July 1999.
Stephen Madden

Another Metrobus and another long trunk route – this time at the outer suburban end rather than in the West End. Route 113 is one of the few long London services that has not been curtailed, and still runs to its full traditional extent, aided no doubt by its long fast stretch along the A41 trunk road. M 956 arrives at Edgware and, unlike the route 82 vehicle, is in full proper Metroline garb. Both routes 82 and 113 were recently retained on re-tender by LT and may soon get new vehicles.
Tony Wilson

The blue skirt livery styling of Metroline is applied in a somewhat modest way on its Routemasters, as exemplified by RML 2649 at Piccadilly Circus on one of Willesden garage's two crew routes into the West End. The side route branding covers only a small section of route 6, but that is because it is the common section with route 98, Metroline's other Routemaster service. *Tony Wilson*

The former London Northern vehicles passed into the Metroline fold in July 1998 but, some eighteen months later, many of them remained in plain drab all-over red. Totally devoid of any relief colour, fleetname or even side adverts, RM 646 presents an unfortunately very down-market appearance on route 10 in Park Lane. *Stephen Madden*

Metroline's purchase of London Northern brought with it some commercial routes in Hertfordshire. The Scania double deckers, a rare type in London, form the allocation on Potters Bar garage's 84 connecting St Albans to Barnet, a route which in earlier years reached much further into Greater London. S 20 calls at London Colney in September 1999. *Tony Wilson*

The blue skirt livery and white fleetname has made a great improvement to the V class of Northern Counties Palatine II bodied Volvo Olympians, inherited from London Suburban Bus via London Northern. Now in their third livery in eight years of life, the class still carries the hard seats that can be seen in this view of V 204 at the Nag's Head, Holloway in October 1999. *Colin Brown*

Dennis Trident deliveries to Metroline in 1999 reached 117 examples, split roughly equally between Plaxton and Alexander bodywork. The latter went to Cricklewood and Harrow Weald garages for routes 16, 140 and 182 but several also appear on the 186, which is one of the original low floor routes of 1993/4 and which often needs a top-up to the LLWs otherwise used thereon. TA 112 turns into Edgware bus station on just such a duty. *Tony Wilson*

The slightly tinted windows on the Plaxton President bodied Tridents, and the use of black on the window and blind-box surrounds make for a somewhat dark picture but with fine contrast to the red, white and blue Metroline livery. Holloway garage now has sixty-five of these fine machines on routes 17, 43 and 134 (also 10 on Sundays) and TP 47 pauses on the Archway Road at Highgate in the mainly fine and sunny month of October 1999. *Colin Brown*

Metroline's first low floor route was the 186 dating back to 1994, and the LLW class of Dennis Lances continue to be the main allocation to date. LLW 34 leaves Edgware on its course in the Harrow direction. Unlike other single deck buses in the fleet, the Metroline fleetname is unusually displayed on the roof line. *Tony Wilson*

One of the original LT minibus routes back in 1972 was the H2. It linked the select Hampstead Garden Suburb with Golders Green Station – and still does – and has been expanded with H1 and H3 variations. The usual allocation is with three Optare MetroRiders and this unique Marshall bodied Mercedes-Benz 811D. All three MetroRiders must be operational on this day as MMS 269 is unusually performing on route 268 in this scene at Golders Green. *Colin Brown*

London Northern's sprightly MAN/ Marshall buses of the MM class are normally to be found on routes 46 and 95. As this book was prepared, just four of the twenty-four in stock had been treated to Metroline company livery, the rest remaining in all-over plain red. On the same August 1999 day as saw the appearance of the MB811D above, route 268 was also host to MM 260, thus providing another unusual sight at Golders Green for the lucky photographer. *Colin Brown*

As may be realised by the views in this book, plenty of the former London Northern buses are still all red. MV 253, one of the five MAN/ Optare Vectas inherited when London Northern took over R & I Buses in 1996, prepares to depart from Brent Cross bus station on route 112. This is a difficult route on which to maintain timekeeping due to the traffic congestion usually experienced on the North Circular Road and at the Hanger Lane gyratory system. *Colin Brown*

The MetroRider is a fairly rare type in London nowadays, although the high fleet number on this example gives a clue to the extent of the breed until fairly recently. Holloway garage still maintain eight of them, all in Metroline livery, for route W5 serving a tortuous series of back roads across Crouch End and Hornsey. However, there must have been a spare one on 25th June 1999 when MRL 213 could be found at Marble Arch on route 274, substituting for the normal Dart. *Stephen Madden*

Four Darts in the Metroline Contract Services fleet carry blue Tesco livery for free services on contract to the supermarket chain. These services are also one of the last few refuges of the earliest Dennis Darts in the DT class. Harrow Weald based DT 122 can usually be found on a service for the store at Pinner Green. *Geoff Rixon*

Seventy-nine Marshall bodied Dart SLFs of the DMS and DML classes came in 1998, and all are in the former London Northern area of Metroline. Most were taken to upgrade several LTB contract routes or to replace older and smaller midibuses such as the last StarRiders and the MW class of Wright bodied MB811Ds. One of the shorter examples, DMS 24, from a batch which replaced MWs, services Barnet's town service 384 in September 1999. *Colin Brown*

Lots of older Darts with the familiar Pointer bodywork can be found in all parts of London, although they have been eclipsed by the later wider low-floor version in recent years. Just about every main operator – and many of the smaller ones – have some of them, and Metroline is no exception. DRL 36 arrives at the Angel, Islington, the terminus of its cross-Camden journey on the 274, which began at Marble Arch and ran past London Zoo, the only LT bus route to do so. *Geoff Rixon*

Metroline, after its assumption of the businesses of several other operators in recent years, has probably one of the most varied fleets of buses in London, with over thirty distinctly different classes. The Northern Counties Paladin bodied Darts normally to be found on route C2 are now in their third livery, the present style being shown on DNL 115 at Oxford Circus. *Colin Lloyd*

The different lengths of Darts have resulted in bus companies having different ideas over how to classify them. Hence one outwardly identical bus can have a totally different coding from another. Metroline's 9.8 metre examples became the EDR (extended DR), the DRL code already having been used for the 9.0 metre version of the 8.5 metre DR. EDR 35 leaves Edgware on route 79, a route that only first saw the class in September 1999 as a result of a re-allocation between garages. *Tony Wilson*

Metroline seem to have had an extraordinarily difficult time in trying to match registration and fleet numbers, with many of the 1999 deliveries being very mixed. Many people rely on the registration to identify a bus at a distance, but they would get it wrong on DLD 117 leaving Brent Cross bus station on route 232. This route was converted from Metrobus to this latest version of the Dart SLF/ Plaxton Pointer 2 buses in the summer of 1999. *Colin Brown*

MITCHAM BELLE

Wimco Group Coaches Ltd, 223 Streatham Road, Mitcham, CR4 2AJ

A very old established coach company, which also specialises in transport for disabled people, won its first LT contract route with the 127 (Tooting & Purley) from 10th April 1999. In previous months, this route had been run by a succession of operators after Londonlinks were unable to continue. Most conveniently, the 127 runs past the garage, and twelve Dart SLFs are in stock to operate it. During June 2000 the company will take over routes 200 and 201 from London General, needing around another two dozen low floor single deckers.

Mitcham Belle is an old-established south London coach operator which won its first LTB contract route from 10th April 1999. Route 127 between Tooting and Purley had been worked by a succession of operators, several of them only temporarily, but soon settled to a much more reliable service under its new stewardship. A 'first day' shot of Dart SLF T152OGC in Carshalton shows the new order, although two more routes (200, 201) were due to join the company's portfolio in June 2000. *Geoff Rixon*

NOSTALGIABUS

Nostalgiabus, Unit 2, Riverside House, 43 Willow Lane, Mitcham, CR4 4NA

Originally set up with operations of vintage-type buses and coaches in mind, the company has been prolific on rail replacement services all over London and has helped out with emergency operations from time to time, notably with the infamous route 60 early in 1999. Routemasters, together with examples of vintage London buses of the RF and GS classes, are indeed operated on commercial and contracted services in Surrey. In London, the company work school journeys on routes 127 and 613, and Olympians are normally used thereon.

Above This company is well known for its 'vintage' fleet and also for its frequent appearance on rail replacement work all over London, and has these features in common with Blue Triangle. It runs a limited amount of LTB contract work, all on schoolday journeys, but also works commercial and schoolday journeys just over the London border in Surrey. RM 2180 crosses Epsom Downs on such a duty, here seen in the livery of its former owner, Timebus. *Gerald Mead*

Opposite Though carrying the poppy red colours of its original operator BTS of Borehamwood, and the inherited BT garage code, the RMLs on route 13 are actually run by Sovereign from Edgware garage. Still looking unchanged after several years, RML 2627 crosses Trafalgar Square in August 1999. As Sovereign do not have sufficient one-person double deckers, Metroline work the evening and Sunday service on the 13, giving an unusual (for London) mix of operators on the same route. *Stephen Madden*

SOVEREIGN

Sovereign Bus & Coach Co. Ltd and Sovereign Buses (London) Ltd, Babbage Road, Stevenage, Herts, SG1 2EQ

Sovereign Bus & Coach was established in January 1989, but now forms part of the Blazefield Group, set out into several small divisions. An associated 'Sovereign Harrow' operation was set up in December 1990 for newly-won locally-based LT contracts, using Mercedes-Benz minibuses. The independent coach company Borehamwood Travel Services dated from August 1984, and BTS ran LT route 292 from 1988 till November 1993, then losing it to Metroline. They also gained the contract to operate crew route 13 (Golders Green to Aldwych) using RMLs leased from London Buses, and later the 114 using Olympians. Blazefield Holdings, the owners of Sovereign, acquired BTS in August 1994 and the trading name was changed from BTS to London Sovereign in September 1996. In late April 1999 the Borehamwood depot was closed due to housing development, and buses were moved to the former London Buses garage at Edgware.

From 21st August 1999 the separate Operator's Licences for Sovereign Harrow and London Sovereign were replaced by one in the name of Sovereign Buses (London) Ltd, and all LT services were then under the same umbrella. As well as Edgware, part of this fleet continues to operate from the Venture garage at 331 Pinner Road, Harrow that had been in use for nearly nine years. However, a maintenance facility was created at Edgware, with Harrow becoming an outstation.

The RMLs on the 13 remain in BTS's poppy red livery, though those poppy red Olympians on the 114 are being gradually refurbished and repainted to Sovereign's blue and cream. These now match the revised version of blue and cream adopted by new Olympians purchased when route 292 was won back from 5th December 1998. Although three Mercedes-Benz remain from the once-large fleet for route 398, the rest of the north-west London fleet consists of 57 new Dart SLFs on routes H10, H11, H12, H13, H17 and 183. Some older Olympians work school journeys on routes 183,606 and 861, and three poppy red liveried Titans act as spares to all routes.

Opposite top At the beginning of 2000, the BTS poppy-red and yellow livery on the older Olympians used on route 114 between Mill Hill and Ruislip was being gradually replaced by the 'Coastliner' version as these vehicles gained internal refurbishment, following the regaining of the LTB route for a further term. No.50 is one of fourteen in the batch, and is seen at South Harrow. *Colin Brown*

Opposite bottom Sovereign has had a presence in Harrow since December 1990, but from 4th September 1999 they won more services, mostly at the expense of Metroline. This brought their London operation to a larger size than their whole operation in Hertfordshire. Fifty-seven brand-new Dart SLF/ Plaxton Pointer 2s were bought to serve the new contracts, and all but three of the Mercedes-Benz midibus fleet were replaced. No.512 represents this large fleet in Eastcote Lane, South Harrow. *Geoff Rixon*

Below Sovereign won route 292 back from 5th December 1998 and, due to the presence of speed humps and tables throughout Borehamwood, only standard floor buses could be operated. Thus what were very nearly the last such double deckers in the London area were introduced, together with the first appearance in Greater London of the fine livery inspired by the 'Yorkshire Coastliner' livery of another of the Blazefield Group's companies. No.64 has been re-registered since it was new, and is seen turning into Edgware bus station in October 1999. *Colin Brown*

QBS
Burnt Oak Queensbury Kenton
Harrow South Harrow Eastcote
RUISLIP STN
114
KANGOL
jD
SPORTS
114
SOVEREIGN
SOVEREIGN
H150 GGS
Leyland

SOVEREIGN
Harrow Weald Hatch End
Pinner Rayners Lane Stn
SOUTH HARROW STATION
H12
SOVEREIGN
DENNIS
PLAXTON
V512 JBH

Deliveries of the Alexander ALX400 bodied Dennis Trident topped 200 at the beginning of the year 2000, and was well on the way to becoming the largest type in the fleet later in the year, being set to take over this mantle from the Titan and Olympian. Early examples entered service in the first months of 1999, with Leyton and Bow garages being the first. Bow garage does not have a TA allocation intended for route 26, but nevertheless Tridents are frequently to be seen on this. TA 45 shows off its far-back positioned central exit door. Later deliveries of TAs have the wheelchair ramp situated there. *Colin Brown*

STAGECOACH

East London Bus & Coach Co. Ltd, 2–4 Clements Road, Ilford, Essex, IG1 1BA
South East London & Kent Bus Co. Ltd, 180 Bromley Road, London, SE26 2XA

Both East London and Selkent were purchased together by Stagecoach Holdings on 6th September 1994, taking a total of 1009 vehicles. Major fleet replacement has occurred in the short period since acquisition, with around 800 new and acquired buses replacing older types over that time. Stagecoach has actively cascaded most of these to other UK subsidiaries. Unlike most London companies where new buses have been almost always linked to new LT contracts, some of the new Stagecoach buses have converted several routes from older types, in the traditional London manner. Vehicles lost their white and grey relief very quickly under Stagecoach ownership, both through full and partial repaints, and gained Stagecoach logos on all-red. However from the end of 1994 East London Routemasters appeared with cream relief bands instead of white, and gold logos, while RMC 1461 has been beautifully restored to its original Green Line colours and appears in daily service on route 15. Selkent's driver training Titans carry corporate Stagecoach national livery. In July 1997 East London took over control of Docklands Transit following its purchase by Stagecoach Holdings, and full integration took place in October 1997.

Fleets of both 'Stagecoach London' companies are integrated under common management, have a common numbering sequence, and transfers north and south of the River occur quite frequently. East London garages are at Barking, Bow, Leyton, Romford, Stratford and Upton Park, and Selkent garages are at Bromley, Catford and Plumstead.

Left More typical of route 26 is the VA class of Alexander bodied Olympians which, like most of Stagecoach London's modern double deckers, are long wheelbase and of high capacity. These features are fairly unusual in London, but make it handy if or when they might be passed on to other provincial Stagecoach companies where such a size is more common. VA 60 is leaving the in-town terminus at Waterloo in June 1999. *Tony Wilson*

Right In a common numbering sequence with the VAs are the Northern Counties bodied VNs. Most of the longer VNs started life with East London and have since gravitated to Selkent, typifying the very common practice of mixing the fleets between the two Stagecoach companies. VN 157 turns out of Whitehall toward Westminster Bridge on the long route 53, which provides a three-to-four-minute peak-hour frequency as far out as Woolwich. *Stephen Madden*

Still a most numerous type, but rapidly declining with the advance of the Trident, is the long-serving Titan, and can be seen in both East London and Selkent territories. Stagecoach buses may be all-over plain unrelieved red, but their fairly frequent repaints mean that they invariably look smart. Selkent's T 771 travels through Dulwich. *Malc McDonald*

The largest concentration of the Scania N113 double decker is with East London. In February 2000 the single door variants were departing for provincial Stagecoach companies, which left just the forty dual-door Northern Counties examples, all based at Upton Park garage. Departing from Stratford, S 51 depicts the correct type on route 238, though the route is due to receive new low floor single-deck buses during summer 2000. *Colin Stannard*

Gold fleetnames, and even cream relief, bring a very traditional London Transport air to Stagecoach's Routemaster fleet. To this day the fleet includes three RMCs (including one in old Green Line colours), five standard RMs and the last RML of all, 2760, still preserved in original condition, and all of these 'specials' perform every weekday on route 15. Perhaps more typical is RML 2392 seen at Hyde Park Corner on route 8. *Stephen Madden*

Tridents of the second tranche delivered over the winter of 1999/2000 carry higher bodywork than the first batch, giving slightly better headroom. Sixty of them provide Selkent's first low floor double deck allocation, operating mainly on routes 96, 122, 177, 199 and 472. Those on the 96 provide the only low floor double deck service into the County of Kent. However, leaving North Greenwich is TA 140 on its way back to Thamesmead. *Colin Stannard*

Mercedes-Benz may have had great hopes for the Vario, but for most operators it has in practice been overtaken by the development of low floor midibus designs such as the Optare Solo and the 'MPD' Dart. The Vario thus remains a rare type in the London area, although Selkent have eighteen on routes 273, 380 and 386. MB 18 travels across lofty Blackheath on route 380, which provides a most circuitous link between Woolwich and Lewisham. *Colin Stannard*

The DAF/ Optare Delta was always a rare beast in London, and was one of the new single-deck bus types being developed in the early 1990s. None of these types ever really caught on in London, and those Deltas that did come all worked on the western and eastern outskirts. Those in the west have all gone, but East London's continue to provide the main service on routes 145 and 169. Delta DA 22 travels through Ilford on the 169. *Laurie Rufus*

A unique type in London is the LV class of twelve Plaxton Verde bodied Dennis Lances at Bromley garage. After some unhappy allocations, they finally found their niche when Kentish Bus gave up route 227 and Selkent took it over. The service needs single-deck buses because of a low bridge at Shortlands. LV 3 prepares to depart from Bromley North. *Colin Lloyd*

The London Buses 1994 experiment with low floor buses affected route 101, and the Scania variation (most were on Dennis Lance chassis) survives with East London, even though similar buses with Arriva left London in 1999. SLW 18 turns at East Ham Town Hall. *Colin Lloyd*

The Alexander Dash bodied Dennis Darts are to be found in small numbers in both East London and Selkent, those in the former having DAL prefix letters and in the latter plain non-prefixed numbers. Otherwise they are identical, and this one carries an incorrect number! Originally a '635' registration could not be obtained so the bus with the last registration of the batch (640) was slipped into the vacant 635 slot. Visual confusion so caused meant that it was subsequently renumbered 640 to match but even here in August 1999 it still had not been physically altered. *Colin Brown*

Stagecoach East London operate two services outside the LT route system to London City Airport, using blue buses from Liverpool Street and green ones from Canning Town. The former route originated with D&J International, a company which ceased operation in 1997. The class code of LCY 9 seen here at Aldgate is derived from the international air industry code (LCY) for London City Airport. *Stephen Madden*

There are lots of SLDs in Stagecoach London fleets, but don't be fooled into believing that they are all the same. There are short and long ones, single- and dual-door ones, some are Alexander and some are Plaxton-bodied. Other companies have lots of different class codes for minuscule differences, but here they are all combined! However, size, length and number of doors often seems to be ignored in day-to-day allocation, but short single-door SLD 79 is here on its correct service 291.
Geoff Rixon

The standard Plaxton Pointer Dart has been prolific in Stagecoach London fleets for some years but in 2000 many have been 'cascaded' onward to provincial Stagecoach companies. The last standard floor Darts delivered to a London company consisted of eighteen in October 1997 for route 106. One of this batch, PD 3, travels through Clapton on its busy course down to Whitechapel. *Colin Lloyd*

The once large class of Mercedes-Benz Optare StarRiders is now down to just seven, and all are with East London. They are kept for route 395 (renumbered from P14 in October 1999) which provides the sole link through the Rotherhithe Tunnel. The Tunnel has a restricted entrance which precludes anything wider than the SR at present. SR 2 exits from the cavernous and new Canada Water bus station south of the River in October 1999.
Colin Lloyd

Fourteen long Plaxton Pointer Dart SLFs entered service in January 1998 on route 235 between Brentford and Sunbury, and immediately presented a most professional image on the service. Restrained route branding is applied to many T-GM buses, and indeed it is rare to see any other than the 'dedicated' buses on any of their routes. R514SJM at Brentford heads back toward Sunbury, which will take it just into the county of Surrey. *Colin Stannard*

TELLINGS-GOLDEN MILLER

Tellings-Golden Miller Ltd, 20A Wintersells Road, Byfleet, Surrey, KT14 7LF
Capital Logistics Ltd, Heathrow Coach Centre, Sipson Road, West Drayton, Middx, UB7 0HN

In June 1985, Tellings Coaches of Byfleet took control of the local bus operations of Golden Miller of Feltham. Although there had been a brief operation on LT routes 116 and 117, it was not until April 1995 that the Tellings-Golden Miller company returned to LT tendered work in a small way with midibus route S3 in the Sutton area, followed by LT route 235 from January 1998.

Much change occurred in 1999, and once Arriva closed its Leatherhead garage from 1st May LT route 465 was handed over to T-GM together with seven Dart SLFs. Then from 3rd July Arriva's small Hounslow garage was closed, and another six LT routes with their various midibuses were taken over. All these buses came in the old London & Country fleet colours and to date the only change made has been to the fleetname. On 1st June 1999 Capital Logistics was sold to Tellings-Golden Miller and both then became constituents of the Status Bus & Coach Group, although both initially retained their trading identities. All this activity meant that five distinct bus liveries were evident! T-GM's normal fleet livery is blue and white with yellow relief.

The Capital Logistics arm of the group operates a large fleet of coaches at both Heathrow and Gatwick Airports, mainly for car park, aircrew and hotel contracts. The firm had themselves entered LT tendered bus work in a small way in August 1993 with LT route H26, and in 1998 LT routes U3, 726 and 60 were gained. However, the 60 was only taken up in its own right after several months of mayhem with a whole series of hired vehicles from many operators.

From 20th November 1999 route H20 came into the fold from London United and further United routes R68 and R70 were then won on LT tender, and were due to be taken up in summer 2000. Route 726 was to be re-equipped with new Volvo B10BLEs after T-GM had won the service on re-tender in their own right.

A series of misfortunes to befall the former London & Country operation in south-west London and north-west Surrey has seen route withdrawals, frequency cuts and garage closures. T-GM has been a main beneficiary and indeed has taken on several of the routes, together with most of the vehicles required. Still bearing L&C's familiar green and red colours, Dart SLF P290FPK carries prominent lettering for its new operator, in Kingston in September 1999. *Stephen Madden*

Two months after Leatherhead's route 465 passed to T-GM, the small Arriva (L&C) depot, along with the vehicles and routes, at Hounslow followed suit in July 1999. East Lancs Dart M523MPF (still displaying part of its former, and incorrect, fleet number), travels along Hounslow High Street on the circuitous H28 service which crosses the Great West Road four times along its course. *Stephen Madden*

Showing how individual vehicles are allocated to specific routes, Vario P703LCF arrives in Kingston on the 512, which is linked with 511 to provide handy connections between the Molesey and Esher areas and Kingston. The routes are contracted to Surrey County Council but have LT ticket availability on the section within the Royal Borough. *Colin Brown*

A picture that is unlikely to be able to be repeated within weeks of this book being published is this view of DAF/ Ikarus J806KHD. The '726 Expresslink' red and white livery dates from 1992 when the route was taken up by London Coaches. The vehicles went with the route when Capital Logistics later won the contract, and then that company was taken over by Tellings-Golden Miller in 1999. New Volvo B10BLEs were due to take over the service in spring 2000. *Stephen Madden*

After seven months of hired vehicles and service disruption, this company's new DAF DB250LFs eventually took over route 60 in March and April 1999. Both Optare Spectra and Plaxton President bodies were mounted, and both are to a fairly high internal specification. The full livery application of 'Connections' title and route branding was intended to be applied to the whole fleet, but the initial enthusiasm immediately waned and, one year further on, most of the buses had still not even received fleetnames. The only bus with full side branding is Spectra T125AUA, seen at Old Coulsdon in April 1999 – note the mistake on the blind whereby the terminal point at Old Coulsdon 'Tudor Rose' is depicted as a 'via' point; no-one has ever bothered to correct this. *Geoff Rixon*

More typical of buses on route 60 is this anonymous Plaxton President T131AUA in High Street, Croydon. Lest we are accused of criticism, more than two years after Arriva's assumption of South London Transport from Cowie, about half of their buses also continue to be similarly anonymous. Though introduced in a very low-key way, Capital Logistics' Presidents were in fact the first of the type to be ordered in the UK, and the first such to enter service. *Colin Brown*

Capital Logistics was a most enthusiastic bidder for LT services in 1998, but this was soured by experiences with route 60. Meanwhile, route U3 between Uxbridge and Heathrow was significantly upgraded from May 1998 with a batch of air-conditioned, double-glazed Optare Excels. R985EWU passes through Harmondsworth village in the first days of service. *David Stewart*

The combination of the various T-GM bus operations early in 2000 was characterised by the introduction of a batch of nine 'MPDs' to replace a selection of hired minibuses and some older MB709Ds. They are allocated to routes H20 and H26, the former a new T-GM and one-time London United route, and the latter a Capital Logistics service. V301MDP is at the Ivybridge Tesco terminal, displaying the temporary blind displays used in the route's first weeks. *Geoff Rixon*

Thorpe's are mainly known in London for their specialised work in the field of accessible transport. They operate the circular Stationlink service, hourly in each direction, SL1 clockwise and SL2 anti-clockwise, linking all main line stations with fully accessible Optare Excels. N200FET at the Angel, Islington is midway between King's Cross and Liverpool Street in this June 1999 scene. *Tony Wilson*

Since 26th September 1998, Thorpe's have operated one mainstream LT service, the 210 between Brent Cross and Finsbury Park which serves the picturesque Hampstead Heath and Highgate Village area on the way. Dart SLF S530JLM at the rather less picturesque Brent Cross shows off the unusual jagged-edge red and yellow colours on this batch of buses. *Laurie Rufus*

THORPE'S

F E Thorpe & Sons Ltd, 272 Latimer Road, North Kensington, London, W10 6QY

Frank E Thorpe & Sons Ltd started as a small private coach company back in 1968, with a fleet of coaches and minibuses on private hire, school and local authority contracts. The company moved into LT work in October 1992 with the winning of the central London inter-station route, marketed as Stationlink. Originally run with three Optare City Pacers, four Optare Excels were bought in 1996 and were the first of the type to appear on the streets of London. LT minibus route C4 (Putney Pier to Hurlingham) was gained from April 1995, and in August 1997 Thorpe took over the LT contracts of Javelin Coaches, Wandsworth with a large group of Mobility Bus routes in west and south-west London. A more mainstream service is route 210, taken over from Grey-Green in September 1998 with a new fleet of Dart SLFs. Vehicles carry a striking red and yellow livery, and a new larger operating base at Unit 5, Fourth Way on the Wembley Stadium trading estate houses the LT bus fleet.

This operator, Travel London being the trading name in this part of the world for Travel West Midlands, was the surprise winner of two central London routes in June 1998. Anyone familiar with TWM's livery can see the similarity of the application, although the colours are reversed to be mainly red for London. Short-length Optare Excel R418HWU rounds Parliament Square on the 211, a route which nowadays covers the former western part of the 11 beyond Fulham. *Geoff Rixon*

Travel London's second route is the C1 and, until Optare Solos were delivered in December 1998, it utilised Wright bodied Volvo B6LEs from parent TWM, and in their livery. As far as London is concerned, this is the only operator of the Solo thus far, so S233EWU buzzing about Victoria is of a rarer type than might be at first imagined. *Stephen Madden*

TRAVEL LONDON

Travel London, Stewarts Lane rail depot, off Dickens Lane, London SW8

Travel London is the trading name of Travel West Midlands in London, part of the National Express Group. They won two LT contract routes C1 and 211 which were taken up in June 1998. Optare Excels run the 211, and Optare Solos the C1, the latter being the only examples of their type in London. Buses are based at Stewarts Lane, but are under threat of moving due to local council pressure.

The last picture but not the least in this book is of Wing's Buses of Uxbridge. They were the last new entrant to the LT Buses tendered route arena in 1999 and thus turned out to be the last new bus operator in Greater London of the 1990s. The company itself has been around for very many years but has always concentrated on coaching and minibus hire. For route U7 they set up a subsidiary – Wing's Buses – and bought three East Lancs Spryte bodied Dart SLFs. Being so far out from central London there was no need for an 80% red livery, so this unusual scheme was a welcome breath of fresh air. V338MBV is at the Charville Lane end of the route in November 1999, but since this picture was obtained the three Darts have acquired fleet numbers, this one being WB 3. *Colin Brown*

WING'S

Wing's Buses Ltd, 127 Waterloo Road, Uxbridge, Middlesex, UB8 2QZ.

The long established coach and minibus firm of Wing's Luxury Travel won its first LT contract route in 1999, taking up the short U7 route from 13th November. Bus subsidiary Wing's Buses was set up to operate the fleet, which consists of three East Lancs bodied Dart SLFs in an unusual three-colour scheme, contrasting with the mainly white coach livery. A further LT service has been won from April 2000, being a link (numbered H50) between Hayes and West Drayton via Stockley Park. This has been specified for air conditioned accessible buses with refinement such as tinted windows and audio-visual passenger information on board. At present, buses operate from the Waterloo Road depot.

TYPE TOTALS

Double Deck Buses

AEC Routemasters	607
AEC Regent(RV)	1
AEC Regent(RT)	4
DAF/Alexander ALX400	158
DAF/Northern Counties	35
DAF/Plaxton President	30
Daimler Fleetline	1
Dennis Arrow/East Lancs	39
Dennis Arrow/Northern Counties	16
Dennis Dominator/Alexander	1
Dennis Dominator/East Lancs	15
Dennis Dominator/Northern Counties	25
Dennis Trident/Alexander ALX400	302
Dennis Trident/East Lancs	24
Dennis Trident/Plaxton President	195
Leyland Atlantean	1
Leyland Titan	429
MCW Metrobus	1110
Optare Spectra	29
Scania/Alexander	10
Scania/Northern Counties	49
Volvo B10M/East Lancs	9
Volvo Citybus/Alexander	49
Volvo Citybus/East Lancs	7
Volvo Citybus/Northern Counties	39
Volvo B7L/Alexander ALX400	46
Volvo B7L/Plaxton President	40

Olympians

Volvo or Leyland /Alexander	229
Volvo or Leyland/Alexander Royale	28
Volvo or Leyland/ECW	167
Volvo or Leyland/East Lancs	74
Volvo or Leyland/Leyland	76
Volvo or Leyland/Northern Counties	538
Volvo or Leyland/Optare	1
Leyland/Roe	4

Single Deck Buses

AEC Regal	1
DAF/East Lancs Myllennium	17
DAF/Ikarus	22
DAF/Optare Delta	29

Dennis Darts

Alexander 9.4m	57
Alexander 9.8m	18
Alexander 10.2m	147
Caetano 10.6m	34
Carlyle 8.5m	31
Duple 8.5m	49
Duple/Carlyle 9m	6
East Lancs 9m	18
East Lancs 10.3m	16
Marshall 8.9m	53
Marshall 9m	4
Marshall 9.3m	185
Marshall 9.8m	3
Marshall 10.2m	167
Northern Counties 9m	65
Plaxton 8.5m	140
Plaxton 8.8m	45
Plaxton 9m	257
Plaxton 9.2m	31
Plaxton 9.3m	39
Plaxton 9.8m	287
Plaxton 10m	134
Plaxton 10.1m	274
Plaxton 10.2m	10
Plaxton 10.6m	47
Plaxton 10.7m	157
Reeve Burgess 8.5	19
Wadham Stringer 9m	3
Wright 8.5m	68
Wright 9m	16
Wright 10.2m	8
Dennis Lance/Alexander	1
Dennis Lance/East Lancs	10
Dennis Lance/Northern Counties	27
Dennis Lance/Plaxton	12
Dennis Lance/Wright	39
Leyland Lynx	21
Leyland National	22
Leyland National Greenway	42
MAN/Marshall	24
MAN/Optare Vectra	13
Marshall Minibus	1
Optare Excel	78
Scania/Van Hool	1
Scania/Wright	16
Volvo B6/Alexander	10
Volvo B6BLE/Wright	19
Volvo B10BLE/Alexander ALX300	7

Minibuses

Fiat/Ducato	4
Freight-Rover/Carlyle	1
Iveco/LHE	1
Iveco/Marshall	4
Iveco/Robin Hood	1
LDV/Crystals	3
MCW Metrorider	7
Mercedes-Benz/Alexander	8
Mercedes-Benz/Crystals	12
Mercedes-Benz/Dormobile	5
Mercedes-Benz/Made-to-Measure	1
Mercedes-Benz/Marshall	12
Mercedes-Benz/Onyx	1
Mercedes-Benz/Phoenix	1
Mercedes-Benz/Plaxton	117
Mercedes-Benz/Reeve Burgess	35
Mercedes-Benz/Robin Hood	4
Mercedes-Benz/U.V.G	3
Mercedes-Benz/Wadham Stringer	6
Mercedes-Benz/Whittaker	1
Mercedes-Benz/Wright	12
Optare MetroRider	64
Optare Solo	10
Optare StarRider	9
Renault-Dodge/Plaxton	3
Renault-Dodge/Wadham Stringer	1

FLEET LISTS

Standard body codes are used in the following fleet lists, showing the body type, seating capacity and entrance position in that order.

Body Type	Single-deck bus	B
	Single-deck coach	C
	Convertible open-top double-deck bus	CO
	Dual-purpose vehicle	DP
	Dual-purpose double-deck vehicle	DPH
	Highbridge double-deck bus	H
	Open-top double-deck bus	O
	Partial open-top double-deck bus	PO
	The further prefix 'F' is used for full-fronted vehicles where this is not normal for the type.	
Seating capacity	For double-deckers the upper-deck capacity is shown first, followed by that for the lower deck. Standee capacities have not been shown as there are sometimes local variations between the licensed capacity of a vehicle and the operational capacity agreed with road staff.	
Seating position	Separate entrance and exit (front and centre) with doors	D
	Front entrance with platform doors	F
	Rear entrance without doors	R
	Rear entrance with platform doors	RD
	The further suffix 'L' indicates a vehicle fitted with a wheelchair tail-lift.	
Fleet number suffixes	Vehicle restricted to staff bus duties	s
	Vehicle restricted to training work	t
	Vehicle unlicensed long-term	u
	Withdrawn	w

AIRLINKS (LT fleet only)

	Volvo Olympian YN3RV18Z4		Alexander Royale	DPH43/9FL	1995/6
N112 UHP	N116 UHP	N120 UHP	N124 YRW	N128 YRW	
N113 UHP	N117 UHP	N121 UHP	N125 YRW	N129 YRW	
N114 UHP	N118 UHP	N122 UHP	N126 YRW	N130 YRW	
N115 UHP	N119 UHP	N123 UHP	N127 YRW		

	Dennis Dart SLF SFD322AR1WGW1		Plaxton Pointer 2 10.7m	B33D	1999
T71 WWV	T73 WWV	T75 WWV			
T72 WWV	T74 WWV	T76 WWV			

ARMCHAIR

MUH 289Xt	Leyland Olympian ONLXB/1R		Eastern Coach Works	H45/32F	1982

	Leyland Olympian ONCL10/1RZ		Alexander RL	H47/30F	1990
G361 YUR	G364 YUR	G368 YUR	G371 YUR		
G362 YUR	G365 YUR	G369 YUR	G372 YUR		
G363 YUR	G366 YUR	G370 YUR			

	Leyland Olympian ON2R50C13Z4		Leyland	H47/31F	1991
H546 GKX	H550 GKX	H554 GKX	H559 GKX		
H547 GKX	H551 GKX	H556 GKX	H561 GKX		
H548 GKX	H552 GKX	H557 GKX	H562 GKX		
H549 GKX	H553 GKX	H558 GKX	H563 GKX		

	Dennis Dart SFD412BR5TGD1		Plaxton Pointer 9.8m	B37F	1996
P27 MLE	P31 MLE	P35 MLE	P157 MLE	P160 MLE	
P28 MLE	P32 MLE	P154 MLE	P158 MLE		
P29 MLE	P34 MLE	P156 MLE	P159 MLE		

	Dennis Dart SLF SFD212BR1TGW1		Plaxton Pointer 10m	B35F	1997
P675 RWU	P680 RWU	P685 RWU	P690 RWU	P695 RWU	
P676 RWU	P681 RWU	P686 RWU	P691 RWU	P696 RWU	
P677 RWU	P682 RWU	P687 RWU	P692 RWU	P697 RWU	
P678 RWU	P683 RWU	P688 RWU	P693 RWU	P698 RWU	
P679 RWU	P684 RWU	P689 RWU	P694 RWU	P699 RWU	

	Volvo Olympian OLY–4953		Northern Counties Palatine II	H47/29F	1997/8
R417 SOY	R419 SOY	R780 SOY	R782 SOY		
R418 SOY	R420 SOY	R781 SOY			

T549 HNH	Dennis Dart SLF SFD612BR1XGW1		Plaxton Pointer 2 8.8m	B29F	1999

	Dennis Dart SLF SFD212BR1WGW (T152 AUA is SLF SFD212BR1XGW1)		Alexander ALX200 10.2m	B27D	1999
T140 AUA	T143 AUA	T146 AUA	T149 AUA	T152 AUA	
T141 AUA	T144 AUA	T147 AUA	T150 AUA		
T142 AUA	T145 AUA	T148 AUA	T151 AUA		

ARRIVA EAST HERTS & ESSEX

Vehicles listed below are those most likely to appear on LT supported services. Additional vehicles of similar types will be seen on peripheral routes in the Waltham Cross, Loughton and Romford areas.

2186–2193		Mercedes-Benz O810 Vario			Plaxton Beaver 2			B27F	1997
2186	R186 DNM	**2188**	R188 DNM	**2190**	R190 DNM	**2192**	R192 DNM		
2187	R187 DNM	**2189**	R189 DNM	**2191**	R191 DNM	**2193**	R193 DNM		

2224	L424 CPB	Mercedes-Benz 709D	Dormobile	B25F	1993
2243	R763 DUB	Mercedes-Benz O810 Vario	Plaxton Beaver 2	B27F	1997

2311–2318		Mercedes-Benz 709D * 2311 is Reeve Burgess Beaver			* Plaxton Beaver			B23F	1989–92
2311	G926 WGS	**2314**	J934 WHJ	**2316**	J936 WHJ	**2318**	J938 WHJ		
2313	J933 WHJ	**2315**	J935 WHJ	**2317**	J937 WHJ				

3388	P258 FPK	Dennis Dart SLF SFD322	Plaxton Pointer 10.6m	B39F	1997
3389	P259 FPK	Dennis Dart SLF SFD322	Plaxton Pointer 10.6m	B39F	1997
3390	P260 FPK	Dennis Dart SLF SFD322	Plaxton Pointer 10.6m	B39F	1997

3404–14		Dennis Dart SFD212BR5TGD2			Plaxton Pointer 9m			B34F	1996
3404	P324 HVX	**3407**	P327 HVX	**3410**	P330 HVX	**3413**	P833 HVX		
3405	P325 HVX	**3408**	P328 HVX	**3411**	P331 HVX	**3414**	P334 HVX		
3406	P326 HVX	**3409**	P329 HVX	**3412**	P332 HVX				

3461–3481		Dennis Dart SLF SFD112			Alexander ALX200 9.4m			B..F	2000
3461	W461 XKX	**3465**	W465 XKX	**3469**	W469 XKX	**3474**	W474 XKX	**3478**	W478 XKX
3462	W462 XKX	**3466**	W466 XKX	**3471**	W471 XKX	**3475**	W475 XKX	**3479**	W479 XKX
3463	W463 XKX	**3467**	W567 XKX	**3472**	W472 XKX	**3476**	W476 XKX	**3481**	W481 XKX
3464	W464 XKX	**3468**	W468 XKX	**3473**	W473 XKX	**3477**	W477 XKX		

3421–31		Dennis Dart SLF SFD322BR1TGW1			Plaxton Pointer 10.6m			B43F	1996
3421	P421 HVX	**3424**	P424 HVX	**3426**	P426 HVX	**3428**	P428 HVX	**3431**	P431 HVX
3422	P423 HVX	**3425**	P425 HVX	**3427**	P427 HVX	**3429**	P429 HVX		

4335–39		DAF SB220LC550			Ikarus Citibus			B48F	1992
4335	J56 GCX	**4336**	J926 CYL	**4337**	J927 CYL	**4339**	K124 TCP		

5250	BYX 240V	MCW Metrobus DR101/12	MCW	H43/30F	1980
5251	KYV 681X	MCW Metrobus DR101/14	MCW	H43/30F	1981
5252	KYO 612X	MCW Metrobus DR101/14	MCW	H43/30F	1981
5253	B283 WUL	MCW Metrobus DR101/17	MCW	H43/30F	1985
5255	B155 WUL	MCW Metrobus DR101/17	MCW	H43/30F	1985
5269	B169 WUL	MCW Metrobus DR101/17	MCW	H43/30F	1985
5348	KYV 786X	MCW Metrobus DR101/14	MCW	H43/30F	1982
5349	GYE 419W	MCW Metrobus DR101/12	MCW	H43/30F	1980
5353	GYE 493W	MCW Metrobus DR101/12	MCW	H43/30F	1980
5363	BYX 233V	MCW Metrobus DR101/12	MCW	H43/30F	1980
5367	GYE 508W	MCW Metrobus DR101/14	MCW	H43/30F	1981
5370	A988 SYF	MCW Metrobus DR101/17	MCW	H43/30F	1984
—	BYX 230V	MCW Metrobus DR101/12	MCW	H43/30F	1980
—	BYX 290V	MCW Metrobus DR101/12	MCW	H43/30F	1980
—	KYV 771X	MCW Metrobus DR101/14	MCW	H43/30F	1982

ARRIVA LONDON

Arriva London North (including Leaside Travel), Arriva London North East and Arriva London South

ADL 1–23 Dennis Dart SLF SFD322BR1XGW1 — Alexander ALX200 10.8m* — * B33D — 1999/2000
* ADL 1–8 are 10.2m and B27D

ADL 1	V701 LWT	**ADL 6**	V606 LGC	**ADL 11**	V611 LGC	**ADL 16**	V616 LGC	**ADL 21**	V621 LGC
ADL 2	V602 LGC	**ADL 7**	V607 LGC	**ADL 12**	V612 LGC	**ADL 17**	V617 LGC	**ADL 22**	V622 LGC
ADL 3	V603 LGC	**ADL 8**	V608 LGC	**ADL 13**	V613 LGC	**ADL 18**	V618 LGC	**ADL 23**	V623 LGC
ADL 4	V604 LGC	**ADL 9**	V609 LGC	**ADL 14**	V614 LGC	**ADL 19**	V619 LGC		
ADL 5	V605 LGC	**ADL 10**	V610 LGC	**ADL 15**	V615 LGC	**ADL 20**	V620 LGC		

AN 262t	KPJ 262W	Leyland Atlantean AN68B/1R	Roe	H43/30F	1981

DBS 1–11 DAF DB250RS505 — Northern Counties Palatine II — H47/30F — 1995

DBS 1	N601 DWY	**DBS 4**	N604 DWY	**DBS 7**	N607 DWY	**DBS 10**	N610 DWY
DBS 2	N602 DWY	**DBS 5**	N605 DWY	**DBS 8**	N608 DWY	**DBS 11**	N611 DWY
DBS 3	N603 DWY	**DBS 6**	N606 DWY	**DBS 9**	N609 DWY		

DBS 12	N612 DWY	DAF DE02RSDB250	Northern Counties Palatine II	H47/30F	1995
DBS 13	N613 DWY	DAF DE02RSDB250	Northern Counties Palatine II	H47/30F	1995
DBS 14	R213 CKO	DAF DE23RSDB250	Northern Counties Palatine II	H43/24D	1998
DBS 15	V715 LWT	DAF DB250RS505	Northern Counties Palatine II	H43/24D	1999

DDL 1–18 Dennis Dart SLF SFD212BR1WGW1 — Plaxton Pointer 2 10.1m — B26D — 1998

DDL 1	S301 JUA	**DDL 5**	S305 JUA	**DDL 9**	S309 JUA	**DDL 13**	S313 JUA	**DDL 17**	S317 JUA
DDL 2	S302 JUA	**DDL 6**	S306 JUA	**DDL 10**	S310 JUA	**DDL 14**	S314 JUA	**DDL 18**	S318 JUA
DDL 3	S303 JUA	**DDL 7**	S307 JUA	**DDL 11**	S311 JUA	**DDL 15**	S315 JUA		
DDL 4	S304 JUA	**DDL 8**	S308 JUA	**DDL 12**	S312 JUA	**DDL 16**	S316 JUA		

DI 4†	P754 RWU	DAF DE33WSSB3000	Ikarus 396	C53F	1997
DIB 1	J929 CYL	DAF SB220LC550	Ikarus Citibus	B48F	1992
DIB 2	J930 CYL	DAF SB220LC550	Ikarus Citibus	B48F	1992
DIB 3	J931 CYL	DAF SB220LC550	Ikarus Citibus	B48F	1992
DIB 4	J413 NCP	DAF SB220LC550	Ikarus Citibus	B48F	1992
DIB 5	J414 NCP	DAF SB220LC550	Ikarus Citibus	B48F	1992

DL 10–19 Dennis Lance 11SDA3113 — East Lancs EL2000 — B49F — 1996

DL 10	N210 TPK	**DL 12**	N212 TPK	**DL 14**	N214 TPK	**DL 16**	N216 TPK	**DL 18**	N218 TPK
DL 11	N211 TPK	**DL 13**	N213 TPK	**DL 15**	N215 TPK	**DL 17**	N217 TPK	**DL 19**	N219 TPK

DLA 1–125 DAF DE02RSDB250 — Alexander ALX400 10.6m — H45/17D* — 1998–99
* DLA 22, 23 and 25 are H45/21D with more examples currently being converted.

Arriva London North East vehicles carry fleet numbers to match their registrations rather than class letters.

DLA 1	R101 GNW	**DLA 13**	S213 JUA	**DLA 25**	S225 JUA	**DLA 37**	S237 JUA	**DLA 49**	S249 JUA
DLA 2	S202 JUA	**DLA 14**	S214 JUA	**DLA 26**	S226 JUA	**238**	S238 JUA	**DLA 50**	S250 JUA
DLA 3	S203 JUA	**DLA 15**	S215 JUA	**DLA 27**	S227 JUA	**239**	S239 JUA	**DLA 51**	S251 JUA
DLA 4	S204 JUA	**DLA 16**	S216 JUA	**DLA 28**	S228 JUA	**240**	S240 JUA	**DLA 52**	S252 JUA
DLA 5	S205 JUA	**DLA 17**	S217 JUA	**DLA 29**	S229 JUA	**241**	S241 JUA	**DLA 53**	S253 JUA
DLA 6	S206 JUA	**DLA 18**	S218 JUA	**DLA 30**	S230 JUA	**242**	S242 JUA	**DLA 54**	S254 JUA
DLA 7	S207 JUA	**DLA 19**	S219 JUA	**DLA 31**	S231 JUA	**243**	S243 JUA	**DLA 55**	S255 JUA
DLA 8	S208 JUA	**DLA 20**	S220 JUA	**DLA 32**	S232 JUA	**244**	S244 JUA	**DLA 56**	S256 JUA
DLA 9	S209 JUA	**DLA 21**	S221 JUA	**DLA 33**	S233 JUA	**245**	S245 JUA	**DLA 57**	S257 JUA
DLA 10	S210 JUA	**DLA 22**	S322 JUA	**DLA 34**	S234 JUA	**246**	S246 JUA	**DLA 58**	S258 JUA
DLA 11	S211 JUA	**DLA 23**	S223 JUA	**DLA 35**	S235 JUA	**247**	S247 JUA	**DLA 59**	S259 JUA
DLA 12	S212 JUA	**DLA 24**	S224 JUA	**DLA 36**	S236 JUA	**DLA 48**	S248 JUA	**DLA 60**	S260 JUA

DLA 61	S261 JUA	**DLA 74**	S274 JUA	**DLA 87**	S287 JUA	**300**	T110 GGO	**313**	T313 FGN
DLA 62	S262 JUA	**DLA 75**	S275 JUA	**DLA 88**	S288 JUA	**301**	T301 FGN	**314**	T314 FGN
DLA 63	S263 JUA	**DLA 76**	S276 JUA	**DLA 89**	S289 JUA	**302**	T302 FGN	**315**	T315 FGN
DLA 64	S264 JUA	**DLA 77**	S277 JUA	**DLA 90**	S290 JUA	**303**	T303 FGN	**DLA 116**	T316 FGN
DLA 65	S265 JUA	**DLA 78**	S278 JUA	**DLA 91**	S291 JUA	**304**	T304 FGN	**DLA 117**	T317 FGN
DLA 66	S266 JUA	**DLA 79**	S279 JUA	**DLA 92**	S292 JUA	**305**	T305 FGN	**DLA 118**	T318 FGN
DLA 67	S267 JUA	**DLA 80**	S280 JUA	**DLA 93**	T293 FGN	**306**	T306 FGN	**DLA 119**	T319 FGN
DLA 68	S268 JUA	**DLA 81**	S281 JUA	**DLA 94**	T294 FGN	**307**	T307 FGN	**DLA 120**	T320 FGN
DLA 69	S269 JUA	**DLA 82**	S282 JUA	**DLA 95**	T295 FGN	**308**	T308 FGN	**DLA 121**	T421 GGO
DLA 70	S270 JUA	**DLA 83**	S283 JUA	**DLA 96**	T296 FGN	**309**	T309 FGN	**DLA 122**	T322 FGN
DLA 71	S271 JUA	**DLA 84**	S284 JUA	**297**	T297 FGN	**310**	T310 FGN	**DLA 123**	T323 FGN
DLA 72	S272 JUA	**DLA 85**	S285 JUA	**298**	T298 FGN	**311**	T311 FGN	**DLA 124**	99 D 53451
DLA 73	S273 JUA	**DLA 86**	S286 JUA	**299**	T299 FGN	**312**	T312 FGN	**DLA 125**	99 D 53440

Note:– At the time of writing, no decision had been made as to whether DLAs 124 and 125 would be taken into stock after a six month loan for evaluation by Dublin Bus.

DLA 126–189 DAF DE02RSDB250 Alexander ALX400 10.2m H43/21D 1999–2000

DLA 126	V326 DGT	**DLA 146**	V346 DGT	**DLA 166**		**DLA 186**		**DLA 206**	
DLA 127	V327 DGT	**DLA 147**	V347 DGT	**DLA 167**		**DLA 187**		**DLA 207**	
DLA 128	V628 LGC	**DLA 148**	V348 DGT	**DLA 168**		**DLA 188**		**DLA 208**	
DLA 129	V329 DGT	**DLA 149**	V349 DGT	**DLA 169**		**DLA 189**		**DLA 209**	
DLA 130	V330 DGT	**DLA 150**	V650 LGC	**DLA 170**		**DLA 190**		**DLA 210**	
DLA 131	V331 DGT	**DLA 151**	V351 DGT	**DLA 171**		**DLA 191**		**DLA 211**	
DLA 132	V332 DGT	**DLA 152**	V352 DGT	**DLA 172**		**DLA 192**		**DLA 212**	
DLA 133	V633 LGC	**DLA 153**	V353 DGT	**DLA 173**		**DLA 193**		**DLA 213**	
DLA 134	V334 DGT	**DLA 154**	V354 DGT	**DLA 174**		**DLA 194**		**DLA 214**	
DLA 135	V335 DGT	**DLA 155**	V355 DGT	**DLA 175**		**DLA 195**		**DLA 215**	
DLA 136	V336 DGT	**DLA 156**	V356 DGT	**DLA 176**		**DLA 196**		**DLA 216**	
DLA 137	V337 DGT	**DLA 157**	V357 DGT	**DLA 177**		**DLA 197**		**DLA 217**	
DLA 138	V338 DGT	**DLA 158**	V358 DGT	**DLA 178**		**DLA 198**		**DLA 218**	
DLA 139	V339 DGT	**DLA 159**		**DLA 179**		**DLA 199**		**DLA 219**	
DLA 140	V640 LGC	**DLA 160**		**DLA 180**		**DLA 200**		**DLA 222**	
DLA 141	V341 DGT	**DLA 161**		**DLA 181**		**DLA 201**		**DLA 221**	
DLA 142	V342 DGT	**DLA 162**		**DLA 182**		**DLA 202**		**DLA 222**	
DLA 143	V343 DGT	**DLA 163**		**DLA 183**		**DLA 203**		**DLA 223**	
DLA 144	V344 DGT	**DLA 164**		**DLA 184**		**DLA 204**			
DLA 145	V345 DGT	**DLA 165**		**DLA 185**		**DLA 205**			

DLP 1–20 DAF DE02RSDB250 Plaxton President 10.5m H45/19D 1998/9

DLP 1	V601 LGC	**DLP 5**	T205 XBV	**DLP 9**	T209 XBV	**DLP 13**	T213 XBV	**DLP 17**	T217 XBV
DLP 2	T202 XBV	**DLP 6**	T206 XBV	**DLP 10**	T210 XBV	**DLP 14**	T214 XBV	**DLP 18**	T218 XBV
DLP 3	T203 XBV	**DLP 7**	T207 XBV	**DLP 11**	T211 XBV	**DLP 15**	T215 XBV	**DLP 19**	T219 XBV
DLP 4	T204 XBV	**DLP 8**	T208 XBV	**DLP 12**	T212 XBV	**DLP 16**	T216 XBV	**DLP 20**	T220 XBV

DP3†	P753 RWU	DAF DE33WSSB3000	Plaxton Premiere 350	C53F	1997
DP 160	M160 SKR	Dennis Dart 9SDL3053	Plaxton Pointer 9m	B35F	1995
DP 161	M161 SKR	Dennis Dart 9SDL3053	Plaxton Pointer 9m	B35F	1995
DP 162	M162 SKR	Dennis Dart 9SDL3053	Plaxton Pointer 9m	B35F	1995
DP 163	M163 SKR	Dennis Dart 9SDL3053	Plaxton Pointer 9m	B35F	1995

DP 301–313 Dennis Dart 9SDL3002* Plaxton Pointer 9m B35F 1991
* DP 302–7 & 313 are 9SDL3011

DP 301	J301 WHJ	**DP 304**	J304 WHJ	**DP 307**	J307 WHJ	**DP 310**	J310 WHJ	**DP 313**	J313 WHJ
DP 302	J302 WHJ	**DP 305**	J305 WHJ	**DP 308**	J308 WHJ	**DP 311**	J311 WHJ		
DP 303	J303 WHJ	**DP 306**	J306 WHJ	**DP 309**	J309 WHJ	**DP 312**	J312 WHJ		

DPL 1†	N551 LUA	DAF DE33WSSB3000	Plaxton Premiere 350	C49FT	1996
DPL 2†	N552 LUA	DAF DE33WSSB3000	Plaxton Premiere 350	C49FT	1996

DPP 416–431 Dennis Dart SLF SFD212BR1VGW1 Plaxton Pointer 10m B36F 1997

DPP 416	R416 COO	**DPP 420**	R420 COO	**DPP 424**	R424 COO	**DPP 428**	R428 COO
DPP 417	R417 COO	**DPP 421**	R421 COO	**DPP 425**	R425 COO	**DPP 429**	R429 COO
DPP 418	R418 COO	**DPP 422**	R422 COO	**DPP 426**	R426 COO	**DPP 430**	R430 COO
DPP 419	R419 COO	**DPP 423**	R423 COO	**DPP 427**	R427 COO	**DPP 431**	R431 COO

DR 28–31 Dennis Dart 8.5SDL3003 Plaxton Pointer 8.5m B28F 1991

DR 28	H128 THE	**DR 29**	H129 THE	**DR 30**	H130 THE	**DR 31**	H131 THE

DRL 38–52 Dennis Dart 9SDL3016 Plaxton Pointer 9m B34F 1992

DRL 38	K538 ORH	**DRL 41**	K541 ORH	**DRL 44**	K544 ORH	**DRL 47**	K547 ORH	**DRL 50**	K550 ORH
DRL 39	K539 ORH	**DRL 42**	K542 ORH	**DRL 45**	K545 ORH	**DRL 48**	K548 ORH	**DRL 51**	K551 ORH
DRL 40	K540 ORH	**DRL 43**	K543 ORH	**DRL 46**	K546 ORH	**DRL 49**	K549 ORH	**DRL 52**	K552 ORH

DRL 147–158 Dennis Dart 9SDL3024 Plaxton Pointer 9m B34F 1993

DRL 147	L247 WAG	**DRL 150**	L150 WAG	**DRL 153**	L153 WAG	**DRL 156**	L156 WAG
DRL 148	L148 WAG	**DRL 151**	L151 WAG	**DRL 154**	L154 WAG	**DRL 157**	L157 WAG
DRL 149	L149 WAG	**DRL 152**	L152 WAG	**DRL 155**	L155 WAG	**DRL 158**	L158 WAG

DRL 201–212 Dennis Dart 9SDL3053 Plaxton Pointer 9m B34F 1995

DRL 201	N701 GUM	**DRL 204**	N704 GUM	**DRL 207**	N707 GUM	**DRL 210**	N710 GUM
DRL 202	N702 GUM	**DRL 205**	N705 GUM	**DRL 208**	N708 GUM	**DRL 211**	N711 GUM
DRL 203	N703 GUM	**DRL 206**	N706 GUM	**DRL 209**	N709 GUM	**DRL 212**	N712 GUM

DRL 213–218 Dennis Dart SLF SFD212BR5TGD1 Plaxton Pointer 9.2m B34F 1996

DRL 213	P913 PWW	**DRL 215**	P915 PWW	**DRL 217**	P917 PWW
DRL 214	P914 PWW	**DRL 216**	P916 PWW	**DRL 218**	P918 PWW

DRN 115–119 Dennis Dart 9SDL3034 Northern Counties Paladin 9m B35F 1994

DRN 115	L115 YVK	**DRN 117**	L117 YVK	**DRN 119**	L119 YVK	**DRN 124**	L124 YVK
DRN 116	L116 YVK	**DRN 118**	L118 YVK	**DRN 122**	L122 VYK		

DS 120–151 Dennis Dart 9SDL3034 Northern Counties Paladin 9m B35F 1994

DS 120	L120 YVK	**DS 123**	L123 YVK	**DS 126**	L126 YVK
DS 121	L121 YVK	**DS 125**	L125 YVK	**DS 151**	L151 YVK

DT 59	H459 UGO	Dennis Dart 8.5SDL3003	Carlyle Dartline 8.5m	B28F	1990
DT 64	H464 UGO	Dennis Dart 8.5SDL3003	Carlyle Dartline 8.5m	B28F	1990
DVH 5†	G905 TYR	DAF MB230LB615	Van Hool Alizee H	C53F	1990
DVH 6†	G906 TYR	DAF MB230LB615	Van Hool Alizee H	C53F	1990
DVH 7†	G907 TYR	DAF MB230LB615	Van Hool Alizee H	C53F	1990
DVH 8†	G908 TYR	DAF MB230LB615	Van Hool Alizee H	C49FT	1990
DW 314	J314 XVX	Dennis Dart 9SDL3011	Wright Handybus 9m	B35F	1992
DW 315	J315 XVX	Dennis Dart 9SDL3011	Wright Handybus 9m	B35F	1992

L 1	A101 SYE	Leyland Olympian ONTL11/1R	Eastern Coach Works	H47/28D	1984
L 2	A102 SYE	Leyland Olympian ONLXB/1R	Eastern Coach Works	H47/28D	1984
L 3	A103 SYE	Leyland Olympian ONLXB/1R	Eastern Coach Works	H47/28D	1984

L 4–259	Leyland Olympian ONLXB/1RH * 166–171 & 189 are DPH42/26D	Eastern Coach Works	H42/26D*	1986–87

L 4	C804 BYY	**L 63**	C63 CHM	**L 166**	D166 FYM	**L 198**	D198 FYM	**L 230**	D230 FYM
L 5	C805 BYY	**L 65**	C65 CHM	**L 167**	D167 FYM	**L 199**	D199 FYM	**L 231**	D231 FYM
L 6	C806 BYY	**L 66**	C66 CHM	**L 168**	D168 FYM	**L 200**	D200 FYM	**L 232**	D232 FYM
L 8	WLT 807	**L 78**	C78 CHM	**L 169**	D169 FYM	**L 201**	D201 FYM	**L 233**	D233 FYM
L 13	VLT 13	**L 79**	C79 CHM	**L 170**	7 CLT	**L 202**	D202 FYM	**L 234**	D234 FYM
L 14	C814 BYY	**L 99**	C99 CHM	**L 171**	D171 FYM	**L 203**	D203 FYM	**L 235**	D235 FYM
L 16	WLT 916	**L 102**	C102 CHM	**L 172**	WLT 372	**L 204**	D204 FYM	**L 236**	D236 FYM
L 17	C817 BYY	**L 113**	C113 CHM	**L 173**	VLT 173	**L 205**	D205 FYM	**L 237**	D237 FYM
L 20	C820 BYY	**L 135**	D135 FYM	**L 174**	D174 FYM	**L 206**	D206 FYM	**L 238**	D238 FYM
L 21	C21 CHM	**L 139**	D139 FYM	**L 175**	D175 FYM	**L 207**	D207 FYM	**L 239**	D239 FYM
L 22	C22 CHM	**L 140**	D140 FYM	**L 176**	D176 FYM	**L 208**	D208 FYM	**L 240**	D240 FYM
L 24	C24 CHM	**L 143**	D143 FYM	**L 177**	D177 FYM	**L 209**	D209 FYM	**L 241**	D241 FYM
L 25	C25 CHM	**L 146**	D146 FYM	**L 178**	D178 FYM	**L 210**	D210 FYM	**L 242**	D242 FYM
L 26	C26 CHM	**L 147**	D147 FYM	**L 179**	D179 FYM	**L 211**	D211 FYM	**L 243**	D243 FYM
L 27	VLT 27	**L 148**	D148 FYM	**L 180**	480 CLT	**L 212**	D212 FYM	**L 244**	VLT 244
L 31	C31 CHM	**L 149**	D149 FYM	**L 181**	D181 FYM	**L 213**	D213 FYM	**L 245**	D245 FYM
L 32	C32 CHM	**L 150**	D150 FYM	**L 182**	D182 FYM	**L 214**	D214 FYM	**L 246**	D246 FYM
L 33	330 CLT	**L 151**	WLT 751	**L 183**	D183 FYM	**L 215**	815 DYE	**L 247**	D247 FYM
L 35	C35 CHM	**L 152**	D152 FYM	**L 184**	D184 FYM	**L 216**	D216 FYM	**L 248**	D248 FYM
L 36	C36 CHM	**L 153**	D153 FYM	**L 185**	D185 FYM	**L 217**	217 CLT	**L 249**	D249 FYM
L 37	C37 CHM	**L 154**	WLT 554	**L 186**	D186 FYM	**L 218**	D218 FYM	**L 250**	D250 FYM
L 38	C38 CHM	**L 155**	D155 FYM	**L 187**	D187 FYM	**L 219**	519 CLT	**L 251**	D251 FYM
L 41	C41 CHM	**L 156**	656 DYE	**L 188**	D188 FYM	**L 220**	D220 FYM	**L 252**	D252 FYM
L 45	C45 CHM	**L 157**	D157 FYM	**L 189**	D189 FYM	**L 221**	D221 FYM	**L 253**	D253 FYM
L 46	C46 CHM	**L 158**	D158 FYM	**L 190**	319 CLT	**L 222**	D222 FYM	**L 254**	D254 FYM
L 47	VLT 47	**L 159**	D159 FYM	**L 191**	D191 FYM	**L 223**	D223 FYM	**L 255**	D255 FYM
L 49	C49 CHM	**L 160**	D160 FYM	**L 192**	D192 FYM	**L 224**	D224 FYM	**L 256**	D256 FYM
L 50	C50 CHM	**L 161**	D161 FYM	**L 193**	D193 FYM	**L 225**	D225 FYM	**L 257**	D257 FYM
L 52	C52 CHM	**L 162**	D162 FYM	**L 194**	D194 FYM	**L 226**	D226 FYM	**L 258**	D258 FYM
L 56	C56 CHM	**L 163**	D163 FYM	**L 195**	D195 FYM	**L 227**	D227 FYM	**L 259**	D259 FYM
L 58	C58 CHM	**L 164**	D164 FYM	**L 196**	D196 FYM	**L 228**	D228 FYM		
L 59	C59 CHM	**L 165**	D165 FYM	**L 197**	D197 FYM	**L 229**	D229 FYM		

L 315–354	Leyland Olympian ON2R50C13Z4	Alexander RH	H43/25D	1992

L 315	J315 BSH	**L 323**	J323 BSH	**L 331**	J331 BSH	**L 339**	J339 BSH	**L 347**	J347 BSH
L 316	J316 BSH	**L 324**	J324 BSH	**L 332**	J332 BSH	**L 340**	J340 BSH	**L 348**	J348 BSH
L 317	J317 BSH	**L 325**	J325 BSH	**L 333**	J433 BSH	**L 341**	J341 BSH	**L 349**	J349 BSH
L 318	J318 BSH	**L 326**	J326 BSH	**L 334**	J334 BSH	**L 342**	J342 BSH	**L 350**	J350 BSH
L 319	J319 BSH	**L 327**	J327 BSH	**L 335**	J335 BSH	**L 343**	J343 BSH	**L 351**	J351 BSH
L 320	J320 BSH	**L 328**	J328 BSH	**L 336**	J336 BSH	**L 344**	J344 BSH	**L 352**	J352 BSH
L 321	J321 BSH	**L 329**	J329 BSH	**L 337**	J337 BSH	**L 345**	J345 BSH	**L 353**	J353 BSH
L 322	J322 BSH	**L 330**	J330 BSH	**L 338**	J338 BSH	**L 346**	J346 BSH	**L 354**	J354 BSH

L 514–556	Leyland Olympian ON2R50C13Z4* * L514/41/3/4/6–54/6 are ONCL10/1RZ	Northern Counties	H47/27D	1990

L 514	G514 VBB	**L 523**	G523 VBB	**L 532**	G532 VBB	**L 541**	G541 VBB	**L 550**	G550 VBB
L 515	G515 VBB	**L 524**	G524 VBB	**L 533**	G533 VBB	**L 542**	G542 VBB	**L 551**	G551 VBB
L 516	G516 VBB	**L 525**	G525 VBB	**L 534**	G534 VBB	**L 543**	G543 VBB	**L 552**	G552 VBB
L 517	G517 VBB	**L 526**	G526 VBB	**L 535**	G535 VBB	**L 544**	G544 VBB	**L 553**	G553 VBB
L 518	G518 VBB	**L 527**	G527 VBB	**L 536**	G536 VBB	**L 545**	G545 VBB	**L 554**	G554 VBB
L 519	G519 VBB	**L 528**	G528 VBB	**L 537**	G537 VBB	**L 546**	G546 VBB	**L 555**	G555 VBB
L 520	G520 VBB	**L 529**	G529 VBB	**L 538**	G538 VBB	**L 547**	G547 VBB	**L 556**	G556 VBB
L 521	G521 VBB	**L 530**	G530 VBB	**L 539**	G539 VBB	**L 548**	G548 VBB		
L 522	G522 VBB	**L 531**	G531 VBB	**L 540**	G540 VBB	**L 549**	G549 VBB		

L611	G611 BPH	Volvo Citybus B10M–50	East Lancs S type	H49/39F	1989

L 694–704		Volvo Olympian YN2RV16Z4			East Lancs E type			H44/30F	1994
L 694	M694 HPF	**L 697**	M697 HPF	**L 700**	M700 HPF	**L 703**	M703 HPF		
L 695	M695 HPF	**L 698**	M698 HPF	**L 701**	M701 HPF	**L 704**	M704 HPF		
L 696	M696 HPF	**L 699**	M699 HPF	**L 702**	M702 HPF				

LDR 1–21		Dennis Dart 9.8SDL3054			Plaxton Pointer 9.8m			B40F	1995
LDR 1	N671 GUM	**LDR 6**	N676 GUM	**LDR 11**	N681 GUM	**LDR 16**	N686 GUM	**LDR 21**	N691 GUM
LDR 2	N672 GUM	**LDR 7**	N677 GUM	**LDR 12**	N682 GUM	**LDR 17**	N687 GUM		
LDR 3	N673 GUM	**LDR 8**	N678 GUM	**LDR 13**	N683 GUM	**LDR 18**	N688 GUM		
LDR 4	N674 GUM	**LDR 9**	N679 GUM	**LDR 14**	N684 GUM	**LDR 19**	N689 GUM		
LDR 5	N675 GUM	**LDR 10**	N680 GUM	**LDR 15**	N685 GUM	**LDR 20**	N690 GUM		

LDR 22–55		Dennis Dart SFD412BR5TGD1			Plaxton Pointer 9.8m			B40F	1996
LDR 22	P822 RWU	**LDR 29**	P829 RWU	**LDR 36**	P836 RWU	**LDR 43**	P843 PWW	**LDR 50**	P850 PWW
LDR 23	P823 RWU	**LDR 30**	P830 RWU	**LDR 37**	P837 RWU	**LDR 44**	P844 PWW	**LDR 51**	P851 PWW
LDR 24	P824 RWU	**LDR 31**	P831 RWU	**LDR 38**	P838 RWU	**LDR 45**	P845 PWW	**LDR 52**	P852 PWW
LDR 25	P825 RWU	**LDR 32**	P832 RWU	**LDR 39**	P839 RWU	**LDR 46**	P846 PWW	**LDR 53**	P853 PWW
LDR 26	P826 RWU	**LDR 33**	P833 RWU	**LDR 40**	P840 PWW	**LDR 47**	P847 PWW	**LDR 54**	P854 PWW
LDR 27	P827 RWU	**LDR 34**	P834 RWU	**LDR 41**	P841 PWW	**LDR 48**	P848 PWW	**LDR 55**	P855 PWW
LDR 28	P828 RWU	**LDR 35**	P835 RWU	**LDR 42**	P842 PWW	**LDR 49**	P849 PWW		

M 6–49		MCW Metrobus DR101/8			MCW			H43/28D	1978/9
M 6t ‡	WYW 6T	**M 14**t	WYW 14T	**M 40**t	WYW 40T				
M 7t	WYW 7T	**M 38**t	WYW 38T	**M 49**t	WYW 49T				

M 60–205		MCW Metrobus DR101/9			MCW			H43/28D	1979
M 60t	WYW 60T	**M 66**t	WYW 66T	**M 149**t	BYX 149V	**M 175**†	BYX 175V		
M 63t	WYW 63T	**M 69**t	WYW 69T	**M 170**†	BYX 170V	**M 205**t	BYX 205V		
M 65t	WYW 65T	**M 132**t	BYX 132V	**M 173**	BYX 173V				

M 266–491		MCW Metrobus DR101/12			MCW			H43/28D	1980
M 266†	BYX 266V	**M 365**	GYE 365W	**M 398**	398 CLT	**M 441**†	GYE 441W	**M 469**t	GYE 469W
M 280t	BYX 280V	**M 372**	GYE 372W	**M 399**	GYE 399W	**M 445**t‡	GYE 445W	**M 478**t	GYE 478W
M 298	BYX 298V	**M 382**t‡	GYE 382W	**M 422**t‡	GYE 422W	**M 450**t‡	GYE 450W	**M 485**t	GYE 485W
M 317‡	EYE 317V	**M 396**	GYE 396W	**M 426**t	GYE 426W	**M 458**	GYE 458W	**M 491**†	GYE 491W

M 511–805		MCW Metrobus DR101/14			MCW			H43/28D	1981/2
M 511	GYE 511W	**M 580**	GYE 580W	**M 629**	KYO 629X	**M 665**	KYV 665X	**M 710**	KYV 710X
M 515	GYE 515W	**M 582**	GYE 582W	**M 630**	KYO 630X	**M 666**	KYV 666X	**M 711**	KYV 711X
M 517	GYE 517W	**M 585**	GYE 585W	**M 633**	KYV 633X	**M 669**	KYV 669X	**M 712**	KYV 712X
M 518t	GYE 518W	**M 590**	GYE 590W	**M 634**	KYV 634X	**M 671**	KYV 671X	**M 713**	KYV 713X
M 529	GYE 529W	**M 591**	GYE 591W	**M 635**	KYV 635X	**M 675**	KYV 675X	**M 714**	KYV 714X
M 530	GYE 530W	**M 593**	GYE 593W	**M 636**	KYV 636X	**M 680**	KYV 680X	**M 715**	KYV 715X
M 535	GYE 535W	**M 600**	GYE 600W	**M 637**	KYV 637X	**M 682**	KYV 682X	**M 716**	KYV 716X
M 537†	GYE 537W	**M 601**	GYE 601W	**M 641**	KYV 641X	**M 684**	KYV 684X	**M 718**	KYV 718X
M 541	GYE 541W	**M 602**	GYE 602W	**M 642**	KYV 642X	**M 688**	KYV 688X	**M 720**	KYV 720X
M 544†	GYE 544W	**M 603**	GYE 603W	**M 644**	KYV 644X	**M 691**	KYV 691X	**M 721**	KYV 721X
M 549l	GYE 549W	**M 609**	KYO 609X	**M 645**	KYV 645X	**M 692**	KYV 692X	**M 722**	KYV 722X
M 555	GYE 555W	**M 610**	KYO 610X	**M 647**	KYV 647X	**M 694**	KYV 694X	**M 723**	KYV 723X
M 562	GYE 562W	**M 617**	KYO 617X	**M 649**†	KYV 649X	**M 699**	KYV 699X	**M 724**	KYV 724X
M 567	GYE 567W	**M 619**	KYO 619X	**M 650**	KYV 650X	**M 700**	KYV 700X	**M 726**	KYV 726X
M 568	GYE 568W	**M 622**	KYO 622X	**M 651**	KYV 651X	**M 701**	KYV 701X	**M 727**	KYV 727X
M 569	GYE 569W	**M 625**†	KYO 625X	**M 652**	KYV 652X	**M 702**	KYV 702X	**M 729**	KYV 729X
M 573†	GYE 573W	**M 626**	KYO 626X	**M 653**	KYV 653X	**M 703**	KYV 703X	**M 731**	KYV 731X
M 575	GYE 575W	**M 627**	KYO 627X	**M 657**	KYV 657X	**M 704**	KYV 704X	**M 732**	KYV 732X
M 577	GYE 577W	**M 628**	KYO 628X	**M 661**	KYV 661X	**M 708**	KYV 708X	**M 733**	KYV 733X

M 736	KYV 736X	M 747	KYV 747X	M 766	KYV 766X	M 778	KYV 778X	M 791	KYV 791X
M 737	KYV 737X	M 750	KYV 750X	M 767	KYV 767X	M 780	KYV 780X	M 793	KYV 793X
M 738	KYV 738X	M 752	KYV 752X	M 768	KYV 768X	M 782	KYV 782X	M 796†	KYV 796X
M 740	KYV 740X	M 753t	KYV 753X	M 770	KYV 770X	M 783	KYV 783X	M 798	KYV 798X
M 741	KYV 741X	M 756	KYV 756X	M 772	KYV 772X	M 784	KYV 784X	M 799	KYV 799X
M 742	KYV 742X	M 757	KYV 757X	M 773	KYV 773X	M 785	KYV 785X	M 803	KYV 803X
M 743	KYV 743X	M 761	KYV 761X	M 774	KYV 774X	M 787	KYV 787X	M 805	KYV 805X
M 744	KYV 744X	M 762	KYV 762X	M 775	KYV 775X	M 788t	KYV 788X		
M 745	KYV 745X	M 765	KYV 765X	M 777†	KYV 777X	M 789	KYV 789X		

M 809–954 MCW Metrobus DR101/16 MCW H43/28D 1983

M 809	OJD 809Y	M 858	OJD 858Y	M 891	OJD 891Y	M 919	A919 SUL	M 939	A939 SUL
M 825	OJD 825Y	M 863	OJD 863Y	M 894	A894 SUL	M 929	A929 SUL	M 948	A948 SUL
M 827	OJD 827Y	M 865	OJD 865Y	M 895	A895 SUL	M 930	A930 SUL	M 954	WLT 954
M 850	OJD 850Y	M 869	OJD 869Y	M 903	A903 SUL	M 936	A936 SUL		

M 959–1036 MCW Metrobus DR101/17 MCW H43/28D 1984

M 959	A959 SYF	M 973	A973 SYF	M 984	A984 SYF	M 1000	A700 THV	M 1036	A736 THV

M 1044	A744 THV	MCW Metrobus DR101/19	MCW	H43/28D	1984
M 1062	B62 WUL	MCW Metrobus DR101/17	MCW	H43/28D	1985
M 1070	B70 WUL	MCW Metrobus DR101/17	MCW	H43/28D	1985
M 1074	B74 WUL	MCW Metrobus DR101/17	MCW	H43/28D	1985
M 1075	B75 WUL	MCW Metrobus DR101/17	MCW	H43/28D	1985

M 1084–1105 MCW Metrobus DR134/1 MCW H43/28D 1985

M 1084	B84 WUL	M 1089	B89 WUL	M 1094	B94 WUL	M 1099	B99 WUL	M 1104	B104 WUL
M 1085	B85 WUL	M 1090	B90 WUL	M 1095	B95 WUL	M 1100	B100 WUL	M 1105	B105 WUL
M 1086	B86 WUL	M 1091	B91 WUL	M 1096	B96 WUL	M 1101	B101 WUL		
M 1087	B87 WUL	M 1092	B92 WUL	M 1097	B97 WUL	M 1102	B102 WUL		
M 1088	B88 WUL	M 1093	B93 WUL	M 1098	B98 WUL	M 1103	B103 WUL		

M 1109–1437 MCW Metrobus DR101/17 MCW H43/28D* 1985/6

* M 1359, 1367 & 1398 are DPH43/28D, 1379 is DPH43/28F, M1437 is DPH43/24F

M 1109	B109 WUL	M 1164	B164 WUL	M 1252	B252 WUL	M 1300	B300 WUL	M 1354	C354 BUV
M 1112	B112 WUL	M 1165	B165 WUL	M 1253	B253 WUL	M 1303	B303 WUL	M 1359	C359 BUV
M 1116	B116 WUL	M 1170	B170 WUL	M 1254	B254 WUL	M 1307	C307 BUV	M 1362	C362 BUV
M 1121	B121 WUL	M 1173	B173 WUL	M 1255	B255 WUL	M 1308	C308 BUV	M 1367†	C367 BUV
M 1123	B123 WUL	M 1175	B175 WUL	M 1265	B265 WUL	M 1309	C309 BUV	M 1379†	VLT 88
M 1124	B124 WUL	M 1176	B176 WUL	M 1276	B276 WUL	M 1310	C310 BUV	M 1398†	C398 BUV
M 1126	B126 WUL	M 1179	B179 WUL	M 1278	B278 WUL	M 1312	C312 BUV	M 1399	C399 BUV
M 1127	B127 WUL	M 1182	B182 WUL	M 1279	B279 WUL	M 1313	C313 BUV	M 1401	C401 BUV
M 1129t	B129 WUL	M 1213	B213 WUL	M 1281	B281 WUL	M 1314	C314 BUV	M 1402	C402 BUV
M 1130	B130 WUL	M 1214	B214 WUL	M 1282	B282 WUL	M 1316	C316 BUV	M 1404	C404 BUV
M 1131	B131 WUL	M 1216	B216 WUL	M 1285	B285 WUL	M 1317	C317 BUV	M 1405	C405 BUV
M 1132	B132 WUL	M 1217	B217 WUL	M 1288	B288 WUL	M 1318	C318 BUV	M 1406	C406 BUV
M 1133	B133 WUL	M 1219	B219 WUL	M 1290	B290 WUL	M 1319	C319 BUV	M 1407	C407 BUV
M 1135	B135 WUL	M 1221	B221 WUL	M 1291	B291 WUL	M 1320	C320 BUV	M 1413	C413 BUV
M 1136	B136 WUL	M 1228	B228 WUL	M 1293	B293 WUL	M 1321	C321 BUV	M 1417	C417 BUV
M 1137	B137 WUL	M 1229	B229 WUL	M 1294	B294 WUL	M 1322	C322 BUV	M 1424	C424 BUV
M 1138	B138 WUL	M 1231	B231 WUL	M 1295	B295 WUL	M 1323	C323 BUV	M 1437†	VLT 12
M 1139	B139 WUL	M 1233	B233 WUL	M 1296	B296 WUL	M 1324	C324 BUV		
M 1140	B140 WUL	M 1239	B239 WUL	M 1297	B297 WUL	M 1326	C326 BUV		
M 1154	B154 WUL	M 1248†	B248 WUL	M 1298	B298 WUL	M 1327	C327 BUV		
M 1162	B162 WUL	M 1249	B249 WUL	M 1299	B299 WUL	M 1332	C332 BUV		

M 1441	A441 UUV	MCW Metrobus DR102/45	MCW	H43/28D	1984
M 1442	A442 UUV	MCW Metrobus DR132/5	MCW	H43/28D	1984

MBT 713u	L713 OVX	Iveco Turbo Daily 59.12	Marshall C31	B18FL	1994
MBT 714u	L714 OVX	Iveco Turbo Daily 59.12	Marshall C31	B18FL	1994
MBT 715u	L715 OVX	Iveco Turbo Daily 59.12	Marshall C31	B18FL	1994
MBT 716u	L716 OVX	Iveco Turbo Daily 59.12	Marshall C31	B18FL	1994
MBV 951	R951 VPU	Mercedes-Benz O814 Vario	Plaxton Beaver 2	B27F	1998

MD 601–612 | Mercedes-Benz 811D | Plaxton Beaver | B28F | 1991

MD 601	J601 WHJ	**MD 605**	J605 WHJ	**MD 608**	J608 WHJ	**MD 611**	J611 WHJ
MD 603	J603 WHJ	**MD 606**	J606 WHJ	**MD 609**	J609 WHJ	**MD 612**	J612 WHJ
MD 604	J604 WHJ	**MD 607**	J607 WHJ	**MD 610**	J610 WHJ		

MR 102	F102 YVP	MCW Metrorider MF150/115	MCW	B25F	1988
MR 104	F104 YVP	MCW Metrorider MF150/116	MCW	DP25F	1988
MR 105	F105 YVP	MCW Metrorider MF150/116	MCW	DP25F	1988
MRL 129s	F129 YVP	MCW Metrorider MF158/16	MCW	B28F	1988
MRL 440	M440 HPF	Optare MetroRider MR17	Optare	B29F	1994
MRL 441	M441 HPF	Optare MetroRider MR17	Optare	B29F	1994
MRL 442	M442 HPF	Optare MetroRider MR17	Optare	B29F	1994
MRL 443	M443 HPF	Optare MetroRider MR17	Optare	B29F	1994
MRL 472	P472 APJ	Optare MetroRider MR17	Optare	B29F	1996

PDL 1–19 | Dennis Dart SLF SFD612 | Plaxton Pointer 2 8.8m | B29F | 2000

PDL 1	V421 DGT	**PDL 5**	V425 DGT	**PDL 9**	V429 DGT	**PDL 13**	V433 DGT	**PDL 17**
PDL 2	V422 DGT	**PDL 6**	V426 DGT	**PDL 10**	V430 DGT	**PDL 14**	V434 DGT	**PDL 18**
PDL 3	V423 DGT	**PDL 7**	V427 DGT	**PDL 11**	V431 DGT	**PDL 15**	V435 DGT	**PDL 19**
PDL 4	V424 DGT	**PDL 8**	V428 DGT	**PDL 12**	V432 DGT	**PDL 16**	V436 DGT	

RM 5–2217 | AEC Routemaster R2RH | Park Royal | H36/28R | 1959–65

RM 5	VLT 5	**RM 385**	WLT 385	**RM 970**	WLT 970	**RM 1398**	KGJ 118A	**RM 1978**	ALD 978B
RM 6	VLT 6	**RM 432**	SVS 617	**RM 997**	WLT 997	**RM 1593**	593 CLT	**RM 2179**	CUV 179C
RM 25	VLT 25	**RM 467**	XVS 651	**RM 1003**	3 CLT	**RM 1725**	725 DYE	**RM 2185**	CUV 185C
RM 275	VLT 275	**RM 531**	WLT 531	**RM 1124**	VYJ 806	**RM 1734**	734 DYE	**RM 2217**	CUV 217C
RM 295u	VLT 295	**RM 664**	WLT 664	**RM 1125**	KGH 858A	**RM 1801**	801 DYE		
RM 311	KGJ 142A	**RM 676**	WLT 676	**RM 1324**	324 CLT	**RM 1811**	EGF 220B		
RM 313u	WSJ 739	**RM 719**	WLT 719	**RM 1330**u	KGH 975A	**RM 1822**	822 DYE		
RM 348	WLT 348	**RM 736**u	XYJ 418	**RM 1361**	VYJ 808	**RM 1872**	ALD 872B		

RMC 1453x	453 CLT	AEC Routemaster R2RH	Park Royal	H32/25RD	1962
RMC 1464x	464 CLT	AEC Routemaster R2RH	Park Royal	O36/25RD	1962

RML 882–901 | AEC Routemaster R2RH | Park Royal | H40/32R | 1961

RML 882	WLT 882	**RML 888**	WLT 888	**RML 895**	WLT 895	**RML 897**	WLT 897
RML 884	WLT 884	**RML 892**	WLT 892	**RML 896**	WLT 896	**RML 901**	WLT 901

RML 2261–2759 | AEC Routemaster R2RH/1 | Park Royal | H40/32R | 1965–68

RML 2261	CUV 261C	**RML 2294**	CUV 294C	**RML 2326**	CUV 326C	**RML 2344**	CUV 344C	**RML 2359**	CUV 359C
RML 2264	CUV 264C	**RML 2301**	CUV 301C	**RML 2328**	CUV 328C	**RML 2346**	CUV 346C	**RML 2366**	JJD 366D
RML 2266	CUV 266C	**RML 2304**	CUV 304C	**RML 2329**	CUV 329C	**RML 2347**	CUV 347C	**RML 2370**	JJD 370D
RML 2267	CUV 267C	**RML 2307**	CUV 307C	**RML 2330**	CUV 330C	**RML 2350**	CUV 350C	**RML 2372**	JJD 372D
RML 2277	CUV 277C	**RML 2315**	CUV 315C	**RML 2333**	CUV 333C	**RML 2351**	CUV 351C	**RML 2373**	JJD 373D
RML 2280	CUV 280C	**RML 2323**	CUV 323C	**RML 2334**	CUV 334C	**RML 2354**	CUV 354C	**RML 2375**	JJD 375D
RML 2287	CUV 287C	**RML 2324**	CUV 324C	**RML 2340**	CUV 340C	**RML 2355**	CUV 355C	**RML 2380**	JJD 380D
RML 2292	CUV 292C	**RML 2325**	CUV 325C	**RML 2343**	CUV 343C	**RML 2356**	CUV 356C	**RML 2382**	JJD 382D

RML 2383	JJD 383D	**RML 2491**	JJD 491D	**RML 2544**	JJD 544D	**RML 2611**	NML 611E	**RML 2688**	SMK 688F
RML 2386	JJD 386D	**RML 2492**	JJD 492D	**RML 2545**	JJD 545D	**RML 2617**	NML 617E	**RML 2692**	SMK 692F
RML 2387	JJD 387D	**RML 2494**	JJD 494D	**RML 2546**	JJD 546D	**RML 2619**	NML 619E	**RML 2708**	SMK 708F
RML 2391	JJD 391D	**RML 2503**	JJD 503D	**RML 2548**	JJD 548D	**RML 2625**	NML 625E	**RML 2715**	SMK 715F
RML 2394	JJD 394D	**RML 2504**	JJD 504D	**RML 2549**	JJD 549D	**RML 2628**	NML 628E	**RML 2716**	SMK 716F
RML 2401	JJD 401D	**RML 2505**	JJD 505D	**RML 2552**	JJD 552D	**RML 2632**	NML 632E	**RML 2718**	SMK 718F
RML 2406	JJD 406D	**RML 2510**	JJD 510D	**RML 2562**	JJD 562D	**RML 2635**	NML 635E	**RML 2726**	SMK 726F
RML 2407	JJD 407D	**RML 2412**	JJD 512D	**RML 2567**	JJD 567D	**RML 2636**	NML 636E	**RML 2730**	SMK 730F
RML 2408	JJD 408D	**RML 2514**	JJD 514D	**RML 2571**	JJD 571D	**RML 2638**	NML 638E	**RML 2741**	SMK 741F
RML 2409	JJD 409D	**RML 2518**	JJD 518D	**RML 2572**	JJD 572D	**RML 2643**	NML 643E	**RML 2742**	SMK 742F
RML 2410	JJD 410D	**RML 2521**	JJD 521D	**RML 2573**	JJD 573D	**RML 2653**	NML 653E	**RML 2746**	SMK 746F
RML 2416	JJD 416D	**RML 2523**	JJD 523D	**RML 2574**	JJD 574D	**RML 2655**	NML 655E	**RML 2747**	SMK 747F
RML 2418	JJD 418D	**RML 2524**	JJD 524D	**RML 2577**	JJD 577D	**RML 2658**	SMK 658F	**RML 2750**	SMK 750F
RML 2434	JJD 434D	**RML 2525**	JJD 525D	**RML 2586**	JJD 586D	**RML 2660**	SMK 660F	**RML 2753**	SMK 753F
RML 2452	JJD 452D	**RML 2526**	JJD 526D	**RML 2588**	JJD 588D	**RML 2666**	SMK 666F	**RML 2754**	SMK 754F
RML 2457	JJD 457D	**RML 2528**	JJD 528D	**RML 2589**	JJD 589D	**RML 2675**	SMK 675F	**RML 2758**	SMK 758F
RML 2460	JJD 460D	**RML 2431**	JJD 531D	**RML 2591**	JJD 591D	**RML 2678**	SMK 678F	**RML 2759**	SMK 759F
RML 2468	JJD 468D	**RML 2533**	JJD 533D	**RML 2595**	JJD 595D	**RML 2682**	SMK 682F		
RML 2477	JJD 477D	**RML 2534**	JJD 534D	**RML 2597**	JJD 597D	**RML 2684**	SMK 684F		
RML 2483	JJD 483D	**RML 2536**	JJD 536D	**RML 2608**	NML 608E	**RML 2685**	SMK 685F		

RV 1x	GJG 750D	AEC Regent V 2D3RA	Park Royal	H40/32F	1966
T 69†	UJN 335V	Leyland Titan TNLXB2RRsp	Park Royal	O44/26D	1979
T 83†	CUL 83V	Leyland Titan TNLXB2RRsp	Park Royal	O44/26D	1979
T 100†	CUL 100V	Leyland Titan TNLXB2RRsp	Park Royal	O44/26D	1979
TPL 1†	124 CLT	Leyland Tiger TRCTL11/3ARZM	Plaxton Paramount 3200 III	C53F	1989
TPL 2†	361 CLT	Leyland Tiger TRCTL11/3ARZM	Plaxton Paramount 3200 III	C53F	1989
TPL 8†	70 CLT	Leyland Tiger TRCL10/3ARZA	Plaxton Paramount 3200 III	C53F	1991
TPL 518†	530 MUY	Leyland Tiger TRCTL11/3ARZ	Plaxton Paramount 3500 III	C51FT	1988

† Leaside Travel livery

VA 115–125 Volvo Citybus B10M-50 Alexander RV H46/29D 1989

VA 115	F115 PHM	**VA 117**	F117 PHM	**VA 119**	F119 PHM	**VA 124**	F124 PHM
VA 116	F116 PHM	**VA 118**	F118 PHM	**VA 123**	F123 PHM	**VA 125**	F125 PHM

VPL 3†	185 CLT	Volvo B10M-61	Plaxton Paramount 3200 II	C53F	1986
VPL 4†	205 CLT	Volvo B10M-61	Plaxton Paramount 3200 II	C53F	1986
VPL 503†	VLT 32	Volvo B10M-60	Plaxton Paramount 3500 III	C49FT	1991

The following vehicles are those with Arriva London North East, formerly Grey-Green

120–158 Volvo Citybus B10M-50 Alexander RV H46/29D 1988–90
(136 is fitted with an East Lancs upper deck following accident damage)

120	F120 PHM	**129**	F129 PHM	**135**	F135 PHM	**141**	F141 PHM	**147**	G147 TYT
121	F121 PHM	**130**	F130 PHM	**136**	F136 PHM	**142**	F142 PHM	**148**	G148 TYT
122	F122 PHM	**131**	F131 PHM	**137**	F137 PHM	**143**	F143 PHM	**155**	H155 XYU
126	F126 PHM	**132**	F132 PHM	**138**	F138 PHM	**144**	F144 PHM	**156**	H156 XYU
127	F127 PHM	**133**	F133 PHM	**139**	F139 PHM	**145**	G145 TYT	**157**	H157 XYU
128	F128 PHM	**134**	F134 PHM	**140**	F140 PHM	**146**	G146 TYT	**158**	H158 XYU

159	L159 GYL	Scania N113DRB	Northern Counties Palatine I	H42/25D	1994
160	L160 GYL	Scania N113DRB	Northern Counties Palatine I	H42/25D	1994
161	L161 GYL	Scania N113DRB	Northern Counties Palatine I	H42/25D	1994

163–172		Volvo B10M-61				East Lancs EL2000 (1992)		H44/30D	1985
163	B863 XYR	**165**	B865 XYR	**167**	B867 XYR	**170**	B870 XYR	**172**	B872 XYR
164	B864 XYR	**166**	B866 XYR	**168**	B868 XYR	**171**	B871 XYR		

178–183		Scania N113DRB				Northern Counties Palatine I		H42/25D	1995/6
178	M178 LYP	**180**	M180 LYP	**182**	N182 OYH				
179	M179 LYP	**181**	N181 OYH	**183**	N183 OYH				

401–415		Leyland Olympian ON2R50C13Z4				Northern Counties		H47/30F	1990
401	H101 GEV	**404**	H104 GEV	**407**	H107 GEV	**410**	H110 GEV	**414**	H114 GEV
402	H102 GEV	**405**	H105 GEV	**408**	H108 GEV	**412**	H112 GEV	**415**	H115 GEV
403	H103 GEV	**406**	H106 GEV	**409**	H109 GEV	**413**	H113 GEV		

721–733		Volvo Citybus B10M-50				Alexander RV		H47/29D	1989
721	F101 TML	**725**	F105 TML	**728**	F108 TML	**732**	F112 TML		
723	F103 TML	**726**	F106 TML	**729**	F109 TML	**733**	F113 TML		
724	F104 TML	**727**	F107 TML	**730**	F110 TML				

934–941		Dennis Dart 9SDL3024				Plaxton Pointer 9m		B31F	1993
934	L934 GYL	**936**	L936 GYL	**938**	L938 GYL	**940**	L940 GYL		
935	L935 GYL	**937**	L937 GYL	**939**	L939 GYL	**941**	L941 GYL		

950	M950 LYR	Dennis Dart 9.8SDL3040				Plaxton Pointer 9.8m		B40F	1995

952–968		Dennis Dart SLF SFD212BR1TGW1				Alexander ALX200 10.2m		B36F	1997
952	P952 RUL	**956**	P956 RUL	**960**	P960 RUL	**964**	P964 RUL	**968**	P968 RUL
953	P953 RUL	**957**	P957 RUL	**961**	P961 RUL	**965**	P965 RUL		
954	P954 RUL	**958**	P958 RUL	**962**	P962 RUL	**966**	P966 RUL		
955	P955 RUL	**959**	P959 RUL	**963**	P963 RUL	**967**	P967 RUL		

969–983		Dennis Dart SLF SFD212BR1WGW1				Alexander ALX200 10.2m		B27D	1998
969	S169 JUA	**972**	S172 JUA	**975**	S175 JUA	**978**	S178 JUA	**981**	S181 JUA
970	S170 JUA	**973**	S173 JUA	**976**	S176 JUA	**979**	S179 JUA	**982**	S182 JUA
971	S171 JUA	**974**	S174 JUA	**977**	S177 JUA	**980**	S180 JUA	**983**	S183 JUA

Previous registrations:–

7 CLT	D170 FYM	**EGF 220B**	811 DYE	**VLT 88**	C379 BUV
70 CLT	H643 GRO	**J354 BSH**	J354 BSH, VLT 32	**VLT 173**	D173 FYM
124 CLT	G661 WMD	**KGH 858A**	125 CLT	**VLT 244**	D244FYM
185 CLT	E892 KYW	**KGJ 118A**	398 CLT	**VYJ 806**	124 CLT
205 CLT	E893 KYW	**KGJ 142A**	WLT 311	**VYJ 808**	361 CLT
217 CLT	D217 FYM	**KGJ 975A**	330 CLT	**WLT 372**	D172 FYM
319 CLT	D190 FYM	**SIB 6713**	UPE 215M	**WLT 554**	D154 FYM
324 CLT	324 CLT, VYJ 807	**SIB 6714**	WPG 216M	**WLT 751**	D151 FYM
330 CLT	C32 CHM	**SVS 617**	WLT 432	**WLT 807**	C808 BYY
361 CLT	G662 WMD	**UJN 335V**	CUL 69V, 70 CLT	**WLT 916**	C816 BYY
398 CLT	GYE 398W	**V601 LGC**	S201 JUA	**WLT 954**	A954 SUL
480 CLT	D180 FYM	**VLT 12**	C437 BUV	**WSJ 739**	WLT 313
519 CLT	D219 FYM	**VLT 13**	C813 BYY	**XYJ 418**	WLT 736
530 MUY	E118 KFV	**VLT 27**	C27 CHM	**XVS 651**	WLT 467
656 DYE	D156 FYM	**VLT 32**	H903 AHS		
815 DYE	D215 FYM	**VLT 47**	C47 CHM		

Special liveries:–

† Leaside Travel (maroon and blue) ‡ All over advertisement x LT style red with cream relief

ARRIVA KENT THAMESIDE

Vehicles listed below are those most likely to be seen on LT supported services. Other vehicles of similar types may be seen on peripheral routes in west Kent.

1444–1814 Optare MetroRider MR17 — Optare — B29F — 1994/6/8

1444	M444 HPF	**1451**	M451 HPF	**1803**	N803 BKN	**1808**	N808 BKN	**1813**	R813 TKO
1445	M445 HPF	**1452**	M452 HPG	**1804**	N804 BKN	**1809**	R809 TKO	**1814**	R814 TKO
1446	M446 HPF	**1453**	M453 HPG	**1805**	N805 BKN	**1810**	R810 TKO		
1447	M447 HPF	**1801**	N801 BKN	**1806**	N806 BKN	**1811**	R811 TKO		
1450	M450 HPF	**1802**	N802 BKN	**1807**	N807 BKN	**1812**	R812 TKO		

1852 N852 YKE Optare MetroRider MR03 — Optare — B25F — 1995

3112–3159 Dennis Dart 9SDL3034 — Northern Counties Paladin 9m — B35F — 1994

3112	L112 YVK	**3133**	L133 YVK	**3140**	L140 YVK	**3148**	L148 YVK	**3156**	L156 YVK
3113	L113 YVK	**3134**	L134 YVK	**3141**	L141 YVK	**3149**	L149 YVK	**3157**	L157 YVK
3128	L128 YVK	**3135**	L135 YVK	**3142**	L142 YVK	**3150**	L150 YVK	**3158**	L158 YVK
3129	L129 YVK	**3136**	L136 YVK	**3143**	L143 YVK	**3152**	L152 YVK	**3159**	L159 YVK
3130	L130 YVK	**3137**	L137 YVK	**3144**	L144 YVK	**3153**	L153 YVK		
3131	L131 YVK	**3138**	L138 YVK	**3145**	L145 YVK	**3154**	L154 YVK		
3132	L132 YVK	**3139**	L139 YVK	**3146**	L146 YVK	**3155**	L155 YVK		

3179	P179 LKL	Dennis Dart SLF SFD322BR1TGW1	Plaxton Pointer 10.6m	B40F	1997
3217	P217 MKL	Dennis Dart SLF SFD322BR1TGW1	Plaxton Pointer 10.6m	B40F	1997

3261–72 Dennis Dart SLF SFD322BR1VGW1 — Plaxton Pointer 10.6m — B39F — 1998

3261	R261 EKO	**3264**	R264 EKO	**3267**	R267 EKO	**3270**	R270 EKO
3262	R262 EKO	**3265**	R265 EKO	**3268**	R268 EKO	**3271**	R271 EKO
3263	R263 EKO	**3266**	R266 EKO	**3269**	R269 EKO	**3272**	R272 EKO

3276–3289 Dennis Dart SLF SFD322BR1WGW1 — Plaxton Pointer 2 10.7m — B37F* — 1999

* 3282–9 are B39F

3276	T276 JKM	**3279**	T279 JKM	**3282**	T282 JKM	**3285**	T285 JKM	**3288**	T288 JKM
3277	T277 JKM	**3280**	T280 JKM	**3283**	T283 JKM	**3286**	T286 JKM	**3289**	T289 JKM
3278	T278 JKM	**3281**	T281 JKM	**3284**	T284 JKM	**3287**	T287 JKM		

3492	RUF 42R	Leyland National 11351/2R	B25DL	1977
3493	THX 202S	Leyland National 10351A/2R	B21DL	1978
3494	YYE 290T	Leyland National 10351A/2R	B21DL	1979

7702–7709 Volvo Citybus B10M–50 — East Lancs S type — H49/39F — 1989/90

7702	G641 CHF	**7706**	G648 EKA	**7708**	G659 DTJ
7703	G642 CHF	**7707**	G649 EKA	**7709**	G660 DTJ

ARRIVA KENT & SUSSEX Route 402

5901–05 Leyland Olympian ON2R50G13Z4* Northern Counties H45/30F 1990
* 5902/4 are ON2R50C13Z4

5901	G901 SKP	**5902**	G902 SKP	**5903**	G903 SKP	**5904**	G904 SKP	**5905**	G905 SKP

ARRIVA SERVING THE SHIRES

Vehicles listed below are only those most likely to be seen on LT supported services.

2171–2198 Mercedes-Benz O814 Vario Plaxton Beaver 2 B27F* 1997/8
* 2196–98 are B31F

2171	R171 VBM	**2173**	R173 VBM	**2175**	R175 VBM	**2197**	R197 DNM
2172	R172 VBM	**2174**	R174 VBM	**2196**	R196 DNM	**2198**	R198 DNM

3258–3260 Volvo B6BLE Wright Crusader 2 B33D 1999

3258	V258 HBH	**3259**	V259 HBH	**3260**	V260 HBH

5077–82 Leyland Olympian ONTL11/1R Eastern Coach Works H43/29F 1985

5077	B273 LPH	**5080**	B270 LPH	**5082**	B272 LPH

5111–25 Leyland Olympian ONCL10/1RZ Leyland H47/31F 1989/90

5111	G281 UMJ	**5114**	G284 UMJ	**5117**	G287 UMJ	**5120**	G290 UMJ	**5123**	G293 UMJ
5112	G282 UMJ	**5115**	G285 UMJ	**5118**	G288 UMJ	**5121**	G291 UMJ	**5124**	G294 UMJ
5113	G283 UMJ	**5116**	G286 UMJ	**5119**	G289 UMJ	**5122**	G292 UMJ	**5125**	G295 UMJ

5126–33 Leyland Olympian ON2R50C13Z4 Leyland H47/29F 1991

5126	H196 GRO	**5128**	H198 GRO	**5132**	H202 GRO
5127	H197 GRO	**5129**	H199 GRO	**5133**	H203 GRO

BLUE TRIANGLE

DB 101	F78 DDA	Leyland Lynx LX2R11C15Z4R	Leyland	B49F	1989
DB 102	F75 DDA	Leyland Lynx LX2R11C15Z4R	Leyland	B49F	1989
DB 103	F77 DDA	Leyland Lynx LX2R11C15Z4R	Leyland	B49F	1989
DB 104	E34 EVW	Leyland Lynx LX112L10ZR1R	Leyland	B49F	1988
DB 105	E968 PME	Leyland Lynx LX112TL11ZR1R	Leyland	B49F	1988
DB 106	E677 DCU	Leyland Lynx LX112L10ZR1	Leyland	B51F	1987
DB 107	E967 PME	Leyland Lynx LX112TL11ZR1R	Leyland	B49F	1988
DB 108	E678 DCU	Leyland Lynx LX112L10ZR1	Leyland	B51F	1987

DL 901–909	Dennis Trident SFD113BR1XGX2	East Lancs Lolyne 9.9m	H45/21D	1999

DL 901	V901 FEC	**DL 903**	V903 FEC	**DL 905**	V905 FEC	**DL 907**	V907 FEC	**DL 909**	V909 FEC
DL 902	V902 FEC	**DL 904**	V904 FEC	**DL 906**	V906 FEC	**DL 908**	V908 FEC		

DMS 2590	THX 590S	Daimler Fleetline FE30ALR	Park Royal	H44/27D	1978
MCW 10	GBU 10V	MCW Metrobus DR/101/6	MCW	H43/30F	1979
MCW 12	WYW 12T	MCW Metrobus DR/101/8	MCW	H43/28D	1978
MCW 19	WYW 19T	MCW Metrobus DR/101/8	MCW	H43/28D	1979
MCW 20	UKA 20V	MCW Metrobus DR/101/3	MCW	H43/30F	1980
MCW 21	UKA 21V	MCW Metrobus DR/101/3	MCW	H43/30F	1980
MCW 27	WYW 27T	MCW Metrobus DR/101/8	MCW	H43/28D	1979
MCW 28	WYW 28T	MCW Metrobus DR/101/8	MCW	H43/28D	1979
MCW 73	ORJ 73W	MCW Metrobus DR/102/21	MCW	H43/30F	1980
MCW 95	ORJ 95W	MCW Metrobus DR/102/21	MCW	H43/30F	1980
MCW 112	BYX 112V	MCW Metrobus DR/101/9	MCW	H43/28D	1979
MCW 146	BYX 146V	MCW Metrobus DR/101/9	MCW	H43/28D	1979
MCW 160	BYX 160V	MCW Metrobus DR/101/9	MCW	H43/28D	1979
MCW 179	BYX 179V	MCW Metrobus DR/101/9	MCW	H43/28D	1979
MCW 195	BYX 195V	MCW Metrobus DR/101/9	MCW	H43/28D	1979
MCW 270	BYX 270V	MCW Metrobus DR/101/12	MCW	H43/28D	1979
MCW 271	BYX 271V	MCW Metrobus DR101/12	MCW	H43/28D	1980
MCW 462	GYE 462W	MCW Metrobus DR101/12	MCW	H43/28D	1980
MCW 463	GYE 463W	MCW Metrobus DR101/12	MCW	H43/28D	1980
MCW 495	MNC 495W	MCW Metrobus DR102/10	MCW	H43/30F	1980
MCW 497	MNC 497W	MCW Metrobus DR102/10	MCW	H43/30F	1980
MCW 501	JUM 501V	MCW Metrobus DR101	MCW	H46/31F	1980
MCW 502	JUM 502V	MCW Metrobus DR101	MCW	H46/31F	1980
MCW 503	GBU 3V	MCW Metrobus DR/101/6	MCW	H43/30F	1979
MCW 514	DAE 514W	MCW Metrobus DR103/4	MCW	H43/30F	1980
MCW 553	C953 LWJ	MCW Metrobus DR102	MCW	DPH42/28F	1986
MCW 555	C955 LWJ	MCW Metrobus DR102	MCW	CH42/28F	1986
MCW 616	KYO 616X	MCW Metrobus DR101/14	MCW	H43/28D	1981
MCW 639	KYV 639X	MCW Metrobus DR101/14	MCW	H43/28D	1981
MCW 712	A712 THV	MCW Metrobus DR101/18	MCW	DPH41/28D	1984
MCW 733	A733 THV	MCW Metrobus DR101/7	MCW	H43/28D	1984
MCW 932	A932 SUL	MCW Metrobus DR101/16	MCW	H43/28D	1983
MCW 981	A981 SYF	MCW Metrobus DR101/17	MCW	H43/28D	1984
RCL 2260	CUV 260C	AEC Routemaster R2RH/3	Park Royal	H36/29RD	1965
RT 2150	KGK 959	AEC Regent III 0961	Weymann	H30/26R	1949
RT 2799	LYR 969	AEC Regent III 0961	Weymann	H30/26R	1952
RT 3062	KXW 171	AEC Regent III 0961	Saunders	H30/26R	1950
RT 3871	LLU 670	AEC Regent III 0961	Park Royal	H30/26R	1950
T 68	CUL 68V	Leyland Titan TNTL11112RRsp	Park Royal	H44/24D	1978
T 96	CUL 96V	Leyland Titan TNTL11112RRsp	Park Royal	H44/24D	1979
T 349	KYV 349X	Leyland Titan TNLXB2RR	Leyland	H44/24D	1981
T 864	A864 SUL	Leyland Titan TNLXB2RR	Leyland	H44/24D	1983
T 908	A908 SUL	Leyland Titan TNLXB2RR	Leyland	H44/24D	1983
T 1055	A655 THV	Leyland Titan TNLXB2RR	Leyland	H44/26D	1983

CONNEX

WYW 54T	MCW Metrobus DR101/8	MCW	H43/28D	1979
BYX 140V	MCW Metrobus DR101/8	MCW	H43/28D	1979
BYX 309V	MCW Metrobus DR101/12	MCW	H43/28D	1980
GYE 565W	MCW Metrobus DR101/14	MCW	H43/28D	1981
KYV 802X	MCW Metrobus DR101/14	MCW	H43/28D	1982
C263 FGG	Leyland National 2 NL116HLXCT/1R		B52F	1986
E751 VJO	MCW MetroRider MF150/26	MCW	B25F	1987
E836 BTN	MCW MetroRider MF150/27	MCW	B25F	1987
G525 VYE	Dennis Dart 8.5SDL3003	Duple Dartline 8.5m	DP21F	1990
G41 VGW	Dennis Dart 8.5SDL3003	Carlyle Dartline 8.5m	DP21F	1990

TA 1–30	Dennis Trident SFD123BR1XGX2 * TA 1–5 are DP45/20D	Alexander ALX400 9.9m	H45/20D*	2000

TA 1	V301 KGW	**TA 7**	V307 KGW	**TA 13**	V313 KGW	**TA 19**	V319 KGW	**TA 26**	V326 KGW
TA 2	V302 KGW	**TA 8**	V308 KGW	**TA 14**	V314 KGW	**TA 20**	V320 KGW	**TA 27**	V327 KGW
TA 3	V303 KGW	**TA 9**	V309 KGW	**TA 15**	V315 KGW	**TA 22**	V322 KGW	**TA 28**	V328 KGW
TA 4	V304 KGW	**TA 10**	V310 KGW	**TA 16**	V316 KGW	**TA 23**	V323 KGW	**TA 29**	V329 KGW
TA 5	V305 KGW	**TA 11**	V311 KGW	**TA 17**	V317 KGW	**TA 24**	V324 KGW	**TA 30**	V330 KGW
TA 6	V306 KGW	**TA 12**	V312 KGW	**TA 18**	V318 KGW	**TA 25**	V325 KGW		

On order:–
Approximately twelve Dennis Dart SLF/Alexander ALX200 for route 322.

CRYSTALS

K286 ESF	Mercedes-Benz 709D	Dormobile Routemaker	B27F	1993
L67 DPE	Mercedes-Benz 709D	Crystals	DP19FL	1994
L76 DPE	Mercedes-Benz 709D	Crystals	DP18FL	1994
L168 EKR	Mercedes-Benz 711D	Crystals	B18FL	1994
M569 TJL	Mercedes-Benz 709D	Crystals	B19FL	1995
N601 JGP	Mercedes-Benz 709D	Crystals	B25F	1995
N602 JGP	Mercedes-Benz 709D	Crystals	B25F	1995
N603 JGP	Mercedes-Benz 709D	Crystals	B25F	1995
N604 JGP	Mercedes-Benz 811D	Crystals	B29F	1995
N605 JGP	Mercedes-Benz 811D	Crystals	B29F	1995
N606 JGP	Mercedes-Benz 811D	Crystals	B29F	1995
P347 HKU	Mercedes-Benz 711D	Crystals	B20FL	1997
P348 HKU	Mercedes-Benz 711D	Crystals	B20FL	1997
S107 HGX	Mercedes-Benz O814 Vario	Plaxton Beaver 2	B27F	1999
S108 HGX	Mercedes-Benz O814 Vario	Plaxton Beaver 2	B27F	1999

On loan:–

S556 BNV	Mercedes-Benz O814 Vario	Plaxton Beaver 2	B31F	1999

Special liveries:–
N601–606 JGP and S107/8 HGX carry blue livery for use in the Orpington area.

EPSOM BUSES

E204 YGC	Mercedes-Benz 709D	Reeve Burgess Beaver	DP25F	1988
E205 YGC	Mercedes-Benz 709D	Reeve Burgess Beaver	DP25F	1988
F207 DGT	Mercedes-Benz 709D	Reeve Burgess Beaver	DP25F	1988
F208 GGH	Mercedes-Benz 709D	Robin Hood	B26F	1988
H210 UGO	Mercedes-Benz 709D	Phoenix	B26F	1990
H947 JPA	Mercedes-Benz 709D	Reeve Burgess Beaver	B25F	1990
K593 BEG	Mercedes-Benz 709D	Marshall C19	B27F	1992
K892 CSX	Dennis Dart 9.8SDL3017	Alexander Dash 9.8m	B40F	1992
K321 GEW	Dennis Dart 9.8SDL3017	Marshall C27 9.8m	B40F	1993
K112 NGK	Dennis Dart 9.8SDL3012	Plaxton Pointer 9.8m	B40F	1993
K113 NGK	Dennis Dart 9.8SDL3012	Plaxton Pointer 9.8m	B40F	1993
L894 NAV	Mercedes-Benz 709D	Marshall C19	B27F	1993
M960 CGF	Dennis Dart 9.8SDL3040	Plaxton Pointer 9.8m	B40F	1994
N401 SPA	Dennis Dart 9.8SDL3054	Plaxton Pointer 9.8m	B40F	1995
N402 SPA	Dennis Dart 9.8SDL3054	Plaxton Pointer 9.8m	B40F	1995
P570 APJ	Mercedes-Benz 709D	Plaxton Beaver	B27F	1997
R211 MGT	Mercedes-Benz O814 Vario	UVG City Star	B27F	1997
R212 MGT	Mercedes-Benz O814 Vario	UVG City Star	B27F	1997
R213 MGT	Mercedes-Benz O814 Vario	UVG City Star	B27F	1997
S451 LGN	Mercedes-Benz O814 Vario	Plaxton Beaver 2	B27F	1998
S452 LGN	Mercedes-Benz O814 Vario	Plaxton Beaver 2	B27F	1998
S453 LGN	Mercedes-Benz O814 Vario	Plaxton Beaver 2	B27F	1998
S454 LGN	Mercedes-Benz O814 Vario	Plaxton Beaver 2	B27F	1998
S455 LGN	Mercedes-Benz O814 Vario	Plaxton Beaver 2	B31F	1998

Dennis Dart SLF SFD612BR1WGW1 — Plaxton Pointer 2 8.8m — B29F — 1998–99

S456 LGN, S457 LGN, S458 LGN, S459 LGN, S460 LGN, S461 LGN, S462 LGN, S463 LGN, S464 LGN, S465 LGN, S466 LGN

T467 EGT	Dennis Dart SLF SFD212	Plaxton Pointer 2 10.1m	B33F	1999
T468 EGT	Dennis Dart SLF SFD212	Plaxton Pointer 2 10.1m	B33F	1999

FIRST CAPITAL

DML 307–329 Dennis Dart SLF SFD212BR1XGW1 — Marshall Capital 10.2m — B28D — 1999

DML 307 V307 GBY, **DML 308** V308 GBY, **DML 309** V309 GBY, **DML 310** V310 GBY, **DML 311** V311 GBY, **DML 312** V312 GBY, **DML 313** V313 GBY, **DML 314** V314 GBY, **DML 315** V315 GBY, **DML 316** V316 GBY, **DML 317** V317 GBY, **DML 318** V318 GBY, **DML 319** V319 GBY, **DML 320** V320 GBY, **DML 321** V421 GBY, **DML 322** V322 GBY, **DML 323** V323 GBY, **DML 324** V324 GBY, **DML 325** V325 GBY, **DML 326** V326 GBY, **DML 327** V327 GBY, **DML 328** V328 GBY, **DML 329** V329 GBY

DMS 330–335 Dennis Dart SLF SFD612BR1XGW1 — Marshall Capital 8.9m — B25F — 1999

DMS 330 V330 GBY, **DMS 331** V331 GBY, **DMS 332** V332 GBY, **DMS 333** V433 GBY, **DMS 334** V334 GBY, **DMS 335** V335 GBY

TN 801–887 Dennis Trident SFD113BR1XGX2 — Plaxton President 9.9m — H39/20D — 1999

TN 801 T801 LLC, **TN 802** T802 LLC, **TN 803** T803 LLC, **TN 804** T804 LLC, **TN 805** T805 LLC, **TN 806** T806 LLC, **TN 807** T807 LLC, **TN 808** T808 LLC, **TN 809** T809 LLC, **TN 810** T810 LLC, **TN 811** T811 LLC, **TN 812** T812 LLC, **TN 813** T813 LLC, **TN 814** T814 LLC, **TN 815** T815 LLC, **TN 816** T816 LLC, **TN 817** T817 LLC, **TN 818** T818 LLC, **TN 819** T819 LLC, **TN 820** T820 LLC, **TN 821** T821 LLC, **TN 822** T822 LLC, **TN 854** T854 KLF, **TN 855** V855 HBY, **TN 856** V856 HBY, **TN 857** V857 HBY, **TN 858** V858 HBY, **TN 859** V859 HBY, **TN 860** T860 KLF, **TN 861** V861 HBY

TN 862	V862 HBY	**TN 868**	T868 KLF	**TN 874**	V874 HBY	**TN 880**	T880 KLF	**TN 886**	V886 HBY
TN 863	V863 HBY	**TN 869**	V869 HBY	**TN 875**	T875 KLF	**TN 881**	T881 KLF	**TN 887**	V887 HBY
TN 864	T864 KLF	**TN 870**	T870 KLF	**TN 876**	T876 KLF	**TN 882**	V882 HBY		
TN 865	T865 KLF	**TN 871**	T871 KLF	**TN 877**	V877 HBY	**TN 883**	T883 KLF		
TN 866	T866 KLF	**TN 872**	V872 HBY	**TN 878**	T878 KLF	**TN 884**	T884 KLF		
TN 867	V867 HBY	**TN 873**	T873 KLF	**TN 879**	T879 KLF	**TN 885**	T885 KLF		

121–128 Leyland Olympian ON2R50C13Z4 — Northern Counties — H47/30F — 1990

121	H141 FLX	**123**	H130 FLX	**125**	H135 FLX	**127**	H137 FLX
122	H142 FLX	**124**	H144 FLX	**126**	H136 FLX	**128**	H145 FLX

129–132 Leyland Olympian ON2R50C13Z4 — Northern Counties — H47/30F — 1991

129	J129 YRM	**130**	J130 YRM	**131**	J131 YRM	**132**	J132 YRM

133	H132 FLX	Leyland Olympian ON2R50C13Z4	Northern Counties	H47/30F	1990
134	J134 YRM	Leyland Olympian ON2R50C13Z4	Northern Counties	H47/30F	1991
135	J135 YRM	Leyland Olympian ON2R50C13Z4	Northern Counties	H47/30F	1991

136–158 Leyland Olympian ON2R50C13Z4 — Leyland — H47/29F — 1991

136	J136 YRM	**141**	J141 YRM	**146**	J146 YRM	**151**	J151 YRM	**156**	J156 YRM
137	J137 YRM	**142**	J142 YRM	**147**	J247 YRM	**152**	J152 YRM	**157**	J157 YRM
138	J138 YRM	**143**	J143 YRM	**148**	J148 YRM	**153**	J153 YRM	**158**	J158 YRM
139	J139 YRM	**144**	J144 YRM	**149**	J149 YRM	**154**	J154 YRM		
140	J140 YRM	**145**	J145 YRM	**150**	J150 YRM	**155**	J155 YRM		

159–165 Leyland Olympian ON2R50C13Z4 — Northern Counties Palatine I — H47/30F — 1992

159	K888 TTT	**161**	K888 TWY	**163**	K888 PFD	**165**	K888 BWU
160	K888 ELR	**162**	K888 LAD	**164**	K888 BFG		

166	K888 TKS	Leyland Olympian ON2RC13Z4	Northern Counties Palatine II	H49/29F	1992
167	L888 YTT	Volvo Olympian YN2RV18Z4	Northern Counties Palatine II	H47/29F	1993
168	L888 TTT	Volvo Olympian YN2RV18Z4	Northern Counties Palatine II	H47/29F	1993
169	E964 PME	Leyland Olympian ONLXB/1RH	Optare	H47/29F	1988
170	E470 SON	MCW Metrobus DR102/63	MCW	H45/30F	1988
171	E461 SON	MCW Metrobus DR102/63	MCW	H45/30F	1988
172	E472 SON	MCW Metrobus DR102/63	MCW	H45/30F	1988
173	H129 FLX	Leyland Olympian ON2R50C13Z4	Northern Counties	H47/30F	1990
178	E478 SON	MCW Metrobus DR102/63	MCW	H45/30F	1988
179	H139 FLX	Leyland Olympian ON2R50C13Z4	Northern Counties	H47/30F	1990
180	H140 FLX	Leyland Olympian ON2R50C13Z4	Northern Counties	H47/30F	1990
181	J181 HME	Dennis Dominator DDA2004	Northern Counties	H45/29F	1991
182	J182 HME	Dennis Dominator DDA2002	Northern Counties	H45/29F	1991
183	B443 CKW	Dennis Dominator DDA901	Alexander RH	H46/32F	1984

191–198 Dennis Dominator DDA1023 — East Lancs S type — H45/31F — 1988

191	F291 PTP	**193**	F293 PTP	**195**	F295 PTP	**197**	F297 PTP
192	F292 PTP	**194u**	F294 PTP	**196**	F296 PTP	**198**	F298 PTP

206–222 Volvo Olympian OLY–4953 — Northern Counties Palatine I — H47/27D — 1998

206	S206 LLO	**210**	S210 LLO	**214**	S214 LLO	**218**	S218 LLO	**222**	S422 LLO
207	S207 LLO	**211**	S211 LLO	**215**	S215 LLO	**219**	S219 LLO		
208	S208 LLO	**212**	S212 LLO	**216**	S216 LLO	**220**	S220 LLO		
209	S209 LLO	**213**	S213 LLO	**217**	S217 LLO	**221**	S221 LLO		

223–238	Volvo Olympian OLY–50	Alexander (Belfast) RH	H47/25D	1997

223	P223 MPU	**227**	P227 MPU	**231**	P231 MPU	**235**	P235 MPU
224	P224 MPU	**228**	P228 MPU	**232**	P232 MPU	**236**	P236 MPU
225	P225 MPU	**229**	P229 MPU	**233**	P233 MPU	**237**	P237 MPU
226	P226 MPU	**230**	P230 MPU	**234**	P234 MPU	**238**	P238 MPU

239–249	Volvo Olympian YN2RV18Z4	Northern Counties Palatine I	H47/27D	1996

239	P239 HMD	**242**	P242 HMD	**245**	P245 HMD	**248**	P248 HMD
240	P240 HMD	**243**	P243 HMD	**246**	P246 HMD	**249**	P249 HMD
241	N241 CMP	**244**	N244 CMP	**247**	N247 CMP		

250	J135 PVC	Leyland Olympian ON2R50C13Z4	Leyland	H47/25D	1991

251–274	Dennis Dominator DDA2001	Northern Counties	H47/29D	1990/1

251	H251 KVX	**257**	H257 KVX	**262**	H262 KVX	**267**	H267 KVX	**272**	H272 KVX
252	H252 KVX	**258**	H258 KVX	**263**	H263 KVX	**268**	H268 KVX	**273**	H273 KVX
253	H253 KVX	**259**	H259 KVX	**264**	H264 KVX	**269**	H269 KVX	**274**	H274 KVX
254	H254 KVX	**260**	H460 KVX	**265**	H265 KVX	**270**	H270 KVX		
255	H255 KVX	**261**	H261 KVX	**266**	H266 KVX	**271**	H271 KVX		

279–294	MCW Metrobus DR102/71	MCW	H46/31F	1988

279	F279 NHJ	**282**	F282 NHJ	**285**	F285 NHJ	**288**	F288 NHJ	**291**	F291 NHJ
280	F280 NHJ	**283**	F283 NHJ	**286**	F286 NHJ	**289**	F289 NHJ	**293**	F293 NHJ
281	F281 NHJ	**284**	F284 NHJ	**287**	F287 NHJ	**290**	F290 NHJ	**294**	F294 NHJ

301	GYE 379W	MCW Metrobus DR101/12	MCW	H43/28D	1980
302	GYE 479W	MCW Metrobus DR101/12	MCW	H43/28D	1980
303	GYE 546W	MCW Metrobus DR101/14	MCW	H43/28D	1980
304	BYX 284V	MCW Metrobus DR101/12	MCW	H43/28D	1980
305	GYE 405W	MCW Metrobus DR101/12	MCW	H43/28D	1980
306	KYO 606X	MCW Metrobus DR101/14	MCW	H43/28D	1980
308	GYE 498W	MCW Metrobus DR101/12	MCW	H43/28D	1980
309	BYX 249V	MCW Metrobus DR101/12	MCW	H43/28D	1980
310	GYE 369W	MCW Metrobus DR101/12	MCW	H43/28D	1980
315	GYE 355W	MCW Metrobus DR101/12	MCW	H43/28D	1980
316	GYE 416W	MCW Metrobus DR101/12	MCW	H43/28D	1980
317	GYE 457W	MCW Metrobus DR101/12	MCW	H43/28D	1980
319	KYV 769X	MCW Metrobus DR101/14	MCW	H43/28D	1980
322	GYE 487W	MCW Metrobus DR101/12	MCW	H43/28D	1980
323	OJD 843Y	MCW Metrobus DR101/16	MCW	H43/28D	1983
324	GYE 348W	MCW Metrobus DR101/12	MCW	H43/28D	1980
325	GYE 465W	MCW Metrobus DR101/12	MCW	H43/28D	1980
327	OJD 872Y	MCW Metrobus DR101/16	MCW	H43/28D	1980
328	GYE 418W	MCW Metrobus DR101/12	MCW	H43/28D	1980
329	A898 SUL	MCW Metrobus DR101/16	MCW	H43/28D	1980
331	A941 SUL	MCW Metrobus DR101/16	MCW	H43/28D	1980
333	GYE 413W	MCW Metrobus DR101/12	MCW	H43/28D	1980
334	GYE 484W	MCW Metrobus DR101/12	MCW	H43/28D	1980
335	OJD 884Y	MCW Metrobus DR101/16	MCW	H43/28D	1980
336	OJD 866Y	MCW Metrobus DR101/16	MCW	H43/28D	1980
337	OJD 887Y	MCW Metrobus DR101/16	MCW	H43/28D	1980
338	GYE 488W	MCW Metrobus DR101/12	MCW	H43/28D	1980

340–348	Dennis Dominator DDA1024	East Lancs S type	H46/33F	1989

340	F140 MBC	**342**	F142 MBC	**345**	F145 MBC	**348**	F148 MBC
341	F141 MBC	**344**u	F144 MBC	**347**	F147 MBC		

350	EYE 340V	MCW Metrobus DR101/12	MCW	H43/28D	1980
351	A751 THV	MCW Metrobus DR101/19	MCW	H43/28D	1984
352	A952 SUL	MCW Metrobus DR101/16	MCW	H43/28D	1983
353	A892 SUL	MCW Metrobus DR101/16	MCW	H43/28D	1983
354	OJD 874Y	MCW Metrobus DR101/16	MCW	H43/28D	1983
357	OJD 857Y	MCW Metrobus DR101/16	MCW	H43/28D	1983
361	OJD 861Y	MCW Metrobus DR101/16	MCW	H43/28D	1983

401–412	Dennis Arrow SFD121BR2SGL6 (408, 410–12 are SFD121BR2TGL6)	Northern Counties Palatine II	H47/33F	1996

401	P401 PLE	**404**	P404 PLE	**407**	P407 PLE	**410**	P410 PLE
402	P402 PLE	**405**	P405 PLE	**408**	P408 PLE	**411**	P411 PLE
403	P403 PLE	**406**	P406 PLE	**409**	P409 PLE	**412**	P412 PLE

413–416	Dennis Arrow SFD121BR2TLG6	Northern Counties Palatine II	H47/35F	1996

413	P413 MTW	**414**	P414 MTW	**415**	P415 MTW	**416**	P416 MTW

417–426	Dennis Arrow SFD121BR3TLG6 (426 is SFD121BR3VGL6)	East Lancs Pyoneer	H49/28D* *418 & 426 are H49/27D	1997/8

417	P417 PVW	**419**	P419 PVW	**421**	P421 PVW	**423**	P423 PVW	**425**	P425 PVW
418	P418 PVW	**420**	P420 PVW	**422**	P422 PVW	**424**	P424 PVW	**426**	R426 SOY

427–454	Dennis Arrow SFD121BR4WGL6 (427 is SFD121BR3VGL6)	East Lancs Pyoneer	H49/27D	1998

427	R427 ULE	**433**	R433 ULE	**439**	R439 ULE	**445**	R445 ULE	**451**	S451 SLL
428	R428 ULE	**434**	R434 ULE	**440**	R440 ULE	**446**	R446 ULE	**452**	S452 SLL
429	R429 ULE	**435**	R435 ULE	**441**	R441 ULE	**447**	R447 ULE	**453**	S453 SLL
430	R430 ULE	**436**	R436 ULE	**442**	R442 ULE	**448**	R448 ULE	**454**	S454 SLL
431	R431 ULE	**437**	R437 ULE	**443**	R443 ULE	**449**	R449 ULE		
432	R432 ULE	**438**	R438 ULE	**444**	R844 YLC	**450**	R450 ULE		

561	F251 NJN	Mercedes-Benz 709D	Reeve Burgess Beaver	B23F	1989
562u	F255 RHK	Mercedes-Benz 709D	Reeve Burgess Beaver	B23F	1990
563	F253 RHK	Mercedes-Benz 709D	Reeve Burgess Beaver	B23F	1990
564t	D764 KWT	Mercedes-Benz 609D	Robin Hood	B20F	1986
565	F245 MVW	Mercedes-Benz 709D	Reeve Burgess Beaver	B23F	1989
566	F256 RHK	Mercedes-Benz 709D	Reeve Burgess Beaver	B23F	1990
567	F257 RHK	Mercedes-Benz 709D	Reeve Burgess Beaver	B23F	1990
568	F258 RHK	Mercedes-Benz 709D	Reeve Burgess Beaver	B23F	1990
569	F246 MVW	Mercedes-Benz 709D	Reeve Burgess Beaver	B23F	1989
570	F254 RHK	Mercedes-Benz 709D	Reeve Burgess Beaver	B23F	1990

571–579	Mercedes-Benz O814 Vario	Marshall Master	B28F	1997/98

571	R411 VPU	**573**	R413 VPU	**575**	R415 VPU	**577**	R417 VPU	**579**	R419 VPU
572	R412 VPU	**574**	R414 VPU	**576**	R416 VPU	**578**	R418 VPU		

581–595	Mercedes-Benz 709D	Reeve Burgess Beaver	B23F	1990–91

581	H301 LPU	**584**	H304 LPU	**588**	H388 MAR	**591**	H391 MAR	**594**	H394 MAR
582	H302 LPU	**585**	H305 LPU	**589**	H389 MAR	**592**	H392 MAR	**595**	H395 MAR
583	H303 LPU	**586**	H306 LPU	**590**	H390 MAR	**593**	H393 MAR		

596	K396 GHJ	Mercedes-Benz 709D	Plaxton Beaver	B23F	1993
601	J601 HMF	Mercedes-Benz 811D	Plaxton Beaver	B28F	1992
602	J602 HMF	Mercedes-Benz 811D	Plaxton Beaver	B28F	1992
603	F803 RHK	Mercedes-Benz 811D	Reeve Burgess Beaver	B31F	1989

604	F804 RHK	Mercedes-Benz 811D	Reeve Burgess Beaver	B31F	1989
605	J605 HMF	Mercedes-Benz 811D	Plaxton Beaver	B28F	1992
607	F802 RHK	Mercedes-Benz 811D	Reeve Burgess Beaver	B31F	1989

610–620		Mercedes-Benz 811D				Plaxton Beaver		B28F	1992
610	J610 HMF	**612**	J612 HMF	**615**	J615 HMF	**617**	J617 HMF	**620**	J620 HMF
611	J611 HMF	**613**	J613 HMF	**616**	J616 HMF	**618**	J618 HMF		

621–630		Optare MetroRider				Optare		B28F	1992
621	J621 HMH	**623**	J623 HMH	**625**	J625 HMH	**627**	J627 HMH	**629**	J629 HMH
622	J622 HMH	**624**	J624 HMH	**626**	J626 HMH	**628**	J628 HMH	**630**	J630 HMH

631	J631 HMH	Mercedes-Benz 811D	Alexander AM	B28F	1992
632	J632 HMH	Mercedes-Benz 811D	Alexander AM	B28F	1992
633	J633 HMH	Mercedes-Benz 811D	Alexander AM	B28F	1992

639–645		Dennis Dart 8.5SDL3003				Wright Handybus 8.5m		B26F	1991
639	JDZ 2339	**641**	JDZ 2341	**643**	JDZ 2343	**645**	JDZ 2373		
640	JDZ 2340	**642**	JDZ 2342	**644**	JDZ 2372				

669	J459 JOW	Dennis Dart 9SDL3011	Wadham Stringer Portsdown 9m	B37F	1991
670	L670 SMC	Dennis Dart 9SDL3034	Northern Counties Paladin 9m	B31F	1994

671–680		Volvo B6–41				Alexander Dash		B31F	1994
671	L671 RMD	**673**	L673 RMD	**675**	L675 RMD	**677**	L677 RMD	**679**	L679 RMD
672	L672 RMD	**674**	L674 RMD	**676**	L676 RMD	**678**	L678 RMD	**680**	L680 RMD

691–696		Dennis Dart 9SDL3016				Plaxton Pointer 9m		B35F	1992
691	K901 CVW	**693**	K903 CVW	**695**	K905 CVW				
692	K902 CVW	**694**	K904 CVW	**696**	K906 CVW				

701–704		Optare Excel L1000				Optare		B33F	1996
701	P701 HMT	**702**	P702 HMT	**703**	P703 HMT	**704**	P704 HMT		

705–717		Dennis Dart SLF SFD212BR1VGW1				East Lancs Spryte 10.3m		B37F	1998
705	R705 VLA	**708**	R708 VLA	**711**	R711 VLA	**714**	R714 VLA	**717**	R717 VLA
706	R706 VLA	**709**	R709 VLA	**712**	R712 VLA	**715**	R715 VLA		
707	R707 VLA	**710**	R710 VLA	**713**	R713 VLA	**716**	R716 VLA		

739u	KRS 539V	Leyland National 2 NL106L11/1R		B44F	1980
744	GUW 454W	Leyland National 2 NL106AL11/2R		B41F	1981
749	B359 LOY	Leyland National 2 NL116L11/3R		B49F	1985
750	NLP 389V	Leyland National 2 NL116L11/3R		B49F	1980

773–786		Dennis Dart SFD412BR5TGD1				Plaxton Pointer 9.8m		B40F	1996
773	N973 EHJ	**776**	N976 EHJ	**779**	N979 EHJ	**782**	N982 EHJ	**785**	N985 EHJ
774	N974 EHJ	**777**	N977 EHJ	**780**	N980 EHJ	**783**	N983 EHJ	**786**	N986 EHJ
775	N975 EHJ	**778**	N978 EHJ	**781**	N981 EHJ	**784**	N984 EHJ		

796	M796 MPM	Dennis Lance 11SDA3101	Alexander PS	B46F	1991
913	ALD 913B	AEC Routemaster R2RH	Park Royal	H36/28R	1964
920	VLT 120	AEC Routemaster R2RH	Park Royal	O36/28R	1959

On order:–

Twenty-two Dennis Trident/Alexander ALX400 10.5m buses for route 25 due spring 2000.
Seven Dennis Dart SLF/Marshall Capital 9.3m buses due spring 2000.
Eleven Dennis Dart SLF/Marshall Capital 10.2m buses due spring 2000.

Previous registrations:–

BYX 284V	BYX 284V, VLT 284
GYE 379W	GYE 379W, WLT 379
GYE 479W	GYE 479W, VLT 179
P401 PLE	P901 HMH
P402 PLE	P902 HMH
P403 PLE	P903 HMH
P404 PLE	P904 HMH
P405 PLE	P905 HMH
P406 PLE	P906 HMH
P407 PLE	P907 HMH
P408 PLE	P908 HMH
P409 PLE	P909 HMH
P410 PLE	P910 HMH
P411 PLE	P911 HMH
P412 PLE	P912 HMH

FIRST CENTREWEST

D 33–41 Dennis Dart SFD412BR5TGD1 Plaxton Pointer 9.8m B37F 1996

D 33	N633 ACF	**D 35**	N635 ACF	**D 37**	N637 ACF	**D 39**	P409 MLA	**D 41**	P411 MLA
D 34	N634 ACF	**D 36**	N636 ACF	**D 38**	P408 MLA	**D 40**	P410 MLA		

D 601–610 Dennis Dart 9.8SDL3054 Plaxton Pointer 9.8m B37F 1996

D 601	N601 XJM	**D 603**	N603 XJM	**D 605**	N605 XJM	**D 607**	N607 XJM	**D 609**	N609 XJM
D 602	N602 XJM	**D 604**	N604 XJM	**D 606**	N606 XJM	**D 608**	N608 XJM	**D 610**	N610 XJM

DM 117–157 Dennis Dart SLF SFD112BR1VGW1 Marshall Capital 9.3m B31F 1997

DM 117	P117 NLW	**DM 126**	P126 NLW	**DM 135**	P135 NLW	**DM 144**	P144 NLW	**DM 153**	P153 NLW
DM 118	P118 NLW	**DM 127**	P127 NLW	**DM 136**	P136 NLW	**DM 145**	P145 NLW	**DM 154**	P154 NLW
DM 119	P119 NLW	**DM 128**	P128 NLW	**DM 137**	P137 NLW	**DM 146**	P146 NLW	**DM 155**	P255 RFL
DM 120	P120 NLW	**DM 129**	P129 NLW	**DM 138**	P138 NLW	**DM 147**	P247 OEW	**DM 156**	P156 NLW
DM 121	P121 NLW	**DM 130**	P130 NLW	**DM 139**	P139 NLW	**DM 148**	P148 NLW	**DM 157**	P157 NLW
DM 122	P122 NLW	**DM 131**	P131 NLW	**DM 140**	P140 NLW	**DM 149**	P149 NLW		
DM 123	P123 NLW	**DM 132**	P132 NLW	**DM 141**	P141 NLW	**DM 150**	P150 NLW		
DM 124	P124 NLW	**DM 133**	P133 NLW	**DM 142**	P142 NLW	**DM 151**	P151 NLW		
DM 125	P125 NLW	**DM 134**	P134 NLW	**DM 143**	P143 NLW	**DM 152**	P152 NLW		

DM 158–164 Dennis Dart SLF SFD112BR1WGW1 (DM 163 is SFD112BR1VGW1) Marshall Capital 9.3m B33F 1997

DM 158	R158 TLM	**DM 160**	R160 TLM	**DM 162**	R162 TLM	**DM 164**	R164 TLM
DM 159	R159 TLM	**DM 161**	R161 TLM	**DM 163**	R163 TLM		

DM 201–234 Dennis Dart SLF SFD112BR1WGW1 Marshall Capital 9.3m B23D 1998

DM 201	R201 TLM	**DM 208**	R208 TLM	**DM 215**	R215 TLM	**DM 222**	R322 TLM	**DM 229**	R229 TLM
DM 202	R202 TLM	**DM 209**	R209 TLM	**DM 216**	R216 TLM	**DM 223**	R223 TLM	**DM 230**	R230 TLM
DM 203	R203 TLM	**DM 210**	R210 TLM	**DM 217**	R217 TLM	**DM 224**	R224 TLM	**DM 231**	R231 TLM
DM 204	R204 TLM	**DM 211**	R211 TLM	**DM 218**	R218 TLM	**DM 225**	R225 TLM	**DM 232**	R232 TLM
DM 205	R205 TLM	**DM 212**	R212 TLM	**DM 219**	R219 TLM	**DM 226**	R226 TLM	**DM 233**	R233 TLM
DM 206	R206 TLM	**DM 213**	R213 TLM	**DM 220**	R220 TLM	**DM 227**	R227 TLM	**DM 234**	R234 TLM
DM 207	R207 TLM	**DM 214**	R214 TLM	**DM 221**	R221 TLM	**DM 228**	R228 TLM		

DM 264–306 Dennis Dart SLF SFD112BR1XGW1 Marshall Capital 9.3m B22D 1999

DM 264	T264 JLD	**DM 273**	T273 JLD	**DM 282**	T282 JLD	**DM 291**	T291 JLD	**DM 300**	T430 JLD
DM 265	T265 JLD	**DM 274**	T274 JLD	**DM 283**	T283 JLD	**DM 292**	T292 JLD	**DM 301**	T301 JLD
DM 266	T266 JLD	**DM 275**	T275 JLD	**DM 284**	T284 JLD	**DM 293**	T293 JLD	**DM 302**	T302 JLD
DM 267	T267 JLD	**DM 276**	T276 JLD	**DM 285**	T285 JLD	**DM 294**	T294 JLD	**DM 303**	T303 JLD
DM 268	T268 JLD	**DM 277**	T277 JLD	**DM 286**	T286 JLD	**DM 295**	T295 JLD	**DM 304**	T304 JLD
DM 269	T269 JLD	**DM 278**	T278 JLD	**DM 287**	T287 JLD	**DM 296**	T296 JLD	**DM 305**	T305 JLD
DM 270	T270 JLD	**DM 279**	T279 JLD	**DM 288**	T288 JLD	**DM 297**	T297 JLD	**DM 306**	T306 JLD
DM 271	T271 JLD	**DM 280**	T280 JLD	**DM 289**	T289 JLD	**DM 298**	T298 JLD		
DM 272	T272 JLD	**DM 281**	T281 JLD	**DM 290**	T290 JLD	**DM 299**	T299 JLD		

DML 165–178 Dennis Dart SLF SFD212BR1VGW1 Marshall Capital 10.2m B35F 1997

DML 165	R165 TLM	**DML 168**	R168 TLM	**DML 171**	R171 TLM	**DML 174**	R174 TLM	**DML 177**	R177 TLM
DML 166	R166 TLM	**DML 169**	R169 TLM	**DML 172**	R172 TLM	**DML 175**	R175 TLM	**DML 178**	R178 TLM
DML 167	R167 TLM	**DML 170**	R170 TLM	**DML 173**	R173 TLM	**DML 176**	R176 TLM		

DML 179–190 Dennis Dart SLF SFD212BR1WGW1 Marshall Capital 10.2m B37F 1998

DML 179	R179 TLM	**DML 182**	R182 TLM	**DML 185**	R185 TLM	**DML 188**	R188 TLM
DML 180	R180 TLM	**DML 183**	R183 TLM	**DML 186**	R186 TLM	**DML 189**	R189 TLM
DML 181	R181 TLM	**DML 184**	R184 TLM	**DML 187**	R187 TLM	**DML 190**	R190 TLM

DML 191–200 Dennis Dart SLF SFD212BR1WGW1 Marshall Capital 10.2m B35F 1998

DML 191	R191 VLD	**DML 193**	R193 VLD	**DML 195**	R195 VLD	**DML 197**	S197 KLM	**DML 199**	S199 KLM
DML 192	R192 VLD	**DML 194**	R194 VLD	**DML 196**	R196 VLD	**DML 198**	S198 KLM	**DML 200**	S220 KLM

DML 235–256 Dennis Dart SLF SFD212BR1WGW1 Marshall Capital 10.2m B29F 1998

DML 235	S235 KLM	**DML 239**	S239 KLM	**DML 243**	S243 KLM	**DML 247**	S247 KLM	**DML 255**	S255 JLP
DML 236	S236 KLM	**DML 240**	S240 KLM	**DML 244**	S244 KLM	**DML 248**	S248 KLM	**DML 256**	S256 JLP
DML 237	S237 KLM	**DML 241**	S241 KLM	**DML 245**	S245 KLM	**DML 253**	S253 JLP		
DML 238	S238 KLM	**DML 242**	S242 KLM	**DML 246**	S246 KLM	**DML 254**	S254 JLP		

DML 336 T336 ALR Dennis Dart SLF SFD212BR1XGW1 Marshall Capital 10.2m B35F 1999

DML 362–380 Dennis Dart SLF SFD212BR1XGW1 Marshall Capital 10.2m B28D 2000

DML 362	W362 VLN	**DML 366**		**DML 370**		**DML 374**		**DML 378**	
DML 363	W363 VLN	**DML 367**		**DML 371**		**DML 375**		**DML 379**	
DML 364	W364 VLN	**DML 368**		**DML 372**		**DML 376**		**DML 380**	
DML 365		**DML 369**		**DML 373**		**DML 377**			

DMS 257–263 Dennis Dart SLF SFD612BR1WGW1 Marshall Capital 8.9m B25F 1999

DMS 257	T257 JLD	**DMS 259**	T259 JLD	**DMS 261**	T261 JLD	**DMS 263**	T263 JLD
DMS 258	T258 JLD	**DMS 260**	T260 JLD	**DMS 262**	T262 JLD		

DMS 337–361 Dennis Dart SLF SFD612BR1XGW1 Marshall Capital 8.9m B25F 1999

DMS 337	T337 ALR	**DMS 342**	T342 ALR	**DMS 347**	V347 DLH	**DMS 352**	V352 DLH	**DMS 357**	V357 DLH
DMS 338	T338 ALR	**DMS 343**	T343 ALR	**DMS 348**	V348 DLH	**DMS 353**	V353 DLH	**DMS 358**	V358 DLH
DMS 339	T339 ALR	**DMS 344**	T344 ALR	**DMS 349**	V349 DLH	**DMS 354**	V354 DLH	**DMS 359**	V359 DLH
DMS 340	T340 ALR	**DMS 345**	V345 DLH	**DMS 350**	V350 DLH	**DMS 355**	V355 DLH	**DMS 360**	V360 DLH
DMS 341	T341 ALR	**DMS 346**	V346 DLH	**DMS 351**	V351 DLH	**DMS 356**	V356 DLH	**DMS 361**	V361 DLH

DP 1–17		Dennis Dart 9SDL3053		Plaxton Pointer 9m		B32F	1995		
DP 1	N801 FLW	**DP 5**	N805 FLW	**DP 9**	N809 FLW	**DP 13**	N813 FLW	**DP 17**	N817 FLW
DP 2	N802 FLW	**DP 6**	N806 FLW	**DP 10**	N810 FLW	**DP 14**	N814 FLW		
DP 3	N803 FLW	**DP 7**	N807 FLW	**DP 11**	N811 FLW	**DP 15**	N815 FLW		
DP 4	N804 FLW	**DP 8**	N808 FLW	**DP 12**	N812 FLW	**DP 16**	N816 FLW		

DW 1–14		Dennis Dart 8.5SDL3003		Wright Handybus 8.5m		DP30F	1990		
DW 1	JDZ 2301	**DW 4**	JDZ 2304	**DW 7**	JDZ 2307	**DW 10**	JDZ 2310	**DW 13**	JDZ 2313
DW 2	JDZ 2302	**DW 5**	JDZ 2305	**DW 8**	JDZ 2308	**DW 11**	JDZ 2311	**DW 14**	JDZ 2314
DW 3	JDZ 2303	**DW 6**	JDZ 2306	**DW 9**	JDZ 2309	**DW 12**	JDZ 2312		

DW 15–24		Dennis Dart 8.5SDL3003		Wright Handybus 8.5m		B26F	1990
DW 15	JDZ 2315	**DW 17**	JDZ 2317	**DW 23**	JDZ 2323		
DW 16	JDZ 2316	**DW 22**	JDZ 2322	**DW 24**	JDZ 2324		

DW 26–32		Dennis Dart 8.5SDL3003		Wright Handybus 8.5m		B30F	1990
DW 26	JDZ 2326	**DW 28**	JDZ 2328	**DW 30**	JDZ 2330	**DW 32**	JDZ 2332
DW 27	JDZ 2327	**DW 29**	JDZ 2329	**DW 31**	JDZ 2331		

DW 75	JDZ 2375	Dennis Dart 8.5SDL3003	Wright Handybus 8.5m	B26F	1990
DW 113	LDZ 9113	Dennis Dart 8.5SDL3010	Wright Handybus 8.5m	B26F	1992
DW 114	LDZ 9114	Dennis Dart 8.5SDL3010	Wright Handybus 8.5m	B26F	1992

DW 115–126		Dennis Dart 8.5SDL3015 (DW 126 is SDL3018)		Wright Handybus 8.5m		B26F	1992
DW 115	LDZ 9115	**DW 118**	LDZ 9118	**DW 121**	LDZ 9121	**DW 124**	LDZ 9124
DW 116	LDZ 9116	**DW 119**	LDZ 9119	**DW 122**	LDZ 9122	**DW 125**	LDZ 9125
DW 117	LDZ 9117	**DW 120**	LDZ 9120	**DW 123**	LDZ 9123	**DW 126**	LDZ 9126

DW 162–170		Dennis Dart 8.5SDL3015 (DW 169 & 170 are B26F)		Wright Handybus 8.5m		B29F	1993		
DW 162	NDZ 3162	**DW 164**	NDZ 3164	**DW 166**	NDZ 3166	**DW 168**	NDZ 3168	**DW 170**	NDZ 3170
DW 163	NDZ 3163	**DW 165**	NDZ 3165	**DW 167**	NDZ 3167	**DW 169**	NDZ 3169		

L 1–6		Dennis Dart SLF SFD212BR1TGW1		Plaxton Pointer 10m		B34F	1996
L 1	P401 MLA	**L 3**	P403 MLA	**L 5**	P405 MLA		
L 2	P402 MLA	**L 4**	P404 MLA	**L 6**	P406 MLA		

LA 24–28		Leyland Olympian ON2R50C13Z4		Alexander RH		H45/29F	1993		
LA 24	L24 GAN	**LA 25**	L25 GAN	**LA 26**	L26 GAN	**LA 27**	L27 GAN	**LA 28**	L28 GAN

LC 1–3		LDV 400		Crystals		DP10FL	1995
LC 1	N921 LUF	**LC 2**	N922 LUF	**LC 3**	N923 LUF		

LLW 11–24		Dennis Lance SLF 11SDA3201		Wright Pathfinder 320		B34D	1993/4		
LLW 11	ODZ 8911	**LLW 14**	ODZ 8914	**LLW 17**	ODZ 8917	**LLW 20**	ODZ 8920	**LLW 23**	ODZ 8923
LLW 12	ODZ 8912	**LLW 15**	ODZ 8915	**LLW 18**	ODZ 8918	**LLW 21**	ODZ 8921	**LLW 24**	ODZ 8924
LLW 13	ODZ 8913	**LLW 16**	ODZ 8916	**LLW 19**	ODZ 8919	**LLW 22**	ODZ 8922		

LLW 31	M221 EAF	Dennis Lance SLF 11SDA3202	Wright Pathfinder 320	B40F	1995

LN 31–43	Leyland Olympian ON2R50C13Z4	Northern Counties	H47/30F	1990

LN 31	H131 FLX	**LN 33**	H133 FLX	**LN 34**	H134 FLX	**LN 38**	H138 FLX	**LN 43**	H143 FLX

LS 504t	GUW 504W	Leyland National 2 NL106AL11/2R (Volvo)		DP43F	1981

M 285–499	MCW Metrobus DR101/12	MCW	H43/28D	1980

M 285	BYX 285V	**M 338**	EYE 338V	**M 368**	GYE 368W	**M 385**	GYE 385W	**M 442**	GYE 442W
M 291	BYX 291V	**M 347**	GYE 347W	**M 370**	GYE 370W	**M 390**	GYE 390W	**M 470**	GYE 470W
M 305	BYX 305V	**M 349**	GYE 349W	**M 371**	GYE 371W	**M 393**	GYE 393W	**M 486**	GYE 486W
M 308	BYX 308V	**M 362**	GYE 362W	**M 374**	GYE 374W	**M 406**	GYE 406W	**M 489**	GYE 489W
M 337	EYE 337V	**M 364**	GYE 364W	**M 383**	GYE 383W	**M 414**	GYE 414W	**M 499**u	GYE 499W

M 523	GYE 523W	MCW Metrobus DR101/14	MCW	H43/28D	1980
M 583	GYE 583W	MCW Metrobus DR101/14	MCW	H43/28D	1980

M 851–943	MCW Metrobus DR101/16	MCW	H43/28D	1983

M 851	OJD 851Y	**M 860**	OJD 860Y	**M 882**	OJD 882Y	**M 938**	A938 SUL
M 859	OJD 859Y	**M 875**	OJD 875Y	**M 883**	OJD 883Y	**M 943**	A943 SUL

M 979	A979 SYF	MCW Metrobus DR101/17	MCW	H43/28D	1984

M 1144–1438	MCW Metrobus DR101/17	MCW	H43/28D	1985/6

M 1144	B144 WUL	**M 1256**	B256 WUL	**M 1338**t	C338 BUV	**M 1382**	C382 BUV	**M 1420**d	C420 BUV
M 1199	B199 WUL	**M 1258**	B258 WUL	**M 1340**t	C340 BUV	**M 1384**t	C384 BUV	**M 1421**	C421 BUV
M 1201	B201 WUL	**M 1259**	B259 WUL	**M 1375**	C375 BUV	**M 1400**	C400 BUV	**M 1422**	C422 BUV
M 1244	B244 WUL	**M 1260**t	B260 WUL	**M 1376**	C376 BUV	**M 1412**t	C412 BUV	**M 1438**	C438 BUV
M 1245	B245 WUL	**M 1267**	B267 WUL	**M 1377**	C377 BUV	**M 1415**	C415 BUV		
M 1246	B246 WUL	**M 1328**t	C328 BUV	**M 1378**	C378 BUV	**M 1418**t	C418 BUV		
M 1247	B247 WUL	**M 1335**t	C335 BUV	**M 1380**t	C380 BUV	**M 1419**t	C419 BUV		

MA 1u	F601 XMS	Mercedes-Benz 811D	Alexander AM	B26F	1988
MT 8	G538 GBD	Mercedes-Benz 709D	Reeve Burgess Beaver	B18FL	1989
RF 326u	MLL 963	AEC Regal IV 9821LT	Metro-Cammell	B39F	1952
RMC 1510	510 CLT	AEC Routemaster R2RH	Park Royal	O32/25RD	1962
RML 885	WLT 885	AEC Routemaster R2RH	Park Royal	H40/32R	1961

RML 2268–2740	AEC Routemaster R2RH/1	Park Royal	H40/32R	1965–67

RML 2268	CUV 268C	**RML 2374**	JJD 374D	**RML 2476**	JJD 476D	**RML 2553**	JJD 553D	**RML 2672**	SMK 672F
RML 2278	CUV 278C	**RML 2378**	JJD 378D	**RML 2480**	JJD 480D	**RML 2555**	JJD 555D	**RML 2677**	SMK 677F
RML 2281	CUV 281C	**RML 2379**	JJD 379D	**RML 2486**	JJD 486D	**RML 2559**	JJD 559D	**RML 2687**	SMK 687F
RML 2291	CUV 291C	**RML 2388**	JJD 388D	**RML 2490**	JJD 490D	**RML 2602**	NML 602E	**RML 2717**	SMK 717F
RML 2309	CUV 309C	**RML 2390**	JJD 390D	**RML 2498**	JJD 498D	**RML 2609**	NML 609E	**RML 2724**	SMK 724F
RML 2313	CUV 313C	**RML 2405**	JJD 405D	**RML 2501**	JJD 501D	**RML 2623**	NML 623E	**RML 2735**	SMK 735F
RML 2352	CUV 352C	**RML 2428**	JJD 428D	**RML 2506**	JJD 506D	**RML 2647**	NML 647E	**RML 2740**	SMK 740F
RML 2357	CUV 357C	**RML 2442**	JJD 442D	**RML 2522**	JJD 522D	**RML 2656**	NML 656E		
RML 2365	JJD 365D	**RML 2467**	JJD 467D	**RML 2530**	JJD 530D	**RML 2664**	SMK 664F		
RML 2369	JJD 369D	**RML 2473**	JJD 473D	**RML 2542**	JJD 542D	**RML 2667**	SMK 667F		

TN 823–853	Dennis Trident SFD113BR1XGX2	Plaxton President 9.9m	H39/20D	1999

TN 823	T823 LLC	**TN 830**	T830 LLC	**TN 837**	T837 LLC	**TN 844**	T844 LLC	**TN 851**	T851 LLC
TN 824	T824 LLC	**TN 831**	T831 LLC	**TN 838**	T838 LLC	**TN 845**	T845 LLC	**TN 852**	T852 LLC
TN 825	T825 LLC	**TN 832**	T832 LLC	**TN 839**	T839 LLC	**TN 846**	T846 LLC	**TN 853**	T853 LLC
TN 826	T826 LLC	**TN 833**	T833 LLC	**TN 840**	T840 LLC	**TN 847**	T847 LLC		
TN 827	T827 LLC	**TN 834**	T834 LLC	**TN 841**	T841 LLC	**TN 848**	T848 LLC		
TN 828	T828 LLC	**TN 835**	T835 LLC	**TN 842**	T842 LLC	**TN 849**	T849 LLC		
TN 829	T829 LLC	**TN 836**	T836 LLC	**TN 843**	T843 LLC	**TN 850**	T850 LLC		

TNL 888–930		Dennis Trident SFD313				Plaxton President 10.5m		H43/24D	2000
TNL 888	V988 HLH	**TNL 897**	V897 HLH	**TNL 906**		**TNL 915**		**TNL 924**	
TNL 889	V889 HLH	**TNL 898**	V898 HLH	**TNL 907**		**TNL 916**		**TNL 925**	
TNL 890	V890 HLH	**TNL 899**	V899 HLH	**TNL 908**		**TNL 917**		**TNL 926**	
TNL 891	V891 HLH	**TNL 900**	V990 HLH	**TNL 909**		**TNL 918**		**TNL 927**	
TNL 892	V892 HLH	**TNL 901**		**TNL 910**		**TNL 919**		**TNL 928**	
TNL 893	V893 HLH	**TNL 902**		**TNL 911**		**TNL 920**		**TNL 929**	
TNL 894	V894 HLH	**TNL 903**		**TNL 912**		**TNL 921**		**TNL 930**	
TNL 895	V895 HLH	**TNL 904**		**TNL 913**		**TNL 922**			
TNL 896	V896 HLH	**TNL 905**		**TNL 914**		**TNL 923**			

V 1–12		Volvo Olympian YN2RV18Z4				Northern Counties Palatine II		H43/29F	1995
V 1	N301 JBV	**V 4**	N304 JBV	**V 7**	N307 JBV	**V 10**	N310 JBV		
V 2	N302 JBV	**V 5**	N305 JBV	**V 8**	N308 JBV	**V 11**	N311 JBV		
V 3	N303 JBV	**V 6**	N306 JBV	**V 9**	N309 JBV	**V 12**	N312 JBV		

V 41–55		Volvo Olympian OLY–50				Northern Counties Palatine II		H43/29F	1996
V 41	P241 UCW	**V 44**	P244 UCW	**V 47**	P247 UCW	**V 50**	P250 UCW	**V 53**	P253 UCW
V 42	P242 UCW	**V 45**	P245 UCW	**V 48**	P248 UCW	**V 51**	P251 UCW	**V 54**	P254 UCW
V 43	P243 UCW	**V 46**	P246 UCW	**V 49**	P249 UCW	**V 52**	P252 UCW	**V 55**	P255 UCW

* VN 88–107		Volvo Olympian OLY–49 * Originally numbered VN 888–907				Northern Counties Palatine I		H47/27D	1999
VN 88	T988 KLF	**VN 92**	T892 KLF	**VN 96**	T896 KLF	**VN 100**	T990 KLF	**VN 104**	T904 KLF
VN 89	T889 KLF	**VN 93**	T893 KLF	**VN 97**	T897 KLF	**VN 101**	T901 KLF	**VN 105**	T905 KLF
VN 90	T890 KLF	**VN 94**	T894 KLF	**VN 98**	T898 KLF	**VN 102**	T902 KLF	**VN 106**	T906 KLF
VN 91	T891 KLF	**VN 95**	T895 KLF	**VN 99**	T899 KLF	**VN 103**	T903 KLF	**VN 107**	T907 KLF

Special liveries:–
The training buses are predominantly yellow.
The LC class and MT 8 carry an all white livery for a London Borough of Richmond Council contract.

FIRST LONDON BUSLINES

D 611–632		Dennis Dart SFD412BR5TGD1				Plaxton Pointer 9.8m		B37F	1996
D 611	N611 XJM	**D 616**	N616 XJM	**D 621**	N621 XJM	**D 626**	N626 XJM	**D 631**	P631 CGM
D 612	N612 XJM	**D 617**	N617 XJM	**D 622**	N622 XJM	**D 627**	P627 CGM	**D 632**	P632 CGM
D 613	N613 XJM	**D 618**	N618 XJM	**D 623**	N623 XJM	**D 628**	P628 CGM		
D 614	N614 XJM	**D 619**	N619 XJM	**D 624**	N624 XJM	**D 629**	P629 CGM		
D 615	N615 XJM	**D 620**	N620 XJM	**D 625**	N625 XJM	**D 630**	P630 CGM		

DML 633–653		Dennis Dart SLF SFD212BR1VGW1		Marshall Capital 10.2m				B37F	1997/98
DML 633	R633 VLX	**DML 637**	R637 VLX	**DML 641**	R641 VLX	**DML 645**	R645 TLM	**DML 650**	R650 TLM
DML 634	R634 VLX	**DML 638**	R638 VLX	**DML 642**	R642 TLM	**DML 646**	R646 TLM	**DML 651**	R651 TLM
DML 635	R835 VLX	**DML 639**	R639 VLX	**DML 643**	R643 TLM	**DML 647**	R647 TLM	**DML 652**	R652 TLM
DML 636	R636 VLX	**DML 640**	R640 VLX	**DML 644**	R644 TLM	**DML 649**	R649 TLM	**DML 653**	R653 TLM

L 7	P407 MLA	Dennis Dart SLF SFD212BR1TGW1	Plaxton Pointer 10m	B34F	1996
L 237	P237 NLW	Dennis Dart SLF SFD212BR1TGW1	Plaxton Pointer 10m	B35F	1996
L 238	P238 NLW	Dennis Dart SLF SFD212BR1TGW1	Plaxton Pointer 10m	B35F	1996
L 239	P239 NLW	Dennis Dart SLF SFD212BR1TGW1	Plaxton Pointer 10m	B35F	1996
RB 551	K651 DBL	Renault-Dodge S75	Plaxton Beaver	B18FL	1992
RB 552	K652 DBL	Renault-Dodge S75	Plaxton Beaver	B18FL	1992
RB 553	K653 DBL	Renault-Dodge S75	Plaxton Beaver	B18FL	1992

FIRST THAMESWAY Routes 193 and Mobility Network

401–410		Mercedes-Benz 711D		Plaxton Beaver				B23F	1996
401	P401 HPU	**403**	P403 HPU	**405**	P405 HPU	**407**	P407 HPU	**409**	P409 HPU
402	P402 HPU	**404**	P404 HPU	**406**	P406 HPU	**408**	P408 HPU	**410**	P410 HPU

851–854		Dennis Dart 9SDL3053		Marshall C36 9m				B17FL	1995
851	N851 CPU	**852**	N852 CPU	**853**	N853 CPU	**854**	N854 CPU		

LONDON CENTRAL & LONDON GENERAL

AV 1–9		Volvo Olympian YN2RC16Z4		Alexander Royale				H45/29F	1995
AV 1	M81 MYM	**AV 3**	M83 MYM	**AV 5**	M85 MYM	**AV 7**	M87 MYM	**AV 9**	WLT 789
AV 2	M82 MYM	**AV 4**	M84 MYM	**AV 6**	M86 MYM	**AV 8**	M91 MYM		

AVL 1–46		Volvo B7L		Alexander ALX400 10.2m				H43/20D	1999/2000
AVL 1	V101 LGC	**AVL 11**	V211 LGC	**AVL 21**	V221 LGC	**AVL 31**	V131 LGC	**AVL 41**	V141 LGC
AVL 2	V102 LGC	**AVL 12**	V112 LGC	**AVL 22**	V122 LGC	**AVL 32**	V132 LGC	**AVL 42**	V142 LGC
AVL 3	V103 LGC	**AVL 13**	V113 LGC	**AVL 23**	V223 LGC	**AVL 33**	V133 LGC	**AVL 43**	V143 LGC
AVL 4	V104 LGC	**AVL 14**	V114 LGC	**AVL 24**	V124 LGC	**AVL 34**	V134 LGC	**AVL 44**	V144 LGC
AVL 5	V105 LGC	**AVL 15**	V115 LGC	**AVL 25**	V125 LGC	**AVL 35**	V135 LGC	**AVL 45**	V145 LGC
AVL 6	V106 LGC	**AVL 16**	V116 LGC	**AVL 26**	V126 LGC	**AVL 36**	V136 LGC	**AVL 46**	V146 LGC
AVL 7	V107 LGC	**AVL 17**	V117 LGC	**AVL 27**	V127 LGC	**AVL 37**	V137 LGC		
AVL 8	V108 LGC	**AVL 18**	V118 LGC	**AVL 28**	V128 LGC	**AVL 38**	V138 LGC		
AVL 9	V109 LGC	**AVL 19**	V119 LGC	**AVL 29**	V129 LGC	**AVL 39**	V139 LGC		
AVL 10	V110 LGC	**AVL 20**	V120 LGC	**AVL 30**	V130 LGC	**AVL 40**	V140 LGC		

DEL 1–11		Dennis Dart 9SDL3034		East Lancs EL2000 9m				B34F	1994
DEL 1	L901 JRN	**DEL 4**	L904 JRN	**DEL 7**	L907 JRN	**DEL 10**	L910 JRN		
DEL 2	L902 JRN	**DEL 5**	L905 JRN	**DEL 8**	L908 JRN	**DEL 11**	L911 JRN		
DEL 3	L903 JRN	**DEL 6**	L906 JRN	**DEL 9**	L909 JRN				

DML 1–29		Dennis Dart SLF SFD112BR1XGW1		Marshall Capital 9.3m				B30F	1999
DML 1	T401 AGP	**DML 7**	T407 AGP	**DML 13**	T413 AGP	**DML 19**	T419 AGP	**DML 25**	T425 AGP
DML 2	T402 AGP	**DML 8**	T408 AGP	**DML 14**	T414 AGP	**DML 20**	T392 AGP	**DML 26**	T426 AGP
DML 3	T403 AGP	**DML 9**	T409 AGP	**DML 15**	T415 AGP	**DML 21**	T421 AGP	**DML 27**	T427 AGP
DML 4	T404 AGP	**DML 10**	T410 AGP	**DML 16**	T416 AGP	**DML 22**	T422 AGP	**DML 28**	T428 AGP
DML 5	T455 AGP	**DML 11**	T411 AGP	**DML 17**	T417 AGP	**DML 23**	T423 AGP	**DML 29**	T429 AGP
DML 6	T406 AGP	**DML 12**	T512 AGP	**DML 18**	T418 AGP	**DML 24**	T424 AGP		

DMS 1–15		Dennis Dart SLF SFD612BR1WGW1		Marshall Capital 8.9m				B28F	1999
DMS 1	T101 KGP	**DMS 4**	T104 KGP	**DMS 7**	T107 KGP	**DMS 10**	T110 KGP	**DMS 13**	T113 KGP
DMS 2	T102 KGP	**DMS 5**	T105 KGP	**DMS 8**	T108 KGP	**DMS 11**	101 CLT	**DMS 14**	T114 KGP
DMS 3	T103 KGP	**DMS 6**	T106 KGP	**DMS 9**	T109 KGP	**DMS 12**	T112 KGP	**DMS 15**	T115 KGP

DPL 1–16		Dennis Dart 9SDL3053		Plaxton Pointer 9m				B35F	1995
DPL 1	M201 EGF	**DPL 5**	M205 EGF	**DPL 9**	M209 EGF	**DPL 13**	M213 EGF		
DPL 2	M202 EGF	**DPL 6**	M206 EGF	**DPL 10**	M210 EGF	**DPL 14**	M214 EGF		
DPL 3	M203 EGF	**DPL 7**	M207 EGF	**DPL 11**	M211 EGF	**DPL 15**	M215 EGF		
DPL 4	M204 EGF	**DPL 8**	M208 EGF	**DPL 12**	M212 EGF	**DPL 16**	M216 EGF		

DR 32–52	Dennis Dart 8.5SDL3003	Plaxton Pointer 8.5 m	B28F	1991

DR 32	WLT 532	**DR 36**	H536 XGK	**DR 41**	H541 XGK	**DR 46**	46 CLT	**DR 51**	H551 XGK
DR 33	H533 XGK	**DR 37**	H537 XGK	**DR 43**	H543 XGK	**DR 47**	H547 XGK	**DR 52**	H552 XGK
DR 34	H534 XGK	**DR 38**	H538 XGK	**DR 44**	H544 XGK	**DR 48**	H548 XGK		
DR 35	H835 XGK	**DR 39**	H539 XGK	**DR 45**	H545 XGK	**DR 49**	H549 XGK		

DR 149–153	Dennis Dart 8.5SDL3015	Plaxton Pointer 8.5 m	B28F	1992

DR 149	K149 LGO	**DR 150**	K150 LGO	**DR 151**	K151 LGO	**DR 152**	K152 LGO	**DR 153**	K153 LGO

DRL 1–15	Dennis Dart 9SDL3011	Plaxton Pointer 9m	B34F	1991

DRL 1	J601 XHL	**DRL 4**	J604 XHL	**DRL 7**	J607 XHL	**DRL 10**	J610 XHL	**DRL 13**	J613 XHL
DRL 2	J602 XHL	**DRL 5**	J605 XHL	**DRL 8**	J608 XHL	**DRL 11**	J611 XHL	**DRL 14**	J614 XHL
DRL 3	J603 XHL	**DRL 6**	J606 XHL	**DRL 9**	J609 XHL	**DRL 12**	J612 XHL	**DRL 15**	J615 XHL

DRL 53–73	Dennis Dart 9SDL3016	Plaxton Pointer 9m	B34F	1992

DRL 53	K853 LGN	**DRL 58**	K858 LGN	**DRL 63**	K863 LGN	**DRL 68**	K868 LGN	**DRL 73**	K873 LGN
DRL 54	K854 LGN	**DRL 59**	K859 LGN	**DRL 64**	K864 LGN	**DRL 69**	K869 LGN		
DRL 55	K855 LGN	**DRL 60**	K860 LGN	**DRL 65**	K865 LGN	**DRL 70**	K870 LGN		
DRL 56	K856 LGN	**DRL 61**	K861 LGN	**DRL 66**	K866 LGN	**DRL 71**	K871 LGN		
DRL 57	K857 LGN	**DRL 62**	K862 LGN	**DRL 67**	K867 LGN	**DRL 72**	K872 LGN		

DRL 74–95	Dennis Dart 9SDL3024	Plaxton Pointer 9m	B32F	1993

DRL 74	K574 MGT	**DRL 79**	K579 MGT	**DRL 84**	K584 MGT	**DRL 89**	K589 MGT	**DRL 94**	K767 OGK
DRL 75	K575 MGT	**DRL 80**	K580 MGT	**DRL 85**	K585 MGT	**DRL 90**	K590 MGT	**DRL 95**	WLT 395
DRL 76	K576 MGT	**DRL 81**	K581 MGT	**DRL 86**	K586 MGT	**DRL 91**	K591 MGT		
DRL 77	K577 MGT	**DRL 82**	K582 MGT	**DRL 87**	K587 MGT	**DRL 92**	K592 MGT		
DRL 78	K578 MGT	**DRL 83**	K583 MGT	**DRL 88**	K588 MGT	**DRL 93**	K593 MGT		

DW 44–58	Dennis Dart 8.5SDL3003	Wright Handybus 8.5m	B30F	1990

DW 44	JDZ 2344	**DW 48**	G551 SGT	**DW 55**	JDZ 2355	**DW 56**	JDZ 2356	**DW 58**	JDZ 2358

DW 127–161	Dennis Dart 8.5SDL3015	Wright Handybus 8.5m	B30F	1992/3

DW 127	K127 LGO	**DW 128**	K128 LGO	**DW 130**	K130 LGO	**DW 131**w	K131 LGO	**DW 132**	K132 LGO

GLS 438–506	Leyland National 2 NL106AL11/2R	East Lancs Greenway (1992–94)	B24D*	1981

* GLS 448, 483–87, 496 are B38D. GLS 459 & 473 are B36D.

GLS 438	GUW 438W	**GLS 452**	GUW 452W	**GLS 471**	GUW 471W	**GLS 483**	83 CLT	**GLS 499**	GUW 499W
GLS 439	GUW 439W	**GLS 455**	GUW 455W	**GLS 473**	GUW 473W	**GLS 486**	186 CLT	**GLS 500**	GUW 500W
GLS 440	GUW 440W	**GLS 459**	GUW 459W	**GLS 474**	GUW 474W	**GLS 487**	WLT 487	**GLS 501**	GUW 501W
GLS 442	GUW 442W	**GLS 460**	GUW 460W	**GLS 476**	GUW 476W	**GLS 490**	GUW 490W	**GLS 502**	GUW 502W
GLS 443	WLT 843	**GLS 463**	WLT 463	**GLS 477**	GUW 477W	**GLS 491**	GUW 491W	**GLS 505**	GUW 505W
GLS 446	GUW 446W	**GLS 466**	GUW 466W	**GLS 478**	GUW 478W	**GLS 492**	GUW 492W	**GLS 506**	GUW 506W
GLS 448	WLT 648	**GLS 467**	WLT 467	**GLS 479**	GUW 479W	**GLS 493**	GUW 493W		
GLS 449	GUW 449W	**GLS 468**	GUW 468W	**GLS 480**	VLT 180	**GLS 496**	WLT 696		
GLS 450	GUW 450W	**GLS 469**	GUW 469W	**GLS 481**	GUW 481W	**GLS 498**	WLT 598		

LDP 1–17	Dennis Dart SLF SFD112BR1TGW1	Plaxton Pointer 9.2m	B32F	1996

LDP 1	P501 RYM	**LDP 5**	P505 RYM	**LDP 9**	WLT 379	**LDP 13**	P513 RYM	**LDP 17**	P517 RYM
LDP 2	P502 RYM	**LDP 6**	P506 RYM	**LDP 10**	P510 RYM	**LDP 14**	P514 RYM		
LDP 3	P503 RYM	**LDP 7**	P507 RYM	**LDP 11**	P511 RYM	**LDP 15**	P515 RYM		
LDP 4	P504 RYM	**LDP 8**	188 CLT	**LDP 12**	P512 RYM	**LDP 16**	P516 RYM		

LDP 18–44		Dennis Dart SLF SFD212BR1TGW1			Plaxton Pointer 10m			B36F	1996
LDP 18	P718 RYL	**LDP 24**	P724 RYL	**LDP 30**	P730 RYL	**LDP 36**	P736 RYL	**LDP 42**	P742 RYL
LDP 19	P719 RYL	**LDP 25**	P725 RYL	**LDP 31**	P731 RYL	**LDP 37**	P737 RYL	**LDP 43**	P743 RYL
LDP 20	P720 RYL	**LDP 26**	P726 RYL	**LDP 32**	P732 RYL	**LDP 38**	P738 RYL	**LDP 44**	P744 RYL
LDP 21	P721 RYL	**LDP 27**	P727 RYL	**LDP 33**	P733 RYL	**LDP 39**	P739 RYL		
LDP 22	P722 RYL	**LDP 28**	P728 RYL	**LDP 34**	P734 RYL	**LDP 40**	P740 RYL		
LDP 23	P723 RYL	**LDP 29**	P729 RYL	**LDP 35**	P735 RYL	**LDP 41**	P741 RYL		

LDP 45–89		Dennis Dart SLF SFD212BR1VGW1			Plaxton Pointer 10m			B36F	1997
LDP 45	R445 LGH	**LDP 55**	R455 LGH	**LDP 64**	R464 LGH	**LDP 73**	R473 LGH	**LDP 83**	R483 LGH
LDP 46	R446 LGH	**LDP 56**	R456 LGH	**LDP 65**	R465 LGH	**LDP 74**	174 CLT	**LDP 84**	R484 LGH
LDP 47	R447 LGH	**LDP 57**	R457 LGH	**LDP 66**	R466 LGH	**LDP 75**	R475 LGH	**LDP 85**	R485 LGH
LDP 48	R448 LGH	**LDP 58**	R458 LGH	**LDP 67**	R467 LGH	**LDP 76**	176 CLT	**LDP 86**	R486 LGH
LDP 49	R449 LGH	**LDP 59**	R459 LGH	**LDP 68**	R468 LGH	**LDP 77**	R477 LGH	**LDP 87**	R487 LGH
LDP 51	R451 LGH	**LDP 60**	R460 LGH	**LDP 69**	R469 LGH	**LDP 78**	R478 LGH	**LDP 88**	R488 LGH
LDP 52	R452 LGH	**LDP 61**	R461 LGH	**LDP 70**	R470 LGH	**LDP 79**	R479 LGH	**LDP 89**	R489 LGH
LDP 53	R453 LGH	**LDP 62**	R462 LGH	**LDP 71**	R471 LGH	**LDP 81**	R481 LGH		
LDP 54	R454 LGH	**LDP 63**	R463 LGH	**LDP 72**	WLT 872	**LDP 82**	R482 LGH		

LDP 90–117		Dennis Dart SLF SFD212AR1WGW1			Plaxton Pointer 2 10.1m			B29D	1998/9
LDP 90	WLT 990	**LDP 96**	S96 EGK	**LDP 103**	S103 EGK	**LDP 109**	S109 EGK	**LDP 115**	S115 EGK
LDP 91	S91 EGK	**LDP 97**	S97 EGK	**LDP 104**	S104 EGK	**LDP 110**	S110 EGK	**LDP 116**	S116 EGK
LDP 92	S92 EGK	**LDP 98**	S98 EGK	**LDP 105**	S105 EGK	**LDP 111**	WLT 311	**LDP 117**	S117 EGK
LDP 93	S93 EGK	**LDP 99**	WLT 599	**LDP 106**	S106 EGK	**LDP 112**	S112 EGK		
LDP 94	S94 EGK	**LDP 101**	S101 EGK	**LDP 107**	S107 EGK	**LDP 113**	S113 EGK		
LDP 95	S95 EGK	**LDP 102**	S102 EGK	**LDP 108**	S108 EGK	**LDP 114**	S114 EGK		

LDP 118–128		Dennis Dart SFD212BR1XGW1			Plaxton Pointer 2 10.1m			B32D	1999
LDP 118	T118 KGP	**LDP 121**	T521 AGP	**LDP 124**	T124 KGP	**LDP 127**	T127 KGP		
LDP 119	T119 KGP	**LDP 122**	T122 KGP	**LDP 125**	T125 KGP	**LDP 128**	T128 KGP		
LDP 120	T120 KGP	**LDP 123**	T523 AGP	**LDP 126**	T126 KGP				

M 47t	WYW 47T	MCW Metrobus DR101/6			MCW			H43/28D	1978

M 171–202		MCW Metrobus DR101/9 * OM171 is O43/27D			MCW			H43/28D*	1979
OM 171	VLT 71	**M 196**	BYX 196V	**M 201**	BYX 201V				
M 177	BYX 177V	**M 198**t	SGK 374V	**M 202**t	BYX 202V				

M 207–490		MCW Metrobus DR101/12 * OM 241 is O43/27D. OM420 is O43/28D			MCW			H43/28D*	1980
M 207	BYX 207V	**M 260**	BYX 260V	**M 297**	BYX 297V	**M 375**	GYE 375W	**M 431**	GYE 431W
M 211	BYX 211V	**M 265**	BYX 265V	**M 302**	BYX 302V	**M 392**	GYE 392W	**M 433**	GYE 433W
M 212	BYX 212V	**M 269**	BYX 269V	**M 307**	BYX 307V	**M 401**	GYE 401W	**M 435**	GYE 435W
M 214	BYX 214V	**M 274**	BYX 274V	**M 323**	EYE 323V	**M 404**	GYE 404W	**M 466**	GYE 466W
M 226	BYX 226V	**M 286**	BYX 286V	**M 331**	EYE 331V	**M 408**	GYE 408W	**M 472**u	GYE 472W
M 239	BYX 239V	**M 288**	BYX 288V	**M 333**	EYE 333V	**M 411**	GYE 411W	**M 475**u	GYE 475W
OM 241	BYX 241V	**M 289**	BYX 289V	**M 350**	GYE 350W	**M 412**	GYE 412W	**M 476**	GYE 476W
M 246	BYX 246V	**M 292**	BYX 292V	**M 354**	GYE 354W	**OM 420**	GYE 420W	**M 477**	GYE 477W
M 256	BYX 256V	**M 293**t	BYX 293V	**M 359**	GYE 359W	**M 423**	GYE 423W	**M 483**	GYE 483W
M 258	BYX 258V	**M 295**	BYX 295V	**M 361**	GYE 361W	**M 430**	GYE 430W	**M 490**t	GYE 490W

M 513–794		MCW Metrobus DR101/14			MCW			H43/28D	1980–81
M 513	GYE 513W	**M 542**	542 CLT	**M 597**	GYE 597W	**M 670**	KYV 670X	**M 725**	KYV 725X
M 514	GYE 514W	**M 556**	GYE 556W	**M 607**	KYO 607X	**M 690**	KYV 690X	**M 760**	KYV 760X
M 516	GYE 516W	**M 566**	GYE 566W	**M 662**	KYV 662X	**M 695**	KYV 695X	**M 763**	KYV 763X
M 532	GYE 532W	**M 589**	GYE 589W	**M 667**	KYV 667X	**M 706**	KYV 706X	**M 794**	KYV 794X

M 806–953 | MCW Metrobus DR101/16 | MCW | H43/28D | 1983

M 806	OJD 806Y	**M 822**	OJD 822Y	**M 846**	OJD 846Y	**M 871**	OJD 871Y	**M 909**	A909 SUL
M 807	OJD 807Y	**M 823**	OJD 823Y	**M 848**	OJD 848Y	**M 873**	OJD 873Y	**M 922**	A922 SUL
M 808	OJD 808Y	**M 826**	OJD 826Y	**M 849**	OJD 849Y	**M 877**	OJD 877Y	**M 923**	A923 SUL
M 811	OJD 811Y	**M 828**	OJD 828Y	**M 852**	OJD 852Y	**M 880**	OJD 880Y	**M 926**	A926 SUL
M 812	OJD 812Y	**M 830**	OJD 830Y	**M 853**	SGC 671Y	**M 888**	OJD 888Y	**M 931**	A931 SUL
M 814	OJD 814Y	**M 833**	OJD 833Y	**M 854**	OJD 854Y	**M 897**	A897 SUL	**M 940**	A940 SUL
M 816	OJD 816Y	**M 834**	OJD 834Y	**M 855**	OJD 855Y	**M 900**	A900 SUL	**M 944**	A944 SUL
M 817	OJD 817Y	**M 837**	OJD 837Y	**M 862**	OJD 862Y	**M 904**	A904 SUL	**M 946**	A946 SUL
M 818	OJD 818Y	**M 838**	OJD 838Y	**M 867**	OJD 867Y	**M 905**	A905 SUL	**M 947**	A947 SUL
M 820	OJD 820Y	**M 842**	OJD 842Y	**M 868**	OJD 868Y	**M 907**	A907 SUL	**M 949**	A949 SUL
M 821	OJD 821Y	**M 845**	OGK 708Y	**M 870**w	OJD 870Y	**M 908**	A908 SUL	**M 953**	A953 SUL

M 965–1440 | MCW Metrobus DR101/17 | MCW | H43/28D* | 1984–86

* M 1432/5/40 are DPH43/28D

M 965	A965 SYF	**M 1108**	B108 WUL	**M 1230**	B230 WUL	**M 1315**	C109 NGH	**M 1391**	C391 BUV
M 970	A970 SYF	**M 1177**	B177 WUL	**M 1232**	B232 WUL	**M 1337**	C337 BUV	**M 1410**t	C410 BUV
M 975	A975 SYF	**M 1180**	B180 WUL	**M 1235**	B235 WUL	**M 1347**	C347 BUV	**M 1411**t	C411 BUV
M 976	A976 SYF	**M 1196**	B196 WUL	**M 1237**	B237 WUL	**M 1357**	C357 BUV	**M 1432**	WLT 432
M 977t	A977 SYF	**M 1203**	B203 WUL	**M 1241**	B241 WUL	**M 1364**	C364 BUV	**M 1433**	C433 BUV
M 978t	A978 SYF	**M 1206**	B206 WUL	**M 1264**	B264 WUL	**M 1370**	C370 BUV	**M 1434**t	WLT 434
M 983	A983 SYF	**M 1211**	B211 WUL	**M 1268**	B268 WUL	**M 1371**t	C371 BUV	**M 1435**	435 CLT
M 991	A991 SYF	**M 1215**	B215 WUL	**M 1301**	B301 WUL	**M 1372**t	772 DYE	**M 1436**t	VLT 136
M 1002	A702 THV	**M 1220**t	B220 WUL	**M 1302**	B302 WUL	**M 1373**t	C373 BUV	**M 1440**	C440 BUV
M 1005	A705 THV	**M 1223**	B223 WUL	**M 1304**	304 CLT	**M 1386**	C386 BUV		
M 1046	VLT 46	**M 1224**	B224 WUL	**M 1305**	B305 WUL	**M 1387**	C387 BUV		
M 1055t	A755 THV	**M 1225**	B225 WUL	**M 1306**	C306 BUV	**M 1388**	C388 BUV		
M 1107	B107 WUL	**M 1226**	B226 WUL	**M 1311**	C311 BUV	**M 1389**t	89 CLT		

MD 1–17 | DAF DE02GSB220LF | East Lancs Myllennium 12m | B33D | 1999

(MDs 8–10 are DAF DE02GGSB220LF)

MD 1	V1 GMT	**MD 5**	V5 GMT	**MD 9**	V9 GMT	**MD 13**	V13 GMT	**MD 17**	V17 GMT
MD 2	V2 GMT	**MD 6**	V6 GMT	**MD 10**	V10 GMT	**MD 14**	V14 GMT		
MD 3	V3 GMT	**MD 7**	V7 GMT	**MD 11**	V11 GMT	**MD 15**	V15 GMT		
MD 4	V4 GMT	**MD 8**	V8 GMT	**MD 12**	V12 GMT	**MD 16**	V16 GMT		

NV 1–27 | Volvo Olympian YN2RV18Z4 | Northern Counties Palatine I | H47/30F | 1995

NV 1	M401 RVU	**NV 7**	M407 RVU	**NV 13**	N413 JBV	**NV 19**	N419 JBV	**NV 25**	N425 JBV
NV 2	2 CLT	**NV 8**	WLT 838	**NV 14**	N414 JBV	**NV 20**	N420 JBV	**NV 26**	N426 JBV
NV 3	M403 RVU	**NV 9**	M409 RVU	**NV 15**	WLT 815	**NV 21**	N421 JBV	**NV 27**	WLT 527
NV 4	M404 RVU	**NV 10**	M410 RVU	**NV 16**	N416 JBV	**NV 22**	N422 JBV		
NV 5	M405 RVU	**NV 11**	N411 JBV	**NV 17**	N417 JBV	**NV 23**	N423 JBV		
NV 6	M406 RVU	**NV 12**	N412 JBV	**NV 18**	N418 JBV	**NV 24**	N424 JBV		

NV 28–48 | Volvo Olympian YN2RV18Z4 | Northern Counties Palatine I | H48/27D | 1996

NV 28	N528 LHG	**NV 33**	N533 LHG	**NV 38**	WLT 688	**NV 43**	N543 LHG	**NV 48**	N548 LHG
NV 29	N529 LHG	**NV 34**	N534 LHG	**NV 39**	N539 LHG	**NV 44**	N544 LHG		
NV 30	N530 LHG	**NV 35**	N535 LHG	**NV 40**	N540 LHG	**NV 45**	N545 LHG		
NV 31	N531 LHG	**NV 36**	N536 LHG	**NV 41**	N541 LHG	**NV 46**	N546 LHG		
NV 32	N532 LHG	**NV 37**	N537 LHG	**NV 42**	N542 LHG	**NV 47**	N547 LHG		

NV 49–99 | Volvo Olympian OLY–4953 | Northern Counties Palatine I | H47/27D* | 1997/98

* NV 58 & 60 are DPH47/27D

NV 49	P549 WGT	**NV 53**	R253 LGH	**NV 57**	R257 LGH	**NV 61**	R261 LGH	**NV 65**	R265 LGH
NV 50	P550 WGT	**NV 54**	R254 LGH	**NV 58**	R258 LGH	**NV 62**	R262 LGH	**NV 66**	R266 LGH
NV 51	R251 LGH	**NV 55**	R255 LGH	**NV 59**	R259 LGH	**NV 63**	R263 LGH	**NV 67**	R267 LGH
NV 52	R252 LGH	**NV 56**	R256 LGH	**NV 60**	260 CLT	**NV 64**	R264 LGH	**NV 68**	WLT 868

NV 69	R269 LGH	**NV 75**	R275 LGH	**NV 82**	R282 LGH	**NV 88**	R288 LGH	**NV 94**	R394 LGH
NV 70	R270 LGH	**NV 76**	R276 LGH	**NV 83**	R283 LGH	**NV 89**	R389 LGH	**NV 95**	R395 LGH
NV 71	R271 LGH	**NV 77**	R277 LGH	**NV 84**	R284 LGH	**NV 90**	R390 LGH	**NV 96**	R396 LGH
NV 72	R272 LGH	**NV 78**	R278 LGH	**NV 85**	R285 LGH	**NV 91**	R391 LGH	**NV 97**	R397 LGH
NV 73	R273 LGH	**NV 79**	R279 LGH	**NV 86**	R286 LGH	**NV 92**	R392 LGH	**NV 98**	R398 LGH
NV 74	R274 LGH	**NV 81**	R281 LGH	**NV 87**	R287 LGH	**NV 93**	R393 LGH	**NV 99**	R399 LGH

NV 101–130 Volvo Olympian YN2RV18Z4 Northern Counties Palatine I H47/27D 1997

NV 101	P901 RYO	**NV 107**	P907 RYO	**NV 113**	P913 RYO	**NV 119**	P919 RYO	**NV 125**	P925 RYO
NV 102	P902 RYO	**NV 108**	698 DYE	**NV 114**	P914 RYO	**NV 120**	P920 RYO	**NV 126**	P926 RYO
NV 103	P903 RYO	**NV 109**	P909 RYO	**NV 115**	P915 RYO	**NV 121**	P921 RYO	**NV 127**	P927 RYO
NV 104	P904 RYO	**NV 110**	P910 RYO	**NV 116**	P916 RYO	**NV 122**	P922 RYO	**NV 128**	P928 RYO
NV 105	P905 RYO	**NV 111**	P911 RYO	**NV 117**	P917 RYO	**NV 123**	P923 RYO	**NV 129**	P929 RYO
NV 106	P906 RYO	**NV 112**	P912 RYO	**NV 118**	P918 RYO	**NV 124**	P924 RYO	**NV 130**	P930 RYO

NV 131–159 Volvo Olympian OLY–4953 Northern Counties Palatine I H47/27D* 1998
* NV 146 is DPH47/26D

NV 131	R331 LGH	**NV 137**	R337 LGH	**NV 144**	R344 LGH	**NV 150**	R550 LGH	**NV 156**	R556 LGH
NV 132	R332 LGH	**NV 138**	R338 LGH	**NV 145**	545 CLT	**NV 151**	R551 LGH	**NV 157**	R557 LGH
NV 133	R433 LGH	**NV 139**	R339 LGH	**NV 146**	WLT 346	**NV 152**	352 CLT	**NV 158**	R558 LGH
NV 134	R334 LGH	**NV 141**	R341 LGH	**NV 147**	R347 LGH	**NV 153**	R553 LGH	**NV 159**	R559 LGH
NV 135	R335 LGH	**NV 142**	R342 LGH	**NV 148**	WLT 548	**NV 154**	R554 LGH		
NV 136	R336 LGH	**NV 143**	R343 LGH	**NV 149**	R549 LGH	**NV 155**	R355 LGH		

NV 161–187 Volvo Olympian OLY–4953 Northern Counties Palatine II DPH47/26D 1997/98

NV 161	R361 LGH	**NV 167**	R367 LGH	**NV 173**	R373 LGH	**NV 179**	VLT 179	**NV 185**	R385 LGH
NV 162	R362 LGH	**NV 168**	R368 LGH	**NV 174**	R374 LGH	**NV 180**	R380 LGH	**NV 186**	R386 LGH
NV 163	R363 LGH	**NV 169**	R369 LGH	**NV 175**	R375 LGH	**NV 181**	R381 LGH	**NV 187**	197 CLT
NV 164	R364 LGH	**NV 170**	WLT 470	**NV 176**	R376 LGH	**NV 182**	R382 LGH		
NV 165	R365 LGH	**NV 171**	R371 LGH	**NV 177**	VLT 277	**NV 183**	R383 LGH		
NV 166	166 CLT	**NV 172**	R372 LGH	**NV 178**	78 CLT	**NV 184**	VLT 284		

PVL 1–17 Volvo B7L Plaxton President H.... 2000

PVL 1	**PVL 9**	**PVL 17**	**PVL 25**	**PVL 33**
PVL 2	**PVL 10**	**PVL 18**	**PVL 26**	**PVL 34**
PVL 3	**PVL 11**	**PVL 19**	**PVL 27**	**PVL 35**
PVL 4	**PVL 12**	**PVL 20**	**PVL 28**	**PVL 36**
PVL 5	**PVL 13**	**PVL 21**	**PVL 29**	**PVL 37**
PVL 6	**PVL 14**	**PVL 22**	**PVL 30**	**PVL 38**
PVL 7	**PVL 15**	**PVL 23**	**PVL 31**	**PVL 39**
PVL 8	**PVL 16**	**PVL 24**	**PVL 32**	**PVL 40**

RM 9–2151 AEC Routemaster R2RH Park Royal H36/28D 1959–65

RM 9	VLT 9	**RM 782**	WLT 782	**RM 1062**	62 CLT	**RM 1305**	305 CLT	**RM 1977**	ALD 977B
RM 71w	UFF 380	**RM 787**	WLT 787	**RM 1082**	82 CLT	**RM 1380**	380 CLT	**RM 1980**	ALD 980B
RM 202	VLT 202	**RM 928**	WLT 928	**RM 1097**	97 CLT	**RM 1400**	KGJ 339A	**RM 2022**	ALM 22B
RM 436	WLT 436	**RM 967**	WLT 967	**RM 1104**	104 CLT	**RM 1621**	KGJ 187A	**RM 2051**	ALM 51B
RM 478	WLT 478	**RM 994**	WLT 994	**RM 1119**	119 CLT	**RM 1666**	KGJ 341A	**RM 2106**	CUV 106C
RM 541	WLT 541	**RM 1002**	OYM 368A	**RM 1168**	168 CLT	**RM 1797**	797 DYE	**RM 2109**	CUV 109C
RM 687	WLT 687	**RM 1033**	DSL 540	**RM 1174**	JSJ 797	**RM 1955**	ALD 955B	**RM 2128**	CUV 128C
RM 758	WLT 758	**RM 1058**	58 CLT	**RM 1260**	JSJ 743	**RM 1962**	ALD 962B	**RM 2151**	CUV 151C

RML 883–899 AEC Routemaster R2RH Park Royal H40/32R 1961

RML 883	WLT 883	**RML 887**	WLT 887	**RML 889**	WLT 889	**RML 894**	WLT 894	**RML 899**	WLT 899

RML 2262–2752		AEC Routemaster R2RH/1		Park Royal				* H40/32R	1965–68

* RML 2516 is H40/32RD and carries fleet number DRM 2516.

RML 2262	CUV 262C	**RML 2345**	CUV 345C	**RML 2465**	JJD 465D	**RML 2564**	JJD 564D	**RML 2631**	NML 631E
RML 2263	CUV 263C	**RML 2358**	CUV 358C	**RML 2466**	JJD 466D	**RML 2568**	JJD 568D	**RML 2637**	NML 637E
RML 2270	CUV 270C	**RML 2360**	CUV 360C	**RML 2469**	JJD 469D	**RML 2570**	JJD 570D	**RML 2640**	NML 640E
RML 2271	CUV 271C	**RML 2361**	CUV 361C	**RML 2472**	JJD 472D	**RML 2575**	JJD 575D	**RML 2644**	NML 644E
RML 2273	CUV 273C	**RML 2362**	CUV 362C	**RML 2474**	JJD 474D	**RML 2576**	JJD 576D	**RML 2648**	NML 648E
RML 2275	CUV 275C	**RML 2363**	CUV 363C	**RML 2475**	JJD 475D	**RML 2578**	JJD 578D	**RML 2654**	NML 654E
RML 2276	CUV 276C	**RML 2364**	JJD 364D	**RML 2482**	JJD 482D	**RML 2580**	JJD 580D	**RML 2669**	SMK 669F
RML 2279	CUV 279C	**RML 2371**	JJD 371D	**RML 2484**	JJD 484D	**RML 2583**	JJD 583D	**RML 2673**	SMK 673F
RML 2283	CUV 283C	**RML 2376**	JJD 376D	**RML 2499**	JJD 499D	**RML 2584**	JJD 584D	**RML 2676**	SMK 676F
RML 2290	CUV 290C	**RML 2381**	JJD 381D	**RML 2502**	JJD 502D	**RML 2587**	JJD 587D	**RML 2680**	SMK 680F
RML 2297	CUV 297C	**RML 2385**	JJD 385D	**RML 2507**	JJD 507D	**RML 2590**	JJD 590D	**RML 2683**	SMK 683F
RML 2302	CUV 302C	**RML 2389**	JJD 389D	**RML 2513**	JJD 513D	**RML 2593**	JJD 593D	**RML 2693**	SMK 693F
RML 2305	CUV 305C	**RML 2396**	JJD 396D	**RML 2515**	JJD 515D	**RML 2596**	JJD 596D	**RML 2711**	SMK 711F
RML 2314	CUV 314C	**RML 2397**	JJD 397D	**DRM 2516**	WLT 516	**RML 2601**	NML 601E	**RML 2712**	SMK 712F
RML 2316	CUV 316C	**RML 2398**	JJD 398D	**RML 2517**	JJD 517D	**RML 2604**	NML 604E	**RML 2714**	SMK 714F
RML 2317	CUV 317C	**RML 2400**	JJD 400D	**RML 2520**	JJD 520D	**RML 2605**	NML 605E	**RML 2725**	SMK 725F
RML 2318	CUV 318C	**RML 2403**	JJD 403D	**RML 2529**	JJD 529D	**RML 2606**	NML 606E	**RML 2732**	SMK 732F
RML 2321	CUV 321C	**RML 2411**	JJD 411D	**RML 2535**	JJD 535D	**RML 2612**	NML 612E	**RML 2733**	SMK 733F
RML 2327	CUV 327C	**RML 2412**	JJD 412D	**RML 2539**	JJD 539D	**RML 2613**	NML 613E	**RML 2736**	SMK 736F
RML 2332	CUV 332C	**RML 2422**	JJD 422D	**RML 2540**	JJD 540D	**RML 2614**	NML 614E	**RML 2745**	SMK 745F
RML 2335	CUV 335C	**RML 2440**	JJD 440D	**RML 2543**	JJD 543D	**RML 2615**	NML 615E	**RML 2752**	SMK 752F
RML 2336	CUV 336C	**RML 2441**	JJD 441D	**RML 2551**	JJD 551D	**RML 2618**	NML 618E		
RML 2338	CUV 338C	**RML 2453**	JJD 453D	**RML 2554**	JJD 554D	**RML 2626**	NML 626E		
RML 2339	CUV 339C	**RML 2454**	JJD 454D	**RML 2556**	JJD 556D	**RML 2629**	NML 629E		
RML 2342	CUV 342C	**RML 2461**	JJD 461D	**RML 2560**	JJD 560D	**RML 2630**	NML 630E		

SC 1w	D585OOV	Freight-Rover Sherpa 374		Carlyle Citibus				B6F	1986

SP 1–25	DAF DB250WB505			Optare Spectra				H44/27F	1992/3
SP 1w	K301 FYG	**SP 7**w	K307 FYG	**SP 12**w	K312 FYG	**SP 18**w	K125 PGO	**SP 23**w	K323 FYG
SP 3w	K303 FYG	**SP 8**w	K308 FYG	**SP 13**w	K313 FYG	**SP 19**w	K124 PGO	**SP 24**w	K324 FYG
SP 4w	K304 FYG	**SP 9**w	K309 FYG	**SP 14**w	K314 FYG	**SP 20**w	K160 PGO	**SP 25**w	K159 PGO
SP 5w	K305 FYG	**SP 10**w	K310 FYG	**SP 15**w	K315 FYG	**SP 21**w	K321 FYG		
SP 6w	K306 FYG	**SP 11**w	K311 FYG	**SP 16**w	K316 FYG	**SP 22**w	K322 FYG		

T 172	CUL 172V	Leyland Titan TNLXB2RRsp		Park Royal				H44/26D	1979

T 329–1120		Leyland Titan TNLXB2RR		Leyland				H44/24D*	1980–84

* T 705, 709, 766, 778, 793 are H44/23D, 799–1120 are H44/26D, 803 is O44/26D, 1060 is H44/24F
(T 875 is used as a mobile rest room for night bus drivers at Victoria Station. Tables and refreshment machines are fitted)

T 329	KYV 329X	**T 718**	OHV 718Y	**T 779**	OHV 779Y	**T 863**	A863 SUL	**T 913**	A913 SYE
T 677t	OHV 677Y	**T 732**	OHV 732Y	**T 782**	OHV 782Y	**T 870**	A870 SUL	**T 914**	A914 SYE
T 678	OHV 678Y	**T 737**	OHV 737Y	**T 787**	OHV 787Y	**T 871**	A871 SUL	**T 917**	A917 SYE
T 679	OHV 679Y	**T 747**	OHV 747Y	**T 793**t	OHV 793Y	**T 875**sp	A875 SUL	**T 919**t	A919 SYE
T 681	OHV 681Y	**T 750**	OHV 750Y	**T 795**	OHV 795Y	**T 888**	A888 SYE	**T 924**	A924 SYE
T 683t	OHV 683Y	**T 752**	OHV 752Y	**T 796**	OHV 796Y	**T 889**	A889 SYE	**T 927**	A927 SYE
T 687	OHV 687Y	**T 757**	OHV 757Y	**T 798**	OHV 798Y	**T 892**	A892 SYE	**T 928**t	A928 SYE
T 693	OHV 693Y	**T 764**	OHV 764Y	**T 799**	OHV 799Y	**T 893**	A893 SYE	**T 929**	A929 SYE
T 694	OHV 694Y	**T 765**	OHV 765Y	**T 803**	OHV 803Y	**T 894**	A894 SYE	**T 930**	A930 SYE
T 704	OHV 704Y	**T 766**	OHV 766Y	**T 806**	OHV 806Y	**T 895**	A895 SYE	**T 931**	A931 SYE
T 705t	OHV 705Y	**T 767**	OHV 767Y	**T 831**t	A831 SUL	**T 897**	A897 SYE	**T 932**w	A932 SYE
T 709	OHV 709Y	**T 773**	OHV 773Y	**T 835**t	A835 SUL	**T 901**	A901 SYE	**T 936**	A936 SYE
T 715	OHV 715Y	**T 774**	OHV 774Y	**T 839**t	A839 SUL	**T 906**	A906 SYE	**T 937**	A937 SYE
T 716	OHV 716Y	**T 775**	OHV 775Y	**T 844**t	A844 SUL	**T 907**	A907 SYE	**T 938**	A938 SYE
T 717	OHV 717Y	**T 778**	OHV 778Y	**T 851**t	A851 SUL	**T 909**	A909 SYE	**T 939**	A939 SYE

T 940	A940 SYE	**T 972**	A972 SYE	**T 1000**	ALM 1B	**T 1042**	A642 THV	**T 1074**	A74 THX
T 942	A942 SYE	**T 973**	A973 SYE	**T 1001**	A601 THV	**T 1043**	A643 THV	**T 1075**	A75 THX
T 943	A943 SYE	**T 974**	A974 SYE	**T 1002**	A602 THV	**T 1044**t	A644 THV	**T 1078**	A78 THX
T 946	A946 SYE	**T 977**	A977 SYE	**T 1004**	A604 THV	**T 1046**	A646 THV	**T 1080**	B80 WUV
T 948	A948 SYE	**T 979**	A979 SYE	**T 1005**	A605 THV	**T 1047**	A647 THV	**T 1082**	B82 WUV
T 952	A952 SYE	**T 980**	A980 SYE	**T 1006**	A606 THV	**T 1051**	A651 THV	**T 1085**	B85 WUV
T 954	A954 SYE	**T 981**	A981 SYE	**T 1010**	A610 THV	**T 1054**	A654 THV	**T 1086**	B86 WUV
T 955	A955 SYE	**T 982**	A982 SYE	**T 1011**	A611 THV	**T 1057**	257 CLT	**T 1087**	B87 WUV
T 956	A956 SYE	**T 983**	A983 SYE	**T 1014**	A614 THV	**T 1060**t	A60 THX	**T 1088**	B88 WUV
T 957	A957 SYE	**T 984**	A984 SYE	**T 1016**	A616 THV	**T 1061**	A61 THX	**T 1090**	B90 WUV
T 958	A958 SYE	**T 985**	A985 SYE	**T 1017**	A617 THV	**T 1062**	A62 THX	**T 1094**	B94 WUV
T 959	A959 SYE	**T 991**	A991 SYE	**T 1018**	A618 THV	**T 1063**	A63 THX	**T 1095**	B95 WUV
T 963	A963 SYE	**T 992**	A992 SYE	**T 1019**	A619 THV	**T 1064**	A64 THX	**T 1098**	B98 WUV
T 967	A967 SYE	**T 993**	A993 SYE	**T 1021**	A621 THV	**T 1068**	A68 THX	**T 1102**	B102 WUV
T 968	A968 SYE	**T 994**	A994 SYE	**T 1033**	A633 THV	**T 1071**	A71 THX	**T 1104**	B104 WUV
T 969	A969 SYE	**T 995**	A995 SYE	**T 1037**	A637 THV	**T 1072**	A72 THX	**T 1107**	B107 WUV
T 970w	A970 SYE	**T 997**	A997 SYE	**T 1040**	A640 THV	**T 1073**	A73 THX	**T 1120**	B120 WUV

T 1129	WDA 4T	Leyland Titan TNLXB1RF	Park Royal	DPH43/29F	1979
TPL 10n	C377 PCD	Leyland Tiger TRCTL11/3RH	Plaxton Paramount 3500 II	C49F	1986
VC 1	G101 NGN	Volvo Citybus B10M–50	Northern Counties	DPH45/35D	1989
VC 2	G102 NGN	Volvo Citybus B10M–50	Northern Counties	DPH45/35D	1989
VC 3	WLT 803	Volvo Citybus B10M–50	Northern Counties	DPH45/35D	1989
VC 4	WLT 474	Volvo Citybus B10M–50	Northern Counties	H45/35D	1989
VC 5	G105 NGN	Volvo Citybus B10M–50	Northern Counties	H45/35D	1989
VC 6	VLT 60	Volvo Citybus B10M–50	Northern Counties	H45/35D	1989

n On long term loan to Nostalgiabus

VC 7–39	Volvo Citybus B10M–50	Northern Counties	H47/35D	1989–91

VC 7	G107 NGN	**VC 14**	614 DYE	**VC 21**	621 DYE	**VC 28**	528 CLT	**VC 35**	G135 PGK
VC 8	G108 NGN	**VC 15**	G115 NGN	**VC 22**	G122 NGN	**VC 29**	229 CLT	**VC 36**	836 DYE
VC 9	G109 NGN	**VC 16**	G116 NGN	**VC 23**	23 CLT	**VC 30**	G130 PGK	**VC 37**	WLT 837
VC 10	G110 NGN	**VC 17**	G117 NGN	**VC 24**	G124 NGN	**VC 31**	G131 PGK	**VC 38**	G138 PGK
VC 11	G647 SGT	**VC 18**	WLT 818	**VC 25**	125 CLT	**VC 32**	G132 PGK	**VC 39**	839 DYE
VC 12	312 CLT	**VC 19**	619 DYE	**VC 26**	G126 NGN	**VC 33**	G133 PGK		
VC 13	G113 NGN	**VC 20**	WLT 920	**VC 27**	G127 NGN	**VC 34**	G134 PGK		

VWL 1	N101HGO	Volvo B6LE–53 (On loan from London Transport)	Wright Crusader	B36F	1995

Previous registrations:–

2 CLT	M402 RVU	**352 CLT**	R552 LGH
23 CLT	G123 NGN	**435 CLT**	C435 BUV
46 CLT	H546 XGK	**528 CLT**	G128 PGK
78 CLT	R378 LGH	**542 CLT**	GYE5 42W
83 CLT	GUW 483W	**545 CLT**	R345 LGH
89 CLT	C389 BUV	**614 DYE**	G114 NGN
125 CLT	G125 NGN	**619 DYE**	G119 NGN
166 CLT	R366 LGH	**621 DYE**	G121 NGN
174 CLT	R474 LGH	**698 DYE**	P908 RYO
176 CLT	R476 LGH	**772 DYE**	C372 BUV
186 CLT	GUW 486W	**836 DYE**	G136 PGK
188 CLT	P508 RYM	**839 DYE**	J139 DGF
197 CLT	R387 LGH	**ALM 1B**	A600 THV
229 CLT	G129 PGK	**C109 NGH**	C315 BUV, VLT 15
257 CLT	A57 THX	**C377 PCD**	C377 PCD, PCN 762, VLT 71
260 CLT	R260 LGH	**DSL 540**	33 CLT
304 CLT	B304 WUL	**G101 NGN**	G101 NGN, 101 CLT
312 CLT	G112 NGN	**G551 SGT**	JDZ 2348, WLT 548

G647 SGT	G111 NGN, WLT 311
GUW 499w	GUW 499W, WLT 599
JSJ 743	260 CLT
JSJ 797	174 CLT
K124 PGO	19 CLT
K125 PGO	18 CLT
K159 PGO	WLT 625
K160 PGO	20 CLT
K767 OGK	K594 MGT, WLT 994
KGJ 187A	621 DYE
KGJ 339A	400 CLT
KGJ 341A	666 DYE
M410 RVU	M410 RVU, WLT 990
N416 JBV	N421 JBV
N420 JBV	N422 JBV
N421 JBV	N424 JBV
N422 JBV	N416 JBV
N423 JBV	N425 JBV
N424 JBV	N426 JBV
N425 JBV	N427 JBV
N426 JBV	N420 JBV
N427 JBV	N423 JBV
N529 LHG	N529 LHG, VLT 29
OGK 708Y	OJD 845Y, 545 CLT
OYM 368A	2 CLT
SGC 671Y	OJD 853Y, VLT 53
SGK 374V	BYX 198V, VLT 98
UFF 380	VLT 71
VLT 9	VLT 9, OYM 374A
VLT 46	A746 THV
VLT 60	G106 NGN
VLT 71	BYX 171V
VLT 136	C436 BUV
VLT 179	R379 LGH
VLT 180	GUW 480W
VLT 277	R377 LGH
VLT 284	R384 LGH
WLT 346	R346 LGH
WLT 379	P509 RYM
WLT 395	K595 MGT
WLT 432	C432 BUV
WLT 434	C434 BUV
WLT 463	GUW 463W
WLT 467	GUW 467W
WLT 470	R370 LGH
WLT 474	G104 NGN
WLT 487	GUW 487W
WLT 516	JJD 516D
WLT 527	N427 JBV
WLT 532	H532 XGK
WLT 548	R348 LGH
WLT 598	GUW 498W
WLT 625	K325 FYG
WLT 648	GUW 448W
WLT 688	N538 LHG
WLT 696	GUW 496W
WLT 789	M89 MYM
WLT 803	G103 NGN
WLT 815	N415 JBV
WLT 818	G118 NGN
WLT 837	G137 PGK
WLT 838	M408 RVU
WLT 843	GUW 443W
WLT 868	R268 LGH
WLT 872	R472 LGH
WLT 920	G120 NGN
WLT 994	WLT 994, VLT 89

Special liveries:–

OMs 171, 241, 420, Ms 1432, 1440, NV 7 and Ts 172 and 803 are red with white or cream relief in differing styles.
Ms 202, 978 and 1389 plus T 1044 carry blue and red livery and are dedicated training buses.

HACKNEY COMMUNITY TRANSPORT

T157 HGT	Fiat/Ducato 3 axle	Rohill	B14FL	1999
T159 HGT	Fiat/Ducato 3 axle	Rohill	B14FL	1999
T247 FLJ	Fiat/Ducato 3 axle	Rohill	B14FL	1999
T248 FLJ	Fiat/Ducato 3 axle	Rohill	B14FL	1999

These vehicles carry red and yellow livery and are used on LT Mobility routes.

HARRIS BUS

302	J582 WVX	Mercedes-Benz 709D	Alexander AM	B25F	1991
303	J583 WVX	Mercedes-Benz 709D	Alexander AM	B25F	1991
310	F310 OVW	MCW MetroRider MF150/112	MCW	B24F	1988
315	J51 GCX	DAF SB220LC550	Ikarus Citibus	B48F	1992
316	J52 GCX	DAF SB220LC550	Ikarus Citibus	B48F	1992
317	P317 KTW	DAF DE02RSDB250	Northern Counties Palatine II	H47/30F	1996
318	P318 KTW	DAF DE02RSDB250	Northern Counties Palatine II	H47/30F	1996
319	M649 RCP	DAF DB250RS505	Northern Counties Palatine II	H47/30F	1995

320–334 Optare Excel L1070 — Optare — B35F — 1996/97

320	P320 KAR	**323**	P323 KAR	**326**	P326 NHJ	**329**	P329 NHJ	**332**	P332 NHJ
321	P321 KAR	**324**	P324 NHJ	**327**	P327 NHJ	**330**	P330 NHJ	**333**	P333 HBC
322	P322 KAR	**325**	P325 NHJ	**328**	P328 NHJ	**331**	P331 NHJ	**334**	P334 NHJ

335	P335 ROO	DAF DB250RS505	Northern Counties Palatine II	H43/25D	1997
336	P336 ROO	DAF DB250RS505	Northern Counties Palatine II	H43/25D	1997
337	P337 ROO	DAF DB250RS505	Northern Counties Palatine II	H43/25D	1997

338–372 Volvo Olympian OLY–56 — East Lancs Pyoneer — H51/28D* — 1997/98
* 351–359 are H51/35F

338	P338 ROO	**345**	P345 ROO	**352**	P352 ROO	**359**	R359 XVX	**366**	R366 DJN
339	P339 ROO	**346**	P346 ROO	**353**	P353 ROO	**360**	R360 DJN	**367**	R367 DJN
340	P340 ROO	**347**	P347 ROO	**354**	R354 XVX	**361**	R361 DJN	**368**	R368 DJN
341	P341 ROO	**348**	P348 ROO	**355**	R355 XVX	**362**	R362 DJN	**369**	R369 DJN
342	P342 ROO	**349**	P349 ROO	**356**	R356 XVX	**363**	R363 DJN	**370**	R370 DJN
343	P343 ROO	**350**	P350 ROO	**357**	R357 XVX	**364**	R364 DJN	**371**	R371 DJN
344	P344 ROO	**351**	P351 ROO	**358**	R358 XVX	**365**	R365 DJN	**372**	R372 DJN

373–380 Optare Excel L1070 — Optare — B35F — 1998

373	R373 DJN	**375**	R375 DJN	**377**	R377 DJN	**379**	R379 DJN		
374	R374 DJN	**376**	R376 DJN	**378**	R378 DJN	**380**	R380 DJN		

381	R381 GTW	DAF DB250RS505 Northern Counties Palatine II	H43/25D	1998
382	R382 GTW	DAF DB250RS505 Northern Counties Palatine II	H43/25D	1998

On loan:–

446	P446 SWX	Optare Excel L1070	Optare	B35F	1997

Special liveries:–
302 LTS Rail advert livery, Ilford Link (317/8,335–359), Lewisham Link (324–332, 334, 360–372), Eltham Link (373–380), Thurrock Link (315/6,320–2), Lakeside Link (381/2).

LIMEBOURNE (Independent Way Ltd)

WYW 73T	MCW Metrobus DR101/9	MCW	H43/28D	1979
BYX 120V	MCW Metrobus DR101/9	MCW	H43/28D	1979
BYX 188V	MCW Metrobus DR101/9	MCW	H43/28D	1979
BYX 237V	MCW Metrobus DR101/12	MCW	H43/28D	1980
BYX 279V	MCW Metrobus DR101/12	MCW	H43/28D	1980
GYE 476W	MCW Metrobus DR101/12	MCW	H43/28D	1980
GYE 477W	MCW Metrobus DR101/12	MCW	H43/28D	1980
KYV 719W	MCW Metrobus DR101/14	MCW	H43/28D	1982

Dennis Dart 8.5SDL3003 — Carlyle Dartline 8.5m — B28F — 1990–91

H89 MOB	H125 MOB	H136 MOB	H156 MOB
H93 MOB	H126 MOB	H141 MOB	H157 NON
H124 MOB	H134 MOB	H142 MOB	

Dennis Dart 8.5SDL3003 — Plaxton Pointer 8.5m — B28F — 1991

H120 THE	H123 THE	H125 THE	H127 THE
H122 THE	H124 THE	H126 THE	H621 TKU

H462 UGO	Dennis Dart 8.5SDL3003	Carlyle Dartline 8.5m	B28F	1990
H468 UGO	Dennis Dart 8.5SDL3003	Carlyle Dartline 8.5m	B28F	1990
H470 UGO	Dennis Dart 8.5SDL3003	Carlyle Dartline 8.5m	B28F	1990

Dennis Dart SLF SFD322BR1WGW1 — Caetano Compass 10.6m — B31D — 1999

T401 LGP	T403 LGP	T406 LGP
T402 LGP	T404 LGP	T407 LGP

* Dennis Dart SLF SFD322BR1WGW1 — Caetano Compass 10.6m — B30D — 1999
* T409–419 LGP are SLF SFD322BR1XGW1T408 LGP

T408 LGP	T411 LGP	T415 LGP	T418 LGP
T409 LGP	T413 LGP	T416 LGP	T419 LGP
T410 LGP	T414 LGP	T417 LGP	

Dennis Dart SLF SFD322BR1XGW1 — Caetano Compass 10.6m — B30D — 1999

T421 LGP	T425 LGP	T429 LGP	T433 LGP	V437 KGF
T422 LGP	T426 LGP	T430 LGP	V434 KGF	
T423 LGP	T427 LGP	T431 LGP	V435 KGF	
T424 LGP	T428 LGP	T432 LGP	V436 KGF	

Named vehicles:–

H 89 Albert Hall
H 93 Barton Hall
H124 Dartington Hall
H125 Haddon Hall
H126 Hazel Hall
H134 Middleton Hall
H136 Mursley Hall
H141 Watcombe Hall
H142 Westminster Hall
H156 Wimpole Hall
H157 Winslow Hall
T401 Tattershall Castle
T402 Corfe Castle
T403 Lindisfarne Castle
T404 Swansea Castle
T406 Powis Castle
T407 Cardiff Castle
T408 Dartmouth Castle
T409 Dorchester Castle
T410 Windsor Castle
T411 Tintagel Castle
T413 Berry Pomeroy Castle
T414 Kingswear Castle
T415 Criccieth Castle
T416 Winchester Castle
T417 Kirby Muxloe Castle
T418 Compton Castle
T419 Barry Castle
T421 Chepstow Castle
T422 Ludlow Castle
T423 Devizes Castle
T424 Carisbrooke Castle
T425 Pendennis Castle
T426 Dover Castle
T427 Urquhart Castle
T428 Sterling Castle
T429 Conwy Castle
T430 Dunster Castle
T431 Totnes Castle
T432 Penrhyn Castle
T433 Lulworth Castle
T434 Portland Castle
T435 Restormel Castle
T436 Okehampton Castle
T437 Monmouth Castle

LONDON TRAVELLER

WYW 76T	MCW Metrobus DR101/8	MCW	H43/28D	1979
BYX 231V	MCW Metrobus DR101/12	MCW	H43/28D	1980
BYX 235V	MCW Metrobus DR101/12	MCW	H43/28D	1980
BYX 259V	MCW Metrobus DR101/12	MCW	H43/28D	1980
BYX 262V	MCW Metrobus DR101/12	MCW	H43/28D	1980
EYE 320V	MCW Metrobus DR101/12	MCW	H43/28D	1980
GOG 228W	MCW Metrobus DR104/8	MCW	H43/30F	1981
GOG 230W	MCW Metrobus DR104/8	MCW	H43/30F	1981
GOG 234W	MCW Metrobus DR104/8	MCW	H43/30F	1981
GOG 235W	MCW Metrobus DR104/8	MCW	H43/30F	1981
GOG 237W	MCW Metrobus DR104/8	MCW	H43/30F	1981
GYE 447W	MCW Metrobus DR101/12	MCW	H43/28D	1981
GYE 527W	MCW Metrobus DR101/14	MCW	H43/28D	1981

R1 LTB	Dennis Arrow SFD121BR3VGL6	East Lancs Pyoneer	CH45/31F	1998

	Volvo B6BLE	East Lancs Spryte	B35D	1999

V501 EFR	V504 EFR	V507 EFR	V510 EFR	V513 EFR
V502 EFR	V505 EFR	V508 EFR	V511 EFR	V514 EFR
V503 EFR	V506 EFR	V509 EFR	V512 EFR	V515 EFR

LONDON UNITED

CD 1–8	Dennis Dart SLF SFD212BR1TGW1	Wright Crusader 10.2m	B32F	1996

CD 1	VDZ 8001	**CD 3**	VDZ 8003	**CD 5**	VDZ 8005	**CD 7**	VDZ 8007
CD 2	VDZ 8002	**CD 4**	VDZ 8004	**CD 6**	VDZ 8006	**CD 8**	VDZ 8008

DA 2w	F551 SHX	DAF SB220LC550	Optare Delta	B49F	1989

DN 1–12	DAF DE23RSDB250	Northern Counties Palatine II	H43/24D	1998

DN 1	R201 CKO	**DN 4**	R204 CKO	**DN 7**	R207 CKO	**DN 10**	R210 CKO
DN 2	R202 CKO	**DN 5**	R205 CKO	**DN 8**	R208 CKO	**DN 11**	R211 CKO
DN 3	R203 CKO	**DN 6**	R206 CKO	**DN 9**	R209 CKO	**DN 12**	R212 CKO

DP 1–11	Dennis Dart SLF SFD322BR1WGW1	Plaxton Pointer 2 10.7m	B36F	1998

DP 1	S301 MKH	**DP 4**	S304 MKH	**DP 7**	S307 MKH	**DP 10**	S310 MKH
DP 2	S302 MKH	**DP 5**	S305 MKH	**DP 8**	S308 MKH	**DP 11**	S311 MKH
DP 3	S303 MKH	**DP 6**	S306 MKH	**DP 9**	S309 MKH		

DP 12–22	Dennis Dart SLF SFD322AR1WGW1	Plaxton Pointer 2 10.7m	B27D	1999

DP12	T412 KAG	**DP15**	T415 KAG	**DP18**	T418 KAG	**DP21**	T421 KAG
DP13	T413 KAG	**DP16**	T416 KAG	**DP19**	T419 KAG	**DP22**	T422 KAG
DP14	T414 KAG	**DP17**	T417 KAG	**DP20**	T420 KAG		

DP 23–33	Dennis Dart SLF SFD322AR1WGW1	Plaxton Pointer 2 10.7m	B34D	1999

DP23	T423 KAG	**DP26**	T426 KAG	**DP29**	T429 KAG	**DP32**	T432 KAG
DP24	T424 KAG	**DP27**	T427 KAG	**DP30**	T430 KAG	**DP33**	T433 KAG
DP25	T425 KAG	**DP28**	T428 KAG	**DP31**	T431 KAG		

DP 34–99 — Dennis Dart SLF SFD322BR1XGW1 — Plaxton Pointer 2 10.7m — B31D — 1999

DP 34	T334 PRH	**DP 48**	T348 PRH	**DP 62**	T362 PRH	**DP 76**	T976 SRH	**DP 90**	V790 FKH
DP 35	T335 PRH	**DP 49**	T349 PRH	**DP 63**	T363 PRH	**DP 77**	T977 SRH	**DP 91**	V791 FKH
DP 36	T336 PRH	**DP 50**	T350 PRH	**DP 64**	T364 PRH	**DP 78**	T978 SRH	**DP 92**	V792 FKH
DP 37	T337 PRH	**DP 51**	T351 PRH	**DP 65**	T365 PRH	**DP 79**	T979 SRH	**DP 93**	V793 FKH
DP 38	T338 PRH	**DP 52**	T352 PRH	**DP 66**	T366 PRH	**DP 80**	T980 SRH	**DP 94**	V794 FKH
DP 39	T339 PRH	**DP 53**	T353 PRH	**DP 67**	T367 PRH	**DP 81**	V781 FKH	**DP 95**	V795 FKH
DP 40	T340 PRH	**DP 54**	T354 PRH	**DP 68**	T368 PRH	**DP 82**	V782 FKH	**DP 96**	V796 FKH
DP 41	T341 PRH	**DP 55**	T355 PRH	**DP 69**	T369 PRH	**DP 83**	V783 FKH	**DP 97**	V797 FKH
DP 42	T342 PRH	**DP 56**	T356 PRH	**DP 70**	T370 PRH	**DP 84**	V784 FKH	**DP 98**	V798 FKH
DP 43	T343 PRH	**DP 57**	T357 PRH	**DP 71**	T371 PRH	**DP 85**	V785 FKH	**DP 99**	V799 FKH
DP 44	T344 PRH	**DP 58**	T358 PRH	**DP 72**	T372 PRH	**DP 86**	V886 FKH		
DP 45	T345 PRH	**DP 59**	T359 PRH	**DP 73**	T373 PRH	**DP 87**	V787 FKH		
DP 46	T346 PRH	**DP 60**	T360 PRH	**DP 74**	T374 PRH	**DP 88**	V788 FKH		
DP 47	T347 PRH	**DP 61**	T361 PRH	**DP 75**	T375 PRH	**DP 89**	V789 FKH		

DPS 1–16 — Dennis Dart SLF SFD212AR1XGW2 — Plaxton Pointer 2 10.1m — B27D — 1999

DPS 1	V801 KAG	**DPS 5**	V805 KAG	**DPS 9**	V809 KAG	**DPS 13**	V813 KAG
DPS 2	V802 KAG	**DPS 6**	V806 KAG	**DPS 10**	V810 KAG	**DPS 14**	V814 KAG
DPS 3	V803 KAG	**DPS 7**	V807 KAG	**DPS 11**	V811 KAG	**DPS 15**	V815 KAG
DPS 4	V904 KAG	**DPS 8**	V808 KAG	**DPS 12**	V812 KAG	**DPS 16**	V816 KAG

DR 1–14 — Dennis Dart 8.5SDL3003 — Reeve Burgess Pointer 8.5m — B28F — 1991

DR 1	H101 THE	**DR 4**	H104 THE	**DR 7**	H107 THE	**DR 10**	H110 THE	**DR 13**	H113 THE
DR 2	H102 THE	**DR 5**	H105 THE	**DR 8**	H108 THE	**DR 11**	WLT 931	**DR 14**	H114 THE
DR 3	H103 THE	**DR 6**	H106 THE	**DR 9**	H109 THE	**DR 12**	H112 THE		

DR 53–57 — Dennis Dart 8.5SDL3010 — Plaxton Pointer 8.5m — B28F — 1991

DR 53	J653 XHL	**DR 54**	J654 XHL	**DR 55**	J655 XHL	**DR 56**	J156 GAT	**DR 57**	J157 GAT

DR 58–141 — Dennis Dart 8.5SDL3010 — Plaxton Pointer 8.5m — B24F — 1991/92

DR 58	J158 GAT	**DR 72**	J372 GKH	**DR 104**	J104 DUV	**DR 118**	J118 DUV	**DR 132**	J132 DUV
DR 59	J159 GAT	**DR 73**	J373 GKH	**DR 105**	J105 DUV	**DR 119**	J119 DUV	**DR 133**	J133 DUV
DR 60	J160 GAT	**DR 74**	J374 GKH	**DR 106**	J106 DUV	**DR 120**	J120 DUV	**DR 134**	J134 DUV
DR 61	J161 GAT	**DR 75**	J375 GKH	**DR 107**	J107 DUV	**DR 121**	J121 DUV	**DR 135**	J135 DUV
DR 62	J362 GKH	**DR 76**	J376 GKH	**DR 108**	J108 DUV	**DR 122**	J122 DUV	**DR 136**	J136 DUV
DR 63	J363 GKH	**DR 77**	J377 GKH	**DR 109**	J109 DUV	**DR 123**	J123 DUV	**DR 137**	J137 DUV
DR 64	J364 GKH	**DR 78**	J378 GKH	**DR 110**	J110 DUV	**DR 124**	J124 DUV	**DR 138**	J138 DUV
DR 65	J365 GKH	**DR 79**	J379 GKH	**DR 111**	WLT 946	**DR 125**	J125 DUV	**DR 139**	J139 DUV
DR 66	J366 GKH	**DR 80**	J380 GKH	**DR 112**	J112 DUV	**DR 126**	J126 DUV	**DR 140**	J140 DUV
DR 67	J367 GKH	**DR 99**	J599 DUV	**DR 113**	J113 DUV	**DR 127**	J127 DUV	**DR 141**	J141 DUV
DR 68	J368 GKH	**DR 100**	VLT 23	**DR 114**	J114 DUV	**DR 128**	J128 DUV		
DR 69	J369 GKH	**DR 101**	J101 DUV	**DR 115**	J115 DUV	**DR 129**	J129 DUV		
DR 70	J370 GKH	**DR 102**	J102 DUV	**DR 116**	J116 DUV	**DR 130**	J130 DUV		
DR 71	J371 GKH	**DR 103**	J103 DUV	**DR 117**	J117 DUV	**DR 131**	J131 DUV		

DRL 96–108 — Dennis Dart 9SDL3024 — Plaxton Pointer 9m — B28F — 1993

DRL 96	K96 SAG	**DRL 99**	K199 SAG	**DRL 102**	K102 SAG	**DRL 105**	K105 SAG	**DRL 108**	K108 SAG
DRL 97	K97 SAG	**DRL 100**	ALM 2B	**DRL 103**	K103 SAG	**DRL 106**	K106 SAG		
DRL 98	K98 SAG	**DRL 101**	K101 SAG	**DRL 104**	K104 SAG	**DRL 107**	K107 SAG		

DRL 159–171	Dennis Dart 9SDL3034 * DRL165–169 are B34F		Plaxton Pointer 9m		B28F*	1993/94

DRL 159 L159 XRH, **DRL 160** L160 XRH, **DRL 161** L161 XRH, **DRL 162** L162 XRH, **DRL 163** L163 XRH, **DRL 164** L164 XRH, **DRL 165** L165 YAT, **DRL 166** L166 YAT, **DRL 167** L167 YAT, **DRL 168** L168 YAT, **DRL 169** L169 YAT, **DRL 170** L170 CKH, **DRL 171** L171 CKH

DT 1–47	Dennis Dart 8.5SDL3003 * DT 29–47 are Carlyle Dartline; DT 42 is B28F	Duple Dartline 8.5m*	DP21F*	1990

DT 1u G501 VYE, **DT 2**u G502 VYE, **DT 5**u G505 VYE, **DT 6**u G506 VYE, **DT 7**u G507 VYE, **DT 9**u G509 VYE, **DT 10**u G510 VYE, **DT 11**u G511 VYE, **DT 12** G512 VYE, **DT 13**u G513 VYE, **DT 14**u G514 VYE, **DT 15** G515 VYE, **DT 17**u G517 VYE, **DT 18**u G518 VYE, **DT 19**u G519 VYE, **DT 20**u G520 VYE, **DT 21**u G521 VYE, **DT 22**u G522 VYE, **DT 23**u G523 VYE, **DT 24**u G524 VYE, **DT 27**u G527 VYE, **DT 29**u G29 TGW, **DT 42**u G42 TGW, **DT 43**u G43 TGW, **DT 45**d G45 TGW, **DT 46**u G46 TGW, **DT 47**u G47 TGW

DT 48–167	Dennis Dart 8.5SDL3003 * DT 75 is B26F	Carlyle Dartline 8.5m	B28F*	1990

DT 48u G48 TGW, **DT 49** G49 TGW, **DT 50**u G50 TGW, **DT 53**u G53 TGW, **DT 56**u G56 TGW, **DT 57**u G57 TGW, **DT 74** H74 MOB, **DT 75**t WLT 329, **DT 80**u 236 CLT, **DT 81**u H81 MOB, **DT 82**u H82 MOB, **DT 86** H86 MOB, **DT 144**u H144 MOB, **DT 145**u H145 MOB, **DT 146**u H146 MOB, **DT 147**u H147 MOB, **DT 148**u H148 MOB, **DT 149**u H149 MOB, **DT 154** H154 MOB, **DT 160**u H160 NON, **DT 164**u WLT 804, **DT 165**u H165 NON, **DT 167**u H167 NON

DT 168	G349 GCK	Dennis Dart 8.5SDL3003	Duple Dartline 8.5m	DP21F	1989

DWL 1–14	Dennis Dart 9SDL3002	Wright Handybus 9m	B35F	1990

DWL 1 JDZ 2401, **DWL 2** JDZ 2402, **DWL 3** JDZ 2403, **DWL 4** JDZ 2404, **DWL 5** JDZ 2405, **DWL 6** JDZ 2406, **DWL 7** JDZ 2407, **DWL 8** JDZ 2408, **DWL 9** JDZ 2409, **DWL 10** JDZ 2410, **DWL 11** JDZ 2411, **DWL 12** JDZ 2412, **DWL 13** JDZ 2413, **DWL 14** JDZ 2414

L 293–305	Leyland Olympian ONCL10/1RZ	Leyland	H47/31F	1989

L 293 G293 UYK, **L 298** G298 UYK, **L 300** G300 UYK, **L 302** G302 UYK, **L 303** G303 UYK, **L 305** G305 UYK

L 308	G308 UYK	Leyland Olympian ON2R50C13Z4	Leyland	H47/31F	1989
L 309	G309 UYK	Leyland Olympian ON2R50C13Z4	Leyland	H47/31F	1989
L 310	G310 UYK	Leyland Olympian ON2R50C13Z4	Leyland	H47/31F	1989

LLW 1–10	Dennis Lance SLF 11SDA3202	Wright Pathfinder 320	B34D	1993/94

LLW 1 ODZ 8901, **LLW 2** ODZ 8902, **LLW 3** ODZ 8903, **LLW 4** ODZ 8904, **LLW 5** ODZ 8905, **LLW 6** ODZ 8906, **LLW 7** ODZ 8907, **LLW 8** ODZ 8908, **LLW 9** ODZ 8909, **LLW 10** ODZ 8910

LS 153t	THX 153S	Leyland National 10351A/2R	(Urban Bus)	B38F	1977
LS 297t	YYE 297T	Leyland National 10351A/2R	(Urban Bus)	B38F	1979
LS 405t	BYW 405V	Leyland National 10351A/2R	(Urban Bus)	B38F	1979
LS 431t	BYW 431V	Leyland National 10351A/2R	(Urban Bus)	B38F	1979

LX 3–8	Leyland Lynx LX2R11C15Z4S		B49F	1989

LX 3 G73 UYV, **LX 4** G74 UYV, **LX 5** G75 UYV, **LX 6** G76 UYV, **LX 7** G77 UYV, **LX 8** G78 UYV

M 13–52 — MCW Metrobus DR101/8 — MCW — H43/28D* — 1978/79
* Training buses are H0/15D

M 13t	WYW 13T	**M 22**t	WYW 22T	**M 36**t	WYW 36T	**M 46**t	WYW 46T
M 17	WYW 17T	**M 30**t	WYW 30T	**M 39**	WYW 39T	**M 52**	WYW 52T
M 21u	WYW 21T	**M 31**t	WYW 31T	**M 43**	WYW 43T		

M 59–204 — MCW Metrobus DR101/9 — MCW — H43/28D* — 1979
* Training buses are H0/15D

M 59	WYW 59T	**M 96**	BYX 96V	**M 131**w	BYX 131V	**M 157**t	BYX 157V	**M 193**t	BYX 193V
M 68	WYW 68T	**M 99**	BYX 99V	**M 134**	BYX 134V	**M 159**t	BYX 159V	**M 203**	BYX 203V
M 86	WYW 86T	**M 100**	BYX 100V	**M 138**	BYX 138V	**M 162**	BYX 162V	**M 204**t	BYX 204V
M 89t	WYW 89T	**M 110**	BYX 110V	**M 147**t	BYX 147V	**M 183**	BYX 183V		
M 93	WYW 93T	**M 122**	BYX 122V	**M 154**	BYX 154V	**M 187**	BYX 187V		

M 206–415 — MCW Metrobus DR101/12 — MCW — H43/28D* — 1980
* Training buses are H0/15D

M 206t	BYX 206V	**M 223**	BYX 223V	**M 264**t	BYX 264V	**M 363**	GYE 363W	**M 387**	GYE 387W
M 221	BYX 221V	**M 227**u	BYX 227V	**M 327**	EYE 327V	**M 366**	GYE 366W	**M 415**	GYE 415W

M 506–697 — MCW Metrobus DR101/14 — MCW — H43/28D — 1981

M 506u	GYE 506W	**M 592**u	GYE 592W	**M 687**	KYV 687X
M 554	GYE 554W	**M 598**	GYE 598W	**M 697**	KYV 697X

M 813–951 — MCW Metrobus DR101/16 — MCW — H43/28D — 1983

M 813u	OJD 813Y	**M 832**u	OJD 832Y	**M 841**	OJD 841Y	**M 864**	OJD 864Y	**M 906**	A906 SUL
M 815	OJD 815Y	**M 835**	OJD 835Y	**M 844**	OJD 844Y	**M 881**	OJD 881Y	**M 920**	A920 SUL
M 831	OJD 831Y	**M 839**	OJD 839Y	**M 856**	OJD 856Y	**M 889**	OJD 889Y	**M 951**	A951 SUL

M 960–1001 — MCW Metrobus DR101/17 — MCW — H43/28D — 1984

M 960	A960 SYF	**M 966**	A966 SYF	**M 980**	A980 SYF	**M 994**	A994 SYF
M 962	A962 SYF	**M 967**	A967 SYF	**M 985**	A985 SYF	**M 999**	A999 SYF
M 963	A963 SYF	**M 969**	A969 SYF	**M 990**	A990 SYF	**M 1001**	A701 THV

M 1006–1029 — MCW Metrobus DR101/18 — MCW — H43/28D* — 1984
* Ms 1011, 1014, 1022 & 1029 are DPH43/28D

M 1006	A706 THV	**M 1013**	A713 THV	**M 1019**	A719 THV	**M 1023**	A723 THV	**M 1028**	A728 THV
M 1008	A708 THV	**M 1014**	A714 THV	**M 1020**	A720 THV	**M 1024**	A724 THV	**M 1029**	A729 THV
M 1010	A710 THV	**M 1015**	A715 THV	**M 1021**	A721 THV	**M 1026**	A726 THV		
M 1011	A711 THV	**M 1016**	A716 THV	**M 1022**	A722 THV	**M 1027**	A727 THV		

M 1030	A730 THV	MCW Metrobus DR101/17	MCW	H43/28D	1984
M 1037	A737 THV	MCW Metrobus DR101/17	MCW	H43/28D	1984
M 1039	A739 THV	MCW Metrobus DR101/17	MCW	H43/28D	1984
M 1048	A748 THV	MCW Metrobus DR101/19	MCW	H43/28D	1984
M 1050	A750 THV	MCW Metrobus DR101/19	MCW	H43/28D	1984
M 1053	A753 THV	MCW Metrobus DR101/19	MCW	H43/28D	1984

M 1064–1439 — MCW Metrobus DR101/17 — MCW — H43/28D — 1984/86

M 1064	B64 WUL	**M 1172**	B172 WUL	**M 1200**	B200 WUL	**M 1257**	B257 WUL	**M 1336**	C336 BUV
M 1069	B69 WUL	**M 1178**	B178 WUL	**M 1207**	B207 WUL	**M 1261**	B261 WUL	**M 1341**	C341 BUV
M 1073	B73 WUL	**M 1184**	B184 WUL	**M 1212**	B212 WUL	**M 1262**	B262 WUL	**M 1343**	C343 BUV
M 1106	B106 WUL	**M 1187**	B187 WUL	**M 1238**	B238 WUL	**M 1266**	B266 WUL	**M 1344**	C344 BUV
M 1110w	B110 WUL	**M 1188**	B188 WUL	**M 1240**	B240 WUL	**M 1269**	B269 WUL	**M 1345**	C345 BUV
M 1125	B125 WUL	**M 1190**	B190 WUL	**M 1242**	B242 WUL	**M 1270**	B270 WUL	**M 1351**	C351 BUV
M 1166	B166 WUL	**M 1191**	B191 WUL	**M 1243**	B243 WUL	**M 1271**	B271 WUL	**M 1352**	C352 BUV
M 1171	B171 WUL	**M 1194**	B194 WUL	**M 1251**	B251 WUL	**M 1272**	B272 WUL	**M 1353**	C353 BUV

M 1356	C356 BUV	**M 1360**	C360 BUV	**M 1363**	C363 BUV	**M 1374**	C374 BUV	**M 1439**	C439 BUV
M 1358	C358 BUV	**M 1361**	C361 BUV	**M 1368**	C368 BUV	**M 1381**	C381 BUV		

MV 1–8 | MAN 11.190 | Optare Vecta | B42F | 1995

MV 1	N281 DWY	**MV 3**	N283 DWY	**MV 5**	N285 DWY	**MV 7**	N287 DWY
MV 2	N282 DWY	**MV 4**	N284 DWY	**MV 6**	N286 DWY	**MV 8**	N288 DWY

RM 2033	ALM 33B	AEC Routemaster R2RH	Park Royal	H36/28R	1964
RM 2078	ALM 78B	AEC Routemaster R2RH	Park Royal	H36/28R	1964
RML 880	WLT 880	AEC Routemaster R2RH	Park Royal	H40/32R	1961
RML 881	HSL 656	AEC Routemaster R2RH	Park Royal	H40/32R	1961
RML 891	HSL 660	AEC Routemaster R2RH	Park Royal	H40/32R	1961

(RMLs 880 and 881 carry fleet numbers ER 880 and 881)

RML 2269–2757 | AEC Routemaster R2RH/1 | Park Royal | H40/32R | 1961

RML 2269	CUV 269C	**RML 2455**	JJD 455D	**RML 2621**	NML 621E	**RML 2702**	SMK 702F	**RML 2739**	SMK 739F
RML 2293	CUV 293C	**RML 2463**	JJD 463D	**RML 2622**	NML 622E	**RML 2704**	SMK 704F	**RML 2744**	SMK 744F
RML 2298	CUV 298C	**RML 2464**	JJD 464D	**RML 2645**	NML 645E	**RML 2707**	SMK 707F	**RML 2751**	SMK 751F
RML 2349	CUV 349C	**RML 2485**	JJD 485D	**RML 2646**	NML 646E	**RML 2720**	SMK 720F	**RML 2757**	SMK 757F
RML 2353	CUV 353C	**RML 2489**	JJD 489D	**RML 2650**	NML 650E	**RML 2721**	SMK 721F		
RML 2414	JJD 414D	**RML 2500**	JJD 500D	**RML 2662**	SMK 662F	**RML 2722**	SMK 722F		
RML 2432	JJD 432D	**RML 2519**	JJD 519D	**RML 2697**	SMK 697F	**RML 2729**	SMK 729S		
RML 2447	JJD 447D	**RML 2600**	NML 600E	**RML 2700**	SMK 700F	**RML 2734**	SMK 734F		

VA 1–10 | Volvo Olympian YN2RV18Z4 | Alexander RH | H45/29F | 1996

VA 1	N131 YRW	**VA 3**	N133 YRW	**VA 5**	N135 YRW	**VA 7**	N137 YRW	**VA 9**	N139 YRW
VA 2	N132 YRW	**VA 4**	N134 YRW	**VA 6**	N136 YRW	**VA 8**	N138 YRW	**VA 10**	N140 YRW

VA 11–54 | Volvo Olympian OLY–4953 | Alexander (Belfast) RH | H47/25D | 1997/98

VA 11	XDZ 5911	**VA 20**	R920 WOE	**VA 29**	R929 WOE	**VA 38**	R938 YOV	**VA 47**	R947 YOV
VA 12	XDZ 5912	**VA 21**	R921 WOE	**VA 30**	R930 YOV	**VA 39**	R939 YOV	**VA 48**	R948 YOV
VA 13	XDZ 5913	**VA 22**	R922 WOE	**VA 31**	R931 YOV	**VA 40**	R940 YOV	**VA 49**	R949 YOV
VA 14	XDZ 5914	**VA 23**	R923 WOE	**VA 32**	R932 YOV	**VA 41**	R941 YOV	**VA 50**	R950 YOV
VA 15	XDZ 5915	**VA 24**	R924 WOE	**VA 33**	R933 YOV	**VA 42**	R942 YOV	**VA 51**	R951 YOV
VA 16	XDZ 5916	**VA 25**	R925 WOE	**VA 34**	R934 YOV	**VA 43**	R943 YOV	**VA 52**	R952 YOV
VA 17	XDZ 5917	**VA 26**	R926 WOE	**VA 35**	R935 YOV	**VA 44**	R944 YOV	**VA 53**	R953 YOV
VA 18	R918 WOE	**VA 27**	R927 WOE	**VA 36**	R936 YOV	**VA 45**	R945 YOV	**VA 54**	R954 YOV
VA 19	R919 WOE	**VA 28**	R928 WOE	**VA 37**	R937 YOV	**VA 46**	R946 YOV		

XL 1–7 | Optare Excel L1000 | Optare | B36F | 1997

XL 1	P151 BUG	**XL 3**	P153 BUG	**XL 6**	P156 BUG
XL 2	P152 BUG	**XL 4**	P154 BUG	**XL 7**	P157 BUG

On order:–

Twenty-six Volvo B7L/Plaxton President and forty-five Volvo B7L/Alexander ALX400 H43/20D double deckers.

Special Liveries:–

DP 12–22 are red, orange and blue with route branding for routes T123 and T4 (Heathrow-Feltham Railair).
DP 23–33 are blue with route branding for routes 555/6/7.
DT 12 is green and carries an all over advert for Marks & Spencer.

Previous registrations:–

ALM 2B	K210 SAG	**H577 MOC**	H577 MOC, WLT 339	**WLT 329**	H575 MOC
236 CLT	H880 LOX	**HSL 656**	WLT 881	**WLT 804**	H264 NON
F551 SHX	F551SHX, A5 LBR	**HSL 660**	WLT 891	**WLT 931**	H611 TKU
G349 GCK	G349 GCK, 500 CLT	**VLT 23**		**WLT 946**	J611 DUV

METROBUS

80	F80 SMC	Leyland Lynx LX112L10ZR1R		B49F	1988
101	K101 JMV	Leyland Lynx II LX2R11V18Z4S		B51F	1992
103	D103 NDW	Leyland Lynx LX112TL11ZR1R		B51F	1987
104	D104 NDW	Leyland Lynx LX112TL11ZR1R		B51F	1987
110	D110 NDW	Leyland Lynx LX112TL11ZR1R		B51F	1987
165	F165 SMT	Leyland Lynx LX112L10Z1S		B49F	1989
166	F166 SMT	Leyland Lynx LX112L10Z1S		B49F	1989
248	B248 NVN	Leyland Olympian ONLXB/1R	ECW	H45/32F	1985
395	C395 DML	Leyland Olympian ONLXB/1R	ECW	H45/32F	1985

301–308 Dennis Dart SLF SFD212BR1TGW1 — Plaxton Pointer 10m — B33F — 1997

301	P301 HDP	**303**	P303 HDP	**305**	P305 HDP	**307**	P307 HDP
302	P302 HDP	**304**	P304 HDP	**306**	P306 HDP	**308**	P308 HDP

312–316 Dennis Dart SLF SFD612BR1XGW1 — Plaxton Pointer 2 8.8m — B29F — 1999

312	T312 SMV	**313**	T313 SMV	**314**	T314 SMV	**315**	T315 SMV	**316**	T316 SMV

322–331 Dennis Dart SLF SFD322BR1XGW1 — Plaxton Pointer 2 10.7m — B31D — 1999

322	V322 KMY	**324**	V324 KMY	**326**	V326 KMY	**328**	V328 KMY	**330**	V330 KMY
323	V323 KMY	**325**	V325 KMY	**327**	V327 KMY	**329**	V329 KMY	**331**	V331 KMY

401–415 Dennis Trident SFD113BR1XGX2 — East Lancs Lolyne 9.9m — H45/24D — 1999

401	T401 SMV	**404**	T404 SMV	**407**	T407 SMV	**410**	T410 SMV	**413**	V413 KMY
402	T402 SMV	**405**	T405 SMV	**408**	T408 SMV	**411**	T411 SMV	**414**	V414 KMY
403	T403 SMV	**406**	T406 SMV	**409**	T409 SMV	**412**	V412 KMY	**415**	V415 KMY

501–510 Optare Excel L1070 — Optare — B35F — 1997

501	P501 OUG	**503**	P503 OUG	**505**	P505 OUG	**507**	P507 OUG	**509**	P509 OUG
502	P502 OUG	**504**	P504 OUG	**506**	P506 OUG	**508**	P508 OUG	**510**	P510 OUG

701–707 Dennis Dart 8.5SDL3010 — Plaxton Pointer 8.5m — B32F* — 1991

701	J701 EMX	**703**	J703 EMX	**705**	J705 EMX	**707**	J707 EMX
702	J702 EMX	**704**	J704 EMX	**706**	J706 EMX		

708–716 Dennis Dart 9SDL3011 — Plaxton Pointer 9m — B35F — 1992

708	K708 KGU	**710**	K710 KGU	**712**	K712 KGU	**714**	K714 KGU	**716**	K716 KGU
709	K709 KGU	**711**	K711 KGU	**713**	K713 KGU	**715**	K715 KGU		

717–720 Dennis Dart 9.8SDL3032 — Plaxton Pointer 9.8m — B35F — 1994

717	L717 OMV	**718**	L718 OMV	**719**	L719 OMV	**720**	L720 OMV

721–726 Dennis Dart 9.8SDL3054 — Plaxton Pointer 9.8m — B35F — 1995

721	M721 CGO	**723**	M723 CGO	**725**	N725 KGF
722	M722 CGO	**724**	M724 CGO	**726**	N726 KGF

729	H908 DTP	Dennis Dart 9SDL3002	Wadham Stringer Portsdown 9m	B35F	1991
730	K488 XPG	Dennis Dart 9.8SDL3017	Plaxton Pointer 9.8m	B40F	1993
731	K831 SFT	Dennis Dart 9.8SDL3017	Plaxton Pointer 9.8m	B40F	1993
732	K832 SFT	Dennis Dart 9.8SDL3017	Plaxton Pointer 9.8m	B40F	1993

734–739	Dennis Dart 9SDL3011	Plaxton Pointer 9m	B35F	1992

734	J224 HGY	**736**	J226 HGY	**738**	J228 HGY
735	J225 HGY	**737**	J227 HGY	**739**	J229 HGY

741–748	Dennis Dart SLF SFD212BR1VGW1 (746–8 are SFD212BR1WGW1)	Plaxton Pointer 10m	B35F	1998

741	R741 BMY	**743**	R743 BMY	**745**	R745 BMY	**747**	R747 FGX
742	R742 BMY	**744**	R744 BMY	**746**	R746 FGX	**748**	R748 FGX

750	M150 HPL	Dennis Dart 9.8SDL3035	Plaxton Pointer 9.8m	B40F	1994
751	M151 HPL	Dennis Dart 9.8SDL3040	Plaxton Pointer 9.8m	B40F	1994
752	J752 PPM	Dennis Dart 9SDL3002	Wadham Stringer Portsdown 9m	B37F	1991
754	L354 FPF	Dennis Dart 9.8SDL3035	Plaxton Pointer 9.8m	B40F	1994
756	L726 DPG	Dennis Dart 9.8SDL3035	Plaxton Pointer 9.8m	B40F	1993
759	N259 PJR	Dennis Dart 9.8SDL3054	Plaxton Pointer 9.8m	B40F	1995
760	N260 PJR	Dennis Dart 9.8SDL3054	Plaxton Pointer 9.8m	B40F	1995
761	N261 PJR	Dennis Dart 9.8SDL3054	Plaxton Pointer 9.8m	B40F	1995

811–816	Leyland Olympian ON2R50C13Z4	Leyland	H47/31F	1990–92

811	H811 AGX	**813**	J813 GGW	**815**	K815 HMV
812	J812 GGW	**814**	K814 HMV	**816**	K816 HMV

817–829	Volvo Olympian YN2RV18Z4	Northern Counties Palatine I	H47/29F	1996

817	P817 SGP	**821**	P821 SGP	**824**	P824 SGP	**828**	P828 SGP
818	P818 SGP	**822**	P822 SGP	**825**	P825 SGP	**829**	P829 SGP
819	P819 SGP	**823**	P823 SGP	**826**	P826 SGP		

830–858	Volvo Olympian OLY–4953	East Lancs Pyoneer	H47/25D	1997/98

830	R830 MFR	**836**	R836 MFR	**843**	R843 MFR	**849**	S849 DGX	**855**	S855 DGX
831	R831 MFR	**837**	R837 MFR	**844**	R844 MFR	**850**	S850 DGX	**856**	S856 DGX
832	R832 MFR	**838**	R838 MFR	**845**	R845 MFR	**851**	S851 DGX	**857**	S857 DGX
833	R833 MFR	**839**	R839 MFR	**846**	S846 DGX	**852**	S852 DGX	**858**	S858 DGX
834	R834 MFR	**841**	R841 MFR	**847**	S847 DGX	**853**	S853 DGX		
835	R835 MFR	**842**	R842 MFR	**848**	S848 DGX	**854**	S854 DGX		

859–866	Volvo Olympian OLY–4953	Northern Counties Palatine I	H47/29F	1998

859	S859 DGX	**861**	S861 DGX	**863**	S863 DGX	**865**	S865 DGX
860	S860 DGX	**862**	S862 DGX	**864**	S864 DGX	**866**	S866 DGX

901–906	Optare MetroRider MR13	Optare	B26F	1996

901	N901 HWY	**903**	N903 HWY	**905**	N905 HWY
902	N902 HWY	**904**	N904 HWY	**906**	N906 HWY

909	F70 RPL	Mercedes-Benz 811D	Optare StarRider	B33F	1989
911	G972 WPA	Optare MetroRider MR03	Optare	B33F	1990
912	H152 UUA	Optare MetroRider MR03	Optare	B26F	1991
913	H161 WWT	Optare MetroRider MR03	Optare	B26F	1991
914	H163 WWT	Optare MetroRider MR03	Optare	B26F	1991
915	H165 WWT	Optare MetroRider MR03	Optare	B26F	1991
916	H172 WWT	Optare MetroRiderMR03	Optare	B26F	1991
917	J326 PPD	Optare MetroRider MR03	Optare	B33F	1991
918	L735 MWW	Optare MetroRider MR13	Optare	B29F	1993
950	S950 VMY	Mercedes-Benz O814 Vario	Plaxton Beaver 2	B24FL	1998
951	S951 VMY	Mercedes-Benz O814 Vario	Plaxton Beaver 2	B24FL	1998
952	S952 VMY	Mercedes-Benz O814 Vario	Plaxton Beaver 2	B24FL	1998

METROLINE

AV 1–22	Volvo Olympian YN2RV18Z4	Alexander RH	H43/25D	1996

AV 1	585 CLT	**AV 6**	P486 MBY	**AV 11**	P491 MBY	**AV 16**	P476 MBY	**AV 21**	P474 MBY
AV 2	P482 MBY	**AV 7**	P487 MBY	**AV 12**	P492 MBY	**AV 17**	P477 MBY	**AV 22**	P475 MBY
AV 3	P483 MBY	**AV 8**	P488 MBY	**AV 13**	P493 MBY	**AV 18**	P478 MBY		
AV 4	P484 MBY	**AV 9**	P489 MBY	**AV 14**	P494 MBY	**AV 19**	P479 MBY		
AV 5	P485 MBY	**AV 10**	P490 MBY	**AV 15**	P495 MBY	**AV 20**	P480 MBY		

AV 23–38	Volvo Olympian OLY–4953	Alexander (Belfast) RH	H43/25D	1998

AV 23	S233 RLH	**AV 27**	S127 RLE	**AV 31**	S131 RLE	**AV 35**	S135 RLE
AV 24	S124 RLE	**AV 28**	S128 RLE	**AV 32**	S132 RLE	**AV 36**	S136 RLE
AV 25	S125 RLE	**AV 29**	S129 RLE	**AV 33**	S133 RLE	**AV 37**	S137 RLE
AV 26	S126 RLE	**AV 30**	S130 RLE	**AV 34**	S134 RLE	**AV 38**	S138 RLE

DAF 539w	H539 YCX	DAF SB220LC550	Ikarus Citibus	B50F	1991
DAF 848w	F848 YJX	DAF SB220LC550	Optare Delta	B49F	1989
DAF 849u	F849 YJX	DAF SB220LC550	Optare Delta	B49F	1989

DC 216–232	Dennis Dart 9SDL3002 * DC 232 is Carlyle Dartline 9m	Duple-Carlyle Dartline 9m*	B36F	1990

DC 216u	G216 LGK	**DC 220**u	G220 LGK	**DC 224**u	G124 RGT	**DC 232**	RIB 7002
DC 219u	G219 LGK	**DC 221**u	G121 RGT	**DC 229**u	G129 RGT		

DL 1–21	Dennis Dart SLF SFD212BR1VGW1	Plaxton Pointer 10m	B36F	1997

DL 1	P201 OLX	**DL 6**	P206 OLX	**DL 11**	P211 OLX	**DL 16**	R116 RLY	**DL 21**	R121 RLY
DL 2	P202 OLX	**DL 7**	P207 OLX	**DL 12**	R112 RLY	**DL 17**	R117 RLY		
DL 3	P203 OLX	**DL 8**	P208 OLX	**DL 13**	R113 RLY	**DL 18**	R118 RLY		
DL 4	P204 OLX	**DL 9**	P209 OLX	**DL 14**	R114 RLY	**DL 19**	R119 RLY		
DL 5	P205 OLX	**DL 10**	P210 OLX	**DL 15**	R115 RLY	**DL 20**	R120 RLY		

DL 75–85	Dennis Dart SLF SFD212BR1WGW1	Plaxton Pointer 2 10.1m	B35F	1998

DL 75	R175 VLA	**DL 78**	R178 VLA	**DL 81**	R181 VLA	**DL 84**	R184 VLA
DL 76	R176 VLA	**DL 79**	R179 VLA	**DL 82**	R182 VLA	**DL 85**	R185 VLA
DL 77	R177 VLA	**DL 80**	R180 VLA	**DL 83**	R183 VLA		

DLD 22–53	Dennis Dart SLF SFD212BR1VGW1	Plaxton Pointer 2 10.1m	B30D	1997

DLD 22	R122 RLY	**DLD 29**	R129 RLY	**DLD 36**	R136 RLY	**DLD 43**	R143 RLY	**DLD 50**	R150 RLY
DLD 23	R123 RLY	**DLD 30**	R130 RLY	**DLD 37**	R137 RLY	**DLD 44**	R144 RLY	**DLD 51**	R151 RLY
DLD 24	R124 RLY	**DLD 31**	R131 RLY	**DLD 38**	R138 RLY	**DLD 45**	R145 RLY	**DLD 52**	R152 RLY
DLD 25	R125 RLY	**DLD 32**	R132 RLY	**DLD 39**	R139 RLY	**DLD 46**	R146 RLY	**DLD 53**	R153 RLY
DLD 26	R126 RLY	**DLD 33**	R133 RLY	**DLD 40**	R140 RLY	**DLD 47**	R147 RLY		
DLD 27	R127 RLY	**DLD 34**	R134 RLY	**DLD 41**	R141 RLY	**DLD 48**	R148 RLY		
DLD 28	R128 RLY	**DLD 35**	R135 RLY	**DLD 42**	R142 RLY	**DLD 49**	R149 RLY		

DLD 54–74	Dennis Dart SLF SFD212BR1WGW1	Plaxton Pointer 2 10.1m	B30D	1998

DLD 54	R154 VLA	**DLD 59**	R159 VLA	**DLD 64**	R164 VLA	**DLD 69**	R169 VLA	**DLD 74**	R174 VLA
DLD 55	R155 VLA	**DLD 60**	R160 VLA	**DLD 65**	R165 VLA	**DLD 70**	R170 VLA		
DLD 56	R156 VLA	**DLD 61**	R161 VLA	**DLD 66**	R166 VLA	**DLD 71**	R171 VLA		
DLD 57	R157 VLA	**DLD 62**	R162 VLA	**DLD 67**	R167 VLA	**DLD 72**	R172 VLA		
DLD 58	R158 VLA	**DLD 63**	R163 VLA	**DLD 68**	R168 VLA	**DLD 73**	R173 VLA		

DLD 86–100	Dennis Dart SLF SFD222AR1WGW1	Plaxton Pointer 2 10.1m	B25D	1998

DLD 86 S286 JLP | **DLD 89** S289 JLP | **DLD 92** S292 JLP | **DLD 95** S295 JLP | **DLD 98** S298 JLP
DLD 87 S287 JLP | **DLD 90** S290 JLP | **DLD 93** S293 JLP | **DLD 96** S296 JLP | **DLD 99** S299 JLP
DLD 88 S288 JLP | **DLD 91** S291 JLP | **DLD 94** S294 JLP | **DLD 97** S297 JLP | **DLD 100** S301 JLP

DLD 108–117	Dennis Dart SLF SFD212BR1XGW1	Plaxton Pointer 2 10.1m	B31D	1999

DLD 108 T48 KLD | **DLD 110** T39 KLD | **DLD 112** T52 KLD | **DLD 114** T54 KLD | **DLD 116** T56 KLD
DLD 109 T49 KLD | **DLD 111** T51 KLD | **DLD 113** T53 KLD | **DLD 115** T35 KLD | **DLD 117** T47 KLD

DLD 118–132	Dennis Dart SLF SFD212BR1XGW1	Plaxton Pointer 2 10.1m	B32D	1999

DLD 118 V118 GBY | **DLD 121** V134 GBY | **DLD 124** V124 GBY | **DLD 127** V127 GBY | **DLD 130** V130 GBY
DLD 119 V119 GBY | **DLD 122** V122 GBY | **DLD 125** V125 GBY | **DLD 128** V128 GBY | **DLD 131** V131 GBY
DLD 120 V120 GBY | **DLD 123** V133 GBY | **DLD 126** V126 GBY | **DLD 129** V129 GBY | **DLD 132** V132 GBY

DLS 1–7	Dennis Dart SLF SFD112BR1WGW1	Plaxton Pointer 9.2m	B32F	1997

DLS 1 P101 OLX | **DLS 3** P103 OLX | **DLS 5** P105 OLX | **DLS 7** P107 OLX
DLS 2 P102 OLX | **DLS 4** P104 OLX | **DLS 6** P106 OLX

DM 242t RIB 8431	Dennis Dart 9.8SDL3035	Marshall C37	B40F	1994

DML 1–18	Dennis Dart SLF SFD212BR1VGW1	Marshall Capital 10.2m	B28D	1998

DML 1 R681 MEW | **DML 5** R685 MEW | **DML 9** R689 MEW | **DML 13** R693 MEW | **DML 17** R697 MEW
DML 2 R682 MEW | **DML 6** R686 MEW | **DML 10** R690 MEW | **DML 14** R694 MEW | **DML 18** R698 MEW
DML 3 R683 MEW | **DML 7** R687 MEW | **DML 11** R691 MEW | **DML 15** R695 MEW
DML 4 R684 MEW | **DML 8** R688 MEW | **DML 12** R692 MEW | **DML 16** R696 MEW

DML 33–47	Dennis Dart SLF SFD212BR1WGW1	Marshall Capital 10.2m	B31F	1998

DML 33 R863 MCE | **DML 36** R866 MCE | **DML 39** R869 MCE | **DML 42** R872 MCE | **DML 45** R875 MCE
DML 34 R864 MCE | **DML 37** R867 MCE | **DML 40** R870 MCE | **DML 43** R873 MCE | **DML 46** R876 MCE
DML 35 R865 MCE | **DML 38** R868 MCE | **DML 41** R871 MCE | **DML 44** R874 MCE | **DML 47** R877 MCE

DML 519–532*	Dennis Dart SLF SFD212BR1WGW1 * Originally numbered DML 19–32	Marshall Capital 10.2m	B31F	1998

DML 519 R619 VEG | **DML 522** R622 VEG | **DML 525** R625 VEG | **DML 528** R638 VEG | **DML 531** R631 VEG
DML 520 R620 VEG | **DML 523** R623 VEG | **DML 526** R626 VEG | **DML 529** R629 VEG | **DML 532** R632 VEG
DML 521 R621 VEG | **DML 524** R624 VEG | **DML 527** R627 VEG | **DML 530** R630 VEG

DML 533 T63 KLD	Dennis Dart SLF SFD212BR1WGW1	Marshall Capital 10.2m	B31F	1999
DML 534 T64 KLD	Dennis Dart SLF SFD212BR1WGW1	Marshall Capital 10.2m	B31F	1999
DML 535 T65 KLD	Dennis Dart SLF SFD212BR1WGW1	Marshall Capital 10.2m	B31F	1999

DMS 1–12	Dennis Dart SLF SFD112BR1VGW1	Marshall Capital 9.3m	B32F	1998

DMS 1 R701 MEW | **DMS 4** R704 MEW | **DMS 7** R707 MEW | **DMS 10** R710 MEW
DMS 2 R702 MEW | **DMS 5** R705 MEW | **DMS 8** R708 MEW | **DMS 11** R711 MEW
DMS 3 R703 MEW | **DMS 6** R706 MEW | **DMS 9** R709 MEW | **DMS 12** R699 MEW

DMS 13–29	Dennis Dart SLF SFD112BR1WGW1 * DMS 28 is B27F	Marshall Capital 9.3m	B32F*	1998

DMS 13 S513 KFL | **DMS 17** S517 KFL | **DMS 21** S521 KFL | **DMS 25** S525 KFL | **DMS 29** S529 KFL
DMS 14 S514 KFL | **DMS 18** S518 KFL | **DMS 22** S522 KFL | **DMS 26** S526 KFL
DMS 15 S515 KFL | **DMS 19** S519 KFL | **DMS 23** S523 KFL | **DMS 27** S527 KFL
DMS 16 S516 KFL | **DMS 20** S520 KFL | **DMS 24** S524 KFL | **DMS 28** S528 KFL

DNL 101–120		Dennis Dart 9SDL3034		Northern Counties Paladin 9m				B34F	1994
DNL 101	L101 HHV	**DNL 105**	L105 HHV	**DNL 109**	L109 HHV	**DNL 114**	L114 HHV	**DNL 118**	L118 HHV
DNL 102	L102 HHV	**DNL 106**	L106 HHV	**DNL 110**	L110 HHV	**DNL 115**	L115 HHV	**DNL 119**	L119 HHV
DNL 103	L103 HHV	**DNL 107**	L107 HHV	**DNL 112**	L112 HHV	**DNL 116**	L116 HHV	**DNL 120**	L120 HHV
DNL 104	L104 HHV	**DNL 108**	L108 HHV	**DNL 113**	L113 HHV	**DNL 117**	L117 HHV		

DP 234–239		Dennis Dart 9SDL3011		Plaxton Pointer 9m		B35F	1992
DP 234	K414 MGN	**DP 236**	K416 MGN	**DP 238**	K418 MGN		
DP 235	RIB 5085	**DP 237**	K417 MGN	**DP 239**	K419 MGN		

DP 240	M498 ALP	Dennis Dart 9SDL3031	Plaxton Pointer 9m	B35F	1995
DP 241	M499 ALP	Dennis Dart 9SDL3031	Plaxton Pointer 9m	B35F	1995

DP 273–276		Dennis Dart SFD212BR5VGD1		Plaxton Pointer 9m				B35F	1997
DP 273	P673 MLE	**DP 274**	P674 MLE	**DP 275**	P675 MLE	**DP 276**	P676 MLE		

DPL 233t	33 LUG	Dennis Dart 9.8SDL3017	Plaxton Pointer 9.8m	B40F	1992

DPL 245–248		Dennis Dart 9.8SDL3054		Plaxton Pointer 9.8m				B40F	1995
DPL 245	M503 ALP	**DPL 246**	M504 ALP	**DPL 247**	M505 ALP	**DPL 248**	M506 ALP		

DR 15–19		Dennis Dart 8.5SDL3003		Reeve Burgess Pointer 8.5m				B28F	1991
DR 15	H115 THE	**DR 16**	H116 THE	**DR 17**	H117 THE	**DR 18**	H118 THE	**DR 19**	H119 THE

DR 40	H540 XGK	Dennis Dart 8.5SDL3003	Plaxton Pointer 8.5m	B28F	1991
DR 42	H542 XGK	Dennis Dart 8.5SDL3003	Plaxton Pointer 8.5m	B28F	1991

DR 81–98		Dennis Dart 8.5SDL3010		Plaxton Pointer 8.5m				B28F	1992
DR 81	J381 GKH	**DR 85**	J385 GKH	**DR 89**	J389 GKH	**DR 93**	J393 GKH	**DR 97**	J397 GKH
DR 82	J382 GKH	**DR 86**	J386 GKH	**DR 90**	J390 GKH	**DR 94**	J394 GKH	**DR 98**	J398 GKH
DR 83	J383 GKH	**DR 87**	J387 GKH	**DR 91**u	J391 GKH	**DR 95**	J395 GKH		
DR 84	J384 GKH	**DR 88**	J388 GKH	**DR 92**	J392 GKH	**DR 96**	J396 GKH		

DR 142–148		Dennis Dart 8.5SDL3015		Plaxton Pointer 8.5m				B28F	1992
DR 142	K242 PAG	**DR 144**	K244 PAG	**DR 146**	K246 PAG	**DR 148**	K248 PAG		
DR 143	K243 PAG	**DR 145**	K245 PAG	**DR 147**	K247 PAG				

DRL 18–37		Dennis Dart 9SDL3016		Plaxton Pointer 9m				B34F	1992
DRL 18	K818 NKH	**DRL 22**	K822 NKH	**DRL 26**	K826 NKH	**DRL 30**	K430 OKH	**DRL 34**	K434 OKH
DRL 19	K819 NKH	**DRL 23**	K823 NKH	**DRL 27**	K827 NKH	**DRL 31**	K431 OKH	**DRL 35**	K435 OKH
DRL 20	K820 NKH	**DRL 24**	K824 NKH	**DRL 28**	K828 NKH	**DRL 32**	K432 OKH	**DRL 36**	K436 OKH
DRL 21	K821 NKH	**DRL 25**	K825 NKH	**DRL 29**	K429 OKH	**DRL 33**	K433 OKH	**DRL 37**	K437 OKH

DT 88–140		Dennis Dart 8.5SDL3003		Carlyle Dartline 8.5m				B28F	1990/91
DT 88u	H588 MOC	**DT 97**	H97 MOB	**DT 107**u	H107 MOB	**DT 133**	H133 MOB	**DT 140**	H140 MOB
DT 90	H890 LOX	**DT 99**u	H899 LOX	**DT 122**u	H122 MOB	**DT 138**	H138 MOB		
DT 92	H92 MOB	**DT 103**	H103 MOB	**DT 123**u	H123 MOB	**DT 139**w	H139 MOB		

EDR 1–9		Dennis Dart 9.8SDL3040			Plaxton Pointer 9.8m			B39F	1994
EDR 1t	M101 BLE	**EDR 3**	M103 BLE	**EDR 5**	M105 BLE	**EDR 7**u	M107 BLE	**EDR 9**u	M109 BLE
EDR 2	M102 BLE	**EDR 4**u	M104 BLE	**EDR 6**u	M106 BLE	**EDR 8**u	M108 BLE		

EDR 10–44		Dennis Dart SFD412BR5TGD1			Plaxton Pointer 9.8m			B39F	1996
EDR 10	P285 MLD	**EDR 17**	P292 MLD	**EDR 24**	P299 MLD	**EDR 31**	P307 MLD	**EDR 38**	P314 MLD
EDR 11	P286 MLD	**EDR 18**	P293 MLD	**EDR 25**	P301 MLD	**EDR 32**	P308 MLD	**EDR 39**	P315 MLD
EDR 12	P287 MLD	**EDR 19**	P294 MLD	**EDR 26**	P302 MLD	**EDR 33**	P309 MLD	**EDR 40**	P316 MLD
EDR 13	P288 MLD	**EDR 20**	P295 MLD	**EDR 27**	P303 MLD	**EDR 34**	P310 MLD	**EDR 41**	P317 MLD
EDR 14	P289 MLD	**EDR 21**	P296 MLD	**EDR 28**	P304 MLD	**EDR 35**	P311 MLD	**EDR 42**	P318 MLD
EDR 15	P290 MLD	**EDR 22**	P297 MLD	**EDR 29**	P305 MLD	**EDR 36**	P312 MLD	**EDR 43**	P319 MLD
EDR 16	P291 MLD	**EDR 23**	P298 MLD	**EDR 30**	P306 MLD	**EDR 37**	P313 MLD	**EDR 44**	P320 MLD

IL 208s	RIB 7004	Iveco Daily 49.10			LHE			B23F	1990
IR 202s	RIB 5082	Iveco Daily 49.10			Robin Hood City Nippy			B23F	1989

LLW 25–38		Dennis Lance SLF 11SDA3202			Wright Pathfinder 320			B34D	1993/94
LLW 25	L25 WLH	**LLW 28**	L28 WLH	**LLW 31**	L31 WLH	**LLW 34**	L34 WLH	**LLW 37**	L37 WLH
LLW 26	L26 WLH	**LLW 29**	L29 WLH	**LLW 32**	L32 WLH	**LLW 35**	L35 WLH	**LLW 38**	L38 WLH
LLW 27	L27 WLH	**LLW 30**	L21 WLH	**LLW 33**	L39 WLH	**LLW 36**	L36 WLH		

LN 1–31		Dennis Lance 11SDA3108			Northern Counties Paladin			B37D	1993
LN 1u	K301 YJA	**LN 8**u	K308 YJA	**LN 14**u	K314 YJA	**LN 21**u	K321 YJA	**LN 29**u	K329 YJA
LN 2u	K302 YJA	**LN 9**t	K309 YJA	**LN 16**u	K316 YJA	**LN 23**u	K323 YJA	**LN 30**u	K330 YJA
LN 3u	K303 YJA	**LN 10**u	K310 YJA	**LN 17**u	K317 YJA	**LN 24**u	K324 YJA	**LN 31**u	K331 YJA
LN 4u	K304 YJA	**LN 11**u	K311 YJA	**LN 18**u	K318 YJA	**LN 25**u	K325 YJA		
LN 5u	K305 YJA	**LN 12**u	K312 YJA	**LN 19**u	K319 YJA	**LN 27**u	K327 YJA		
LN 6u	K306 YJA	**LN 13**u	K313 YJA	**LN 20**u	K320 YJA	**LN 28**u	K328 YJA		

M 1–5		MCW Metrobus DR101/3			MCW			H43/28D	1978
M 1t	THX 101S	**M 3**t	THX 103S	**M 4**t	THX 104S	**M 5**t	THX 105S		

M 18–42		MCW Metrobus DR101/8			MCW			H43/28D	1978–79
M 18	WYW 18T	**M 25**u	WYW 25T	**M 33**w	WYW 33T	**M 41**	WYW 41T	**M 42**u	WYW 42T

M 58–194		MCW Metrobus DR101/8			MCW			H43/28D	1979
M 58	WYW 58T	**M 90**u	WYW 90T	**M 113**w	BYX 113V	**M 166**	BYX 166V	**M 184**	BYX 184V
M 79u	WYW 79T	**M 97**w	BYX 97V	**M 119**	BYX 119V	**M 167**	BYX 167V	**M 192**	BYX 192V
M 83	WYW 83T	**M 102**t	BYX 102V	**M 137**	BYX 137V	**M 169**	BYX 169V	**M 194**	BYX 194V
M 87w	WYW 87T	**M 111**t	BYX 111V	**M 151**	BYX 151V	**M 178**	BYX 178V		

M 229–482		MCW Metrobus DR101/12			MCW			H43/28D	1980
M 229w	BYX 229V	**M 335**	EYE 335V	**M 407**	GYE 407W	**M 446**t	GYE 446W	**M 461**	GYE 461W
M 238w	BYX 238V	**M 342**	EYE 342V	**M 409**t	GYE 409W	**M 448**	GYE 448W	**M 468**t	GYE 468W
M 272w	BYX 272V	**M 352**	GYE 352W	**M 428**t	GYE 428W	**M 449**	GYE 449W	**M 481**w	GYE 481W
M 300	BYX 300V	**M 367**t	GYE 367W	**M 429**	GYE 429W	**M 453**	GYE 453W	**M 482**	GYE 482W
M 306	BYX 306V	**M 373**	GYE 373W	**M 432**	GYE 432W	**M 455**	GYE 455W		
M 324	EYE 324V	**M 391**	GYE 391W	**M 436**	GYE 436W	**M 459**w	GYE 459W		
M 326	EYE 326V	**M 403**	GYE 403W	**M 440**	GYE 440W	**M 460**	GYE 460W		

M 550–696		MCW Metrobus DR101/14			MCW			H43/28D	1981–82
M 550	GYE 550W	**M 574**w	GYE 574W	**M 618**	KYO 618X	**M 655**	KYV 655X	**M 683**	KYV 683X
M 572t	GYE 572W	**M 595**	GYE 595W	**M 621**	KYO 621X	**M 678**t	KYV 678X	**M 696**	KYV 696X

M 810–955 MCW Metrobus DR101/16 — MCW — H43/28D — 1983

M 810	OJD 810Y	M 878	OJD 878Y	M 910	A910 SUL	M 921	A921 SUL	M 935	A935 SUL
M 819u	WLT 342	M 879	OJD 879Y	M 911	A911 SUL	M 924	A924 SUL	M 937	A937 SUL
M 824	OJD 824Y	M 890	OJD 890Y	M 912	A912 SUL	M 925	A925 SUL	M 945	A945 SUL
M 829	OJD 829Y	M 896	A896 SUL	M 915	A915 SUL	M 928	A928 SUL	M 950	A950 SUL
M 876	OJD 876Y	M 899	A899 SUL	M 916	A916 SUL	M 934	A934 SUL	M 955	A955 SUL

M 956–1043 MCW Metrobus DR101/17 — MCW — H43/28D — 1984

M 956	A956 SYF	M 971	A971 SYF	M 995u	A995 SYF	M 1034	A734 THV	M 1042	A742 THV
M 957	A957 SYF	M 974	A974 SYF	M 997	A997 SYF	M 1035	A735 THV	M 1043	A743 THV
M 961t	A961 SYF	M 982	A982 SYF	M 1004	A704 THV	M 1038	A738 THV		
M 964	A964 SYF	M 987	A987 SYF	M 1031	A731 THV	M 1040	A740 THV		
M 968	A968 SYF	M 993	A993 SYF	M 1032	A732 THV	M 1041	A741 THV		

M 1045t	A745 THV	MCW Metrobus DR101/19	MCW	DPH43/28D	1984
M 1047	A747 THV	MCW Metrobus DR101/19	MCW	H43/28D	1984
M 1052	A752 THV	MCW Metrobus DR101/19	MCW	H43/28D	1984

M 1056–1431 MCW Metrobus DR101/17 — MCW — H43/28D* — 1985
* Ms 1185, 1236,1393 & 1396 are DPH43/28D

M 1056	B56 WUL	M 1113	B113 WUL	M 1161	B161 WUL	M 1250	B250 WUL	M 1369	C369 BUV
M 1057	B57 WUL	M 1114	B114 WUL	M 1163	B163 WUL	M 1273	WLT 902	M 1383	C383 BUV
M 1058	B58 WUL	M 1115	B115 WUL	M 1167	B167 WUL	M 1274	B274 WUL	M 1385	C385 BUV
M 1059	B59 WUL	M 1118	B118 WUL	M 1168	B168 WUL	M 1277	B277 WUL	M 1390	C390 BUV
M 1060	B60 WUL	M 1119	B119 WUL	M 1174	B174 WUL	M 1284	B284 WUL	M 1392t	C392 BUV
M 1061	B61 WUL	M 1120	B120 WUL	M 1181	B181 WUL	M 1287	B287 WUL	M 1393t‡	C393 BUV
M 1063	B63 WUL	M 1141	B141 WUL	M 1183	B183 WUL	M 1292	B292 WUL	M 1394	C394 BUV
M 1065	B65 WUL	M 1142	B142 WUL	M 1185	WLT 893	M 1325	C325 BUV	M 1395	C395 BUV
M 1066	B66 WUL	M 1143	B143 WUL	M 1186	B186 WUL	M 1329	C329 BUV	M 1396t	C396 BUV
M 1067t	B67 WUL	M 1145	B145 WUL	M 1189	B189 WUL	M 1330	C330 BUV	M 1397	C397 BUV
M 1068	B68 WUL	M 1146	B146 WUL	M 1192	B192 WUL	M 1331	C331 BUV	M 1403	C403 BUV
M 1071	B71 WUL	M 1147	B147 WUL	M 1193	B193 WUL	M 1333	C333 BUV	M 1408	C408 BUV
M 1072	B72 WUL	M 1148	B148 WUL	M 1195	B195 WUL	M 1334	C334 BUV	M 1414	C414 BUV
M 1076	B76 WUL	M 1149	B149 WUL	M 1197	B197 WUL	M 1339	C339 BUV	M 1416	C416 BUV
M 1077	B77 WUL	M 1150	B150 WUL	M 1198	B198 WUL	M 1342	C342 BUV	M 1423	C423 BUV
M 1078	B78 WUL	M 1151	B151 WUL	M 1202u	B202 WUL	M 1346	C346 BUV	M 1425	C425 BUV
M 1079	B79 WUL	M 1153	B153 WUL	M 1204	B204 WUL	M 1348	C348 BUV	M 1426	C426 BUV
M 1080t	B80 WUL	M 1156	B156 WUL	M 1205	B205 WUL	M 1349	C349 BUV	M 1427	C427 BUV
M 1081	B81 WUL	M 1157	B157 WUL	M 1208	B208 WUL	M 1350	C350 BUV	M 1428	C428 BUV
M 1082	B82 WUL	M 1158	B158 WUL	M 1218	B218 WUL	M 1355	C355 BUV	M 1429	WLT 826
M 1083	B83 WUL	M 1159	B159 WUL	M 1234	B234 WUL	M 1365	C365 BUV	M 1430	C430 BUV
M 1111	B111 WUL	M 1160	B160 WUL	M 1236	WLT 646	M 1366	C366 BUV	M 1431	C431 BUV

MC 1	P481 HEG	Marshall Minibus	Marshall	B29F	1996

MM 254–268 MAN 11.220 — Marshall C37 — B38F — 1996

MM 254	N121 XEG	MM 257	N124 XEG	MM 260	N127 XEG	MM 263	N130 XEG	MM 266	N133 XEG
MM 255	N122 XEG	MM 258	N125 XEG	MM 261	N128 XEG	MM 264	N131 XEG	MM 267	N134 XEG
MM 256	N123 XEG	MM 259	N126 XEG	MM 262	N129 XEG	MM 265	N132 XEG	MM 268	N135 XEG

MM 270–278 MAN 11.220 — Marshall Capital — B38F — 1996

MM 270	P470 JEG	MM 272	P472 JEG	MM 274	P474 JEG	MM 276	P476 JEG	MM 278	P478 JEG
MM 271	P471 JEG	MM 273	P473 JEG	MM 275	P475 JEG	MM 277	P477 JEG		

MMS 269	N161 YEG	Mercedes-Benz 811D	Marshall C16	B26F	1996
MR 87	F87 GGC	Mercedes-Benz 811D	Robin Hood	C29F	1989
MR 90	F90 GGC	Mercedes-Benz 811D	Robin Hood	C29F	1989

MRL 213–222	Optare MetroRider MR03	Optare	B26F	1991/93

MRL 213 J213 BWU · **MRL 215** J215 BWU · **MRL 217** J217 BWU · **MRL 219** J219 BWU · **MRL 221** J221 BWU · **MRL 222** K422 HWY

MRL 223 P448 SWX	Optare MetroRider MR13	Optare	B29F	1997
MRL 224 P449 SWX	Optare MetroRider MR13	Optare	B29F	1997

MV 249–253	MAN 11.190	Optare Vecta	B42F	1995

MV 249 M507 ALP · **MV 250** M508 ALP · **MV 251** N701 FLN · **MV 252** N702 FLN · **MV 253** N703 FLN

MW 21–37	Mercedes-Benz 811D	Wright Nimbus	B26F	1993

MW 21w NDZ 7921 · **MW 22**w NDZ 7922 · **MW 23**w NDZ 7923 · **MW 24**w NDZ 7924 · **MW 25**w NDZ 7925 · **MW 29**w NDZ 7929 · **MW 31**w NDZ 7931 · **MW 32**w NDZ 7932 · **MW 35**w NDZ 7935 · **MW 36**w K510 FYN · **MW 37**w K476 FYN

OM 243 M501 ALP	Optare MetroRider MR33	Optare	B25F	1995
OM 244 M502 ALP	Optare MetroRider MR33	Optare	B25F	1995
OM 279 P509 NWU	Optare MetroRider MR13	Optare	B25F	1996

RM 70–1979	AEC Routemaster R2RH * RM 644 is O36/28RD	Park Royal	H36/28R*	1959–65

RM 70 VLT 70 · **RM 268** VLT 268 · **RM 446** WLT 446 · **RM 644** WLT 644 · **RM 646** KFF 257 · **RM 1348** 348 CLT · **RM 1799** 799 DYE · **RM 1971** ALD 971B · **RM 1979** ALD 979B

RMC 1513 513 CLT	AEC Routemaster R2RH	Park Royal	O32/62	1962
RML 893 KFF276	AEC Routemaster R2RH	Park Royal	H40/32R	1961
RML 902 ALC464A	AEC Routemaster R2RH	Park Royal	H40/32R	1961
RML 903 WLT903	AEC Routemaster R2RH	Park Royal	H40/32R	1961

RML 2274–2755	AEC Routemaster R2RH/1	Park Royal	H40/32R	1965–68

RML 2274 CUV 274C	**RML 2367** JJD 367D	**RML 2478** JJD 478D	**RML 2599** NML 599E	**RML 2698** SMK 698F
RML 2282 CUV 282C	**RML 2368** JJD 368D	**RML 2479** JJD 479D	**RML 2603** NML 603E	**RML 2699** SMK 699F
RML 2284 CUV 284C	**RML 2377** JJD 377D	**RML 2508** JJD 508D	**RML 2620** NML 620E	**RML 2701** SMK 701F
RML 2285 CUV 285C	**RML 2384** JJD 384D	**RML 2509** JJD 509D	**RML 2633** NML 633E	**RML 2703** SMK 703F
RML 2288 CUV 288C	**RML 2393** JJD 393D	**RML 2511** JJD 511D	**RML 2634** NML 634E	**RML 2706** SMK 706F
RML 2289 CUV 289C	**RML 2395** JJD 395D	**RML 2532** JJD 532D	**RML 2649** NML 649E	**RML 2710** SMK 710F
RML 2295 CUV 295C	**RML 2413** JJD 413D	**RML 2537** JJD 537D	**RML 2651** NML 651E	**RML 2713** SMK 713F
RML 2296 CUV 296C	**RML 2419** JJD 419D	**RML 2547** JJD 547D	**RML 2652** NML 652E	**RML 2727** SMK 727F
RML 2299 CUV 299C	**RML 2430** JJD 430D	**RML 2558** JJD 558D	**RML 2659** SMK 659F	**RML 2728** SMK 728F
RML 2308 CUV 308C	**RML 2431** JJD 431D	**RML 2561** JJD 561D	**RML 2679** SMK 679F	**RML 2731** SMK 731F
RML 2310 CUV 310C	**RML 2439** JJD 439D	**RML 2566** JJD 566D	**RML 2681** SMK 681F	**RML 2737** SMK 737F
RML 2312 CUV 312C	**RML 2443** JJD 443D	**RML 2579** JJD 579D	**RML 2689** SMK 689F	**RML 2755** SMK 755F
RML 2331 CUV 331C	**RML 2446** JJD 446D	**RML 2585** JJD 585D	**RML 2690** SMK 690F	
RML 2348 CUV 348C	**RML 2471** JJD 471D	**RML 2594** JJD 594D	**RML 2695** SMK 695F	

S 11–20	Scania N113DRB	Alexander RH	H47/31F	1991

S 11 J811 HMC · **S 12** J812 HMC · **S 13** J813 HMC · **S 14** J814 HMC · **S 15** J815 HMC · **S 16** J816 HMC · **S 17** J817 HMC · **S 18** J818 HMC · **S 19** J819 HMC · **S 20** J820 HMC

TA 66–107		Dennis Trident SFD111BR1XGX2				Alexander ALX400 9.9m		H45/19D	1999
TA 66	T61 KLD	**TA 77**	T87 KLD	**TA 88**	T188 CLO	**TA 99**	T199 CLO	**TA 110**	V310 GLB
TA 67	T67 KLD	**TA 78**	T78 KLD	**TA 89**	T189 CLO	**TA 100**	T218 CLO	**TA 111**	V311 GLB
TA 68	T68 KLD	**TA 79**	T79 KLD	**TA 90**	T190 CLO	**TA 101**	T201 CLO	**TA 112**	V312 GLB
TA 69	T69 KLD	**TA 80**	T89 KLD	**TA 91**	T191 CLO	**TA 102**	T202 CLO	**TA 113**	V313 GLB
TA 70	T37 KLD	**TA 81**	T38 KLD	**TA 92**	T192 CLO	**TA 103**	V303 GLB	**TA 114**	V314 GLB
TA 71	T41 KLD	**TA 82**	T182 CLO	**TA 93**	T193 CLO	**TA 104**	T204 CLO	**TA 115**	V315 GLB
TA 72	T72 KLD	**TA 83**	T183 CLO	**TA 94**	T194 CLO	**TA 105**	T205 CLO	**TA 116**	V316 GLB
TA 73	T43 KLD	**TA 84**	T184 CLO	**TA 95**	T195 CLO	**TA 106**	T206 CLO	**TA 117**	V317 GLB
TA 74	T74 KLD	**TA 85**	T185 CLO	**TA 96**	T196 CLO	**TA 107**	T207 CLO		
TA 75	T75 KLD	**TA 86**	T186 CLO	**TA 97**	T197 CLO	**TA 108**	V308 GLB		
TA 76	T76 KLD	**TA 87**	T187 CLO	**TA 98**	T199 CLO	**TA 109**	V309 GLB		

TP 1–65		Dennis Trident SFD111BR1XGX2 Plaxton President 9.9m* * TP 2–31 are SFD111BR1WGX2						H45/22D	1999
TP 1	T101 KLD	**TP 14**	T114 KLD	**TP 27**	T127 KLD	**TP 40**	T140 CLO	**TP 53**	V753 HBY
TP 2	T102 KLD	**TP 15**	T115 KLD	**TP 28**	T128 KLD	**TP 41**	T141 CLO	**TP 54**	V754 HBY
TP 3	T103 KLD	**TP 16**	T116 KLD	**TP 29**	T129 KLD	**TP 42**	T142 CLO	**TP 55**	V755 HBY
TP 4	T104 KLD	**TP 17**	T117 KLD	**TP 30**	T97 KLD	**TP 43**	T143 CLO	**TP 56**	V756 HBY
TP 5	T105 KLD	**TP 18**	T118 KLD	**TP 31**	T98 KLD	**TP 44**	T144 CLO	**TP 57**	V757 HBY
TP 6	T106 KLD	**TP 19**	T119 KLD	**TP 32**	T132 CLO	**TP 45**	T145 CLO	**TP 58**	V758 HBY
TP 7	T107 KLD	**TP 20**	T120 KLD	**TP 33**	T133 CLO	**TP 46**	T146 CLO	**TP 59**	V759 HBY
TP 8	T108 KLD	**TP 21**	T71 KLD	**TP 34**	T134 CLO	**TP 47**	V307 GLB	**TP 60**	V760 HBY
TP 9	T109 KLD	**TP 22**	T122 KLD	**TP 35**	T135 CLO	**TP 48**	T148 CLO	**TP 61**	V761 HBY
TP 10	T110 KLD	**TP 23**	T73 KLD	**TP 36**	T136 CLO	**TP 49**	V749 HBY	**TP 62**	V762 HBY
TP 11	T81 KLD	**TP 24**	T124 KLD	**TP 37**	T137 CLO	**TP 50**	V750 HBY	**TP 63**	V763 HBY
TP 12	T112 KLD	**TP 25**	T125 KLD	**TP 38**	T138 CLO	**TP 51**	V751 HBY	**TP 64**	V764 HBY
TP 13	T113 KLD	**TP 26**	T126 KLD	**TP 39**	T139 CLO	**TP 52**	V752 HBY	**TP 65**	V765 HBY

V 201–217		Volvo Olympian YN2RV18Z4				Northern Counties Palatine II		H47/25D	1993/4
V 201	L201 SKD	**V 205**	L205 SKD	**V 209**	L209 SKD	**V 214**	L214 TWM		
V 202	L202 SKD	**V 206**	L206 SKD	**V 210**	L210 SKD	**V 215**	L215 TWM		
V 203	L203 SKD	**V 207**	L207 SKD	**V 212**	L212 TWM	**V 216**	L216 TWM		
V 204	L204 SKD	**V 208**	L208 SKD	**V 213**	L213 TWM	**V 217**	L217 TWM		

On order:–

Seventeen Dennis Dart SLF/Plaxton Pointer 2 buses for route C2 from June 2000.

Special liveries:–

DR 94 is white with branding for Safeway supermarket.
DR 95 and DTs 88, 92, 103 and 122 are all blue and carry allover adverts for Tesco.
LN 25 is all white.
M 1393 is in orange livery and advertises 'The Ultimate People Carrier' for promotion of bus travel.

Previous registrations:–

33 LUG	J823 GGF	**RIB 7004**	G208 LGK
585 CLT	P481 MBY	**RIB 8431**	L416 PAR
ALC 464A	WLT 902	**V303 GLB**	T203 CLO
K476 FYN	NDZ 7937	**V307 GLB**	T147 CLO
K510 FYN	NDZ 7936	**WLT 342**	OJD 819Y
KFF 257	WLT 646	**WLT 646**	B236 WUL
KFF 276	WLT 893	**WLT 826**	C429 BUV
RIB 5082	F202 HGN	**WLT 893**	B185 WUL
RIB 5085	K415 MGN	**WLT 902**	B273 WUL
RIB 7002	CMN 12A, H403 HOY		

MITCHAM BELLE

	Dennis Dart SLF SFD322BR1XGW1		Plaxton Pointer 2 10.7m	B30D	1999
T151 OGC	T154 OGC	T158 OGC	T876 HGT		
T152 OGC	T156 OGC	T159 OGC	T877 HGT		
T153 OGC	T157 OGC	T875 HGT	T880 HGT		

SOVEREIGN

RML 2265–2756	AEC Routemaster R2RH/1		Park Royal		H40/32R	1965–68

RML 2265 CUV 265C	**RML 2487** JJD 487D	**RML 2569** JJD 569D	**RML 2663** SMK 663F	**RML 2694** SMK 694F
RML 2322 CUV 322C	**RML 2527** JJD 527D	**RML 2582** JJD 582D	**RML 2668** SMK 668F	**RML 2719** SMK 719F
RML 2341 CUV 341C	**RML 2538** JJD 538D	**RML 2598** JJD 598D	**RML 2674** SMK 674F	**RML 2756** SMK 756F
RML 2404 JJD 404D	**RML 2563** JJD 563D	**RML 2627** NML 627E	**RML 2686** SMK 686F	

29	H139 GGS	Leyland Olympian ON2R50C13Z4	Northern Counties	H47/30F	1991
30	H140 GGS	Leyland Olympian ON2R50C13Z4	Northern Counties	H47/30F	1991
33	BPF 133Y	Leyland Olympian ONTL11/1R	Roe	H43/29F	1983
37	BPF 137Y	Leyland Olympian ONTL11/1R	Roe	H43/29F	1983
38	A138 DPE	Leyland Olympian ONTL11/1R	Roe	H43/29F	1983
40	A140 DPE	Leyland Olympian ONTL11/1R	Roe	H43/29F	1983

41–52		Leyland Olympian ON2R50C13Z4		Northern Counties		H47/30F	1991
41	H141 GGS	**44**	H144 GGS	**47**	H147 GGS	**50**	H150 GGS
42	H142 GGS	**45**	H145 GGS	**48**	H148 GGS	**51**	H151 GGS
43	H143 GGS	**46**	H146 GGS	**49**	H149 GGS	**52**	H152 GGS

53–64		Volvo Olympian OLY–4953		Northern Counties Palatine I		H43/29F	1998
53	S53 VNM	**56**	S56 VNM	**58**	S58 VNM	**63**	S63 WNM
54	S54 VNM	**57**	S57 VNM	**59**	S59 VNM	**64**	S64 WNM

459	M459 UUR	Mercedes-Benz 811D	Plaxton Beaver	B31F	1995
460	M460 UUR	Mercedes-Benz 811D	Plaxton Beaver	B31F	1995
461	M461 UUR	Mercedes-Benz 811D	Plaxton Beaver	B31F	1995

503–557		Dennis Dart SLF SFD212BR1XGW1		Plaxton Pointer 2 10.1m				B31D	1999
503	T503 JPP	**515**	V515 JBH	**526**	V526 JBH	**537**	V537 JBH	**549**	V549 JBH
504	T504 JPP	**516**	V516 JBH	**527**	V527 JBH	**538**	V538 JBH	**550**	V550 JBH
506	V506 JBH	**517**	V517 JBH	**528**	V528 JBH	**539**	V539 JBH	**551**	V551 JBH
507	V507 JBH	**518**	V518 JBH	**529**	V529 JBH	**540**	V540 JBH	**552**	V552 JBH
508	V508 JBH	**519**	V519 JBH	**530**	V530 JBH	**542**	V542 JBH	**553**	V553 JBH
509	V509 JBH	**520**	V520 JBH	**531**	V531 JBH	**543**	V543 JBH	**554**	V554 JBH
510	V510 JBH	**521**	V521 JBH	**532**	V532 JBH	**544**	V544 JBH	**556**	V556 JBH
511	V511 JBH	**522**	V522 JBH	**533**	V533 JBH	**545**	V545 JBH	**557**	V557 JBH
512	V512 JBH	**523**	V523 JBH	**534**	V534 JBH	**546**	V546 JBH		
513	V513 JBH	**524**	V524 JBH	**535**	V535 JBH	**547**	V547 JBH		
514	V514 JBH	**525**	V525 JBH	**536**	V536 JBH	**548**	V548 JBH		

558–562		Dennis Dart SLF SFD112BR1XGW1		Plaxton Pointer 2 9.3m				B29F	1999
558	V558 JBH	**559**	V559 JBH	**560**	V560 JBH	**561**	V561 JBH	**562**	V562 JBH

706	OHV 706Y	Leyland Titan TNLXB2RR	Leyland	H44/28F	1983
720	NUW 620Y	Leyland Titan TNLXB2RR	Leyland	H44/28F	1982
757	WYV 57T	Leyland Titan TNLXB2RRsp	Park Royal	H44/28F	1979

STAGECOACH EAST LONDON & STAGECOACH SELKENT

DA 10	G684 KNW	DAF SB220LC550	Optare Delta	B40D	1989

DA 11–35 DAF SB220LC550 | Optare Delta | B40D | 1992/93

DA 13 & 15 are currently on loan to Stagecoach South [Hampshire Bus]

DA 11	J711 CYG	**DA 16**	J716 CYG	**DA 21**	J721 CYG	**DA 26**	J726 CYG	**DA 31**	K631 HWX
DA 12	J712 CYG	**DA 17**	J717 CYG	**DA 22**	J722 CYG	**DA 27**	J727 CYG	**DA 32**	K632 HWX
DA 13	472 YMF	**DA 18**	J718 CYG	**DA 23**	J723 CYG	**DA 28**	J728 CYG	**DA 33**	K633 HWX
DA 14	J714 CYG	**DA 19**	J719 CYG	**DA 24**	J724 CYG	**DA 29**	J729 CYG	**DA 34**	K634 HWX
DA 15	YLJ 332	**DA 20**	J720 CYG	**DA 25**	J725 CYG	**DA 30**	K630 HWX	**DA 35**	K635 HWX

DRL 112–134 Dennis Dart 9SDL3024 | Plaxton Pointer 9m | B34F | 1993

DRL 112	K112 SRH	**DRL 125**	K125 SRH	**DRL 128**	K128 SRH	**DRL 131**	K131 SRH	**DRL 134**	K134 SRH
DRL 117	K117 SRH	**DRL 126**	K126 SRH	**DRL 129**	K129 SRH	**DRL 132**	K132 SRH		
DRL 121	K121 SRH	**DRL 127**	K127 SRH	**DRL 130**	K130 SRH	**DRL 133**	K133 SRH		

J5	M105 CCD	Dennis Javelin 11SDL2133	Plaxton Premier Interurban	C47F	1995
J6	M106 CCD	Dennis Javelin 11SDL2133	Plaxton Premier Interurban	C47F	1995
J8	M108 CCD	Dennis Javelin 11SDL2133	Plaxton Premier Interurban	C47F	1995

LCY 1–9 Dennis Dart SLF SFD212BR1VGW1 | Alexander ALX200 10.2m | B29DL | 1997

LCY 1	P801 NJN	**LCY 3**	P803 NJN	**LCY 5**	P805 NJN	**LCY 7**	P807 NJN	**LCY 9**	R209 XNO
LCY 2	P802 NJN	**LCY 4**	P804 NJN	**LCY 6**	P806 NJN	**LCY 8**	R208 XNO		

LCY 10	S410 TNO	Dennis Dart SLF SFD212BR1WGW1	Alexander ALX200 10.2m	B29DL	1998
LCY 11	S411 TNO	Dennis Dart SLF SFD212BR1WGW1	Alexander ALX200 10.2m	B29DL	1998

LV 1–12 Dennis Lance 11SDA3108 | Plaxton Verde | B42D | 1994

LV 1	L201 YAG	**LV 4**	L204 YAG	**LV 7**	L207 YAG	**LV 10**u	L210 YAG
LV 2	L202 YAG	**LV 5**	L205 YAG	**LV 8**	L208 YAG	**LV 11**	L211 YAG
LV 3u	L203 YAG	**LV 6**	L206 YAG	**LV 9**	L209 YAG	**LV 12**	WLT 461

MB 1–18 Mercedes-Benz O814 Vario | Plaxton Beaver 2 | B29F | 1997

MB 1	R501 YWC	**MB 5**	R505 YWC	**MB 9**	R509 YWC	**MB 13**	R513 YWC	**MB 17**	R517 YWC
MB 2	R502 YWC	**MB 6**	R506 YWC	**MB 10**	R510 YWC	**MB 14**	R514 YWC	**MB 18**	R518 YWC
MB 3	R503 YWC	**MB 7**	R507 YWC	**MB 11**	R511 YWC	**MB 15**	R515 YWC		
MB 4	R504 YWC	**MB 8**	R508 YWC	**MB 12**	R512 YWC	**MB 16**	R516 YWC		

PD 1–18 Dennis Dart SFD412BR5VGD1 | Plaxton Pointer 9.8m | B37D | 1997

PD 1	R701 YWC	**PD 5**	R705 YWC	**PD 9**	R709 YWC	**PD 13**	R713 YWC	**PD 17**	R717 YWC
PD 2	R702 YWC	**PD 6**	R706 YWC	**PD 10**	R710 YWC	**PD 14**	R714 YWC	**PD 18**	R718 YWC
PD 3	R703 YWC	**PD 7**	R707 YWC	**PD 11**	R711 YWC	**PD 15**	R715 YWC		
PD 4	R704 YWC	**PD 8**	R708 YWC	**PD 12**	R712 YWC	**PD 16**	R716 YWC		

PD 59–103 Dennis Dart 9.8SDL3054 | Plaxton Pointer 9.8m | B37D | 1995

PD 59	M59 VJO	**PD 69**	M69 VJO	**PD 85**	M85 WBW	**PD 93**	M93 WBW	**PD 101**	M101 WBW
PD 63	M63 VJO	**PD 71**	M71 VJO	**PD 86**	M86 WBW	**PD 94**	M94 WBW	**PD 102**	M102 WBW
PD 64	M64 VJO	**PD 73**	M73 VJO	**PD 87**	M87 WBW	**PD 95**	M95 WBW	**PD 103**	M103 WBW
PD 65	M65 VJO	**PD 81**	M81 WBW	**PD 89**	M89 WBW	**PD 96**	M96 WBW		
PD 67	M67 VJO	**PD 82**	M82 WBW	**PD 91**	M91 WBW	**PD 97**	M97 WBW		
PD 68	M68 VJO	**PD 83**	M83 WBW	**PD 92**	M92 WBW	**PD 98**	M98 WBW		

PD 418–425	Dennis Dart 9.8SDL3054	Plaxton Pointer 9.8m	B40F	1996

PD 418	N418 MBW	**PD 420**	N420 MBW	**PD 422**	N422 MBW	**PD 423**	N423 MBW	**PD 425**	N425 MBW

PD 709–722	Dennis Dart 9.8SDL3035	Plaxton Pointer 9.8m	B37D	1994

PD 709	L709 JUD	**PD 712**	L712 JUD	**PD 715**	L715 JUD	**PD 718**	L718 JUD	**PD 721**	L721 JUD
PD 710	L710 JUD	**PD 713**	L713 JUD	**PD 716**	L716 JUD	**PD 719**	L719 JUD	**PD 722**	L722 JUD
PD 711	L711 JUD	**PD 714**	L714 JUD	**PD 717**	L717 JUD	**PD 720**	L720 JUD		

RM 613	WLT 613	AEC Routemaster R2RH	Park Royal	H36/28R	1960
RM 980	USK 625	AEC Routemaster R2RH	Park Royal	H36/28R	1961
RM 1289	XSL 596A	AEC Routemaster R2RH	Park Royal	H36/28R	1962
RM 1527	527 CLT	AEC Routemaster R2RH	Park Royal	H36/28R	1963
RM 1599	YTS 820A	AEC Routemaster R2RH	Park Royal	H36/28R	1963
RMC 1456	LFF 875	AEC Routemaster R2RH	Park Royal	H32/25RD	1961
RMC 1461	461 CLT	AEC Routemaster R2RH	Park Royal	H32/25RD	1961
RMC 1485	485 CLT	AEC Routemaster R2RH	Park Royal	H32/25RD	1961
RML 886	WLT 886	AEC Routemaster R2RH	Park Royal	H40/32R	1961
RML 890	XFF 814	AEC Routemaster R2RH	Park Royal	H40/32R	1961
RML 898	XFF 813	AEC Routemaster R2RH	Park Royal	H40/32R	1961

RML 2272–2760	AEC Routemaster R2RH/1	Park Royal	H40/32R	1965–68

RML 2272	CUV 272C	**RML 2437**	JJD 437D	**RML 2495**	JJD 495D	**RML 2624**	NML 624E	**RML 2709**	SMK 709F
RML 2286	CUV 286C	**RML 2444**	JJD 444D	**RML 2496**	JJD 496D	**RML 2639**	NML 639E	**RML 2723**	SMK 723F
RML 2300	CUV 300C	**RML 2445**	JJD 445D	**RML 2497**	JJD 497D	**RML 2641**	NML 641E	**RML 2738**	SMK 738F
RML 2303	CUV 303C	**RML 2450**	JJD 450D	**RML 2541**	JJD 541D	**RML 2642**	NML 642E	**RML 2743**	SMK 743F
RML 2311	CUV 311C	**RML 2451**	JJD 451D	**RML 2550**	JJD 550D	**RML 2657**	NML 657E	**RML 2748**	SMK 748F
RML 2392	JJD 392D	**RML 2456**	JJD 456D	**RML 2565**	JJD 565D	**RML 2661**	SMK 661F	**RML 2749**	SMK 749F
RML 2399	JJD 399D	**RML 2462**	JJD 462D	**RML 2581**	JJD 581D	**RML 2665**	SMK 665F	**RML 2760**	SMK 760F
RML 2402	JJD 402D	**RML 2470**	JJD 470D	**RML 2592**	JJD 592D	**RML 2670**	SMK 670F		
RML 2415	JJD 415D	**RML 2481**	JJD 481D	**RML 2607**	NML 607E	**RML 2671**	SMK 671F		
RML 2429	JJD 429D	**RML 2488**	JJD 488D	**RML 2610**	NML 610E	**RML 2696**	SMK 696F		
RML 2435	JJD 435D	**RML 2493**	JJD 493D	**RML 2616**	NML 616E	**RML 2705**	SMK 705F		

S32–71	Scania N113DRB	Northern Counties	H44/25D	1991/92

S 32	J132 HMT	**S 40**	J140 HMT	**S 48**	K848 LMK	**S 56**	K856 LMK	**S 64**	K864 LMK
S 33	J133 HMT	**S 41**	J141 HMT	**S 49**	K849 LMK	**S 57**	K857 LMK	**S 65**	K865 LMK
S 34	J134 HMT	**S 42**	J142 HMT	**S 50**	K850 LMK	**S 58**	K858 LMK	**S 66**	K866 LMK
S 35	J135 HMT	**S 43**	J143 HMT	**S 51**	K851 LMK	**S 59**	K859 LMK	**S 67**	K867 LMK
S 36	J136 HMT	**S 44**	J144 HMT	**S 52**	K852 LMK	**S 60**	K860 LMK	**S 68**	K868 LMK
S 37	J137 HMT	**S 45**	J145 HMT	**S 53**	K853 LMK	**S 61**	K861 LMK	**S 69**	K869 LMK
S 38	J138 HMT	**S 46**	K846 LMK	**S 54**	K854 LMK	**S 62**	K862 LMK	**S 70**	K870 LMK
S 39	J139 HMT	**S 47**	K847 LMK	**S 55**	K855 LMK	**S 63**	K863 LMK	**S 71**	K871 LMK

SLD 1–29	Dennis Dart SLF SFD212BR1TGW1	Alexander ALX200 10.2m	B36F	1996/97

SLD 1	P21 HMF	**SLD 7**	P27 HMF	**SLD 13**	P613 SEV	**SLD 19**	R119 VPU	**SLD 25**	R125 VPU
SLD 2	P31 HMF	**SLD 8**	P28 HMF	**SLD 14**	R114 VPU	**SLD 20**	R120 VPU	**SLD 26**	R126 VPU
SLD 3	P23 HMF	**SLD 9**	P29 HMF	**SLD 15**	R115 VPU	**SLD 21**	R121 VPU	**SLD 27**	R127 VPU
SLD 4	P24 HMF	**SLD 10**	P610 SEV	**SLD 16**	R116 VPU	**SLD 22**	R122 VPU	**SLD 28**	R128 VPU
SLD 5	P25 HMF	**SLD 11**	P611 SEV	**SLD 17**	R117 VPU	**SLD 23**	R123 VPU	**SLD 29**	R129 VPU
SLD 6	P26 HMF	**SLD 12**	R712 XAR	**SLD 18**	R118 VPU	**SLD 24**	R124 VPU		

SLD 30–41	Dennis Dart SLF SFD212BR1VGW1	Alexander ALX200 10.2m	B30D	1998

SLD 30	R930 FOO	**SLD 33**	R933 FOO	**SLD 36**	R936 FOO	**SLD 39**	R939 FOO
SLD 31	R931 FOO	**SLD 34**	R934 FOO	**SLD 37**	R937 FOO	**SLD 40**	R940 FOO
SLD 32	R932 FOO	**SLD 35**	R935 FOO	**SLD 38**	R938 FOO	**SLD 41**	R941 FOO

SLD 42–58		Dennis Dart SLF SFD112BR1VGW1				Alexander ALX200 9.4m		B29F	1998
SLD 42	R942 FOO	**SLD 46**	R946 FOO	**SLD 50**	R950 FOO	**SLD 54**	R454 FVX	**SLD 58**	R458 FVX
SLD 43	R943 FOO	**SLD 47**	R947 FOO	**SLD 51**	R451 FVX	**SLD 55**	R455 FVX		
SLD 44	R944 FOO	**SLD 48**	R948 FOO	**SLD 52**	R452 FVX	**SLD 56**	R456 FVX		
SLD 45	R945 FOO	**SLD 49**	R949 FOO	**SLD 53**	R453 FVX	**SLD 57**	R457 FVX		

SLD 59–78		Dennis Dart SLF SFD212BR1WGW1				Alexander ALX200 10.2m		B33F	1998/9
SLD 59	S459 BWC	**SLD 63**	S463 BWC	**SLD 67**	S467 BWC	**SLD 71**	S471 BWC	**SLD 75**	S475 BWC
SLD 60	S460 BWC	**SLD 64**	S464 BWC	**SLD 68**	S468 BWC	**SLD 72**u	S472 BWC	**SLD 76**u	S476 BWC
SLD 61	S461 BWC	**SLD 65**	S465 BWC	**SLD 69**	S469 BWC	**SLD 73**	S473 BWC	**SLD 77**	S477 BWC
SLD 62	S462 BWC	**SLD 66**	S466 BWC	**SLD 70**	S470 BWC	**SLD 74**	S474 BWC	**SLD 78**	S478 BWC

SLD 79–88		Dennis Dart SLF SFD112BR1WGW1				Alexander ALX200 9.4m		B29F	1999
SLD 79	S479 BWC	**SLD 81**	S481 BWC	**SLD 83**	S483 BWC	**SLD 85**	S485 BWC	**SLD 87**	S487 BWC
SLD 80	S480 BWC	**SLD 82**	S482 BWC	**SLD 84**	S484 BWC	**SLD 86**	S486 BWC	**SLD 88**	S488 BWC

SLD 89–95		Dennis Dart SLF SFD212BR1WGW1				Alexander ALX200 10.2m		B33F	1999
SLD 89	S489 BWC	**SLD 91**	S491 BWC	**SLD 93**	S493 BWC	**SLD 95**	S495 BWC		
SLD 90	S490 BWC	**SLD 92**	S492 BWC	**SLD 94**	S494 BWC				

SLD 96–106		Dennis Dart SLF SFD112BR1WGW1				Alexander ALX200 9.4m		B29F	1999
SLD 96	S496 BWC	**SLD 99**	S499 BWC	**SLD 102**	S102 WHK	**SLD 105**	S105 WHK		
SLD 97	S497 BWC	**SLD 100**	WLT 898	**SLD 103**	S103 WHK	**SLD 106**	S106 WHK		
SLD 98	S498 BWC	**SLD 101**	S101 WHK	**SLD 104**	S104 WHK				

SLD 107–110		Dennis Dart SLF SFD212BR1XGW1				Plaxton Pointer 2 10.1m		B33F	1999
SLD 107	V107 MVX	**SLD 108**	V108 MVX	**SLD 109**	V109 MVX	**SLD 110**	V110 MVX		

SLD 111–138		Dennis Dart SLF SFD212BR1XGW1				Plaxton Pointer 2 10.1m		B31D	1999
SLD 111	V173 MVX	**SLD 117**	V117 MVX	**SLD 123**	V175 MVX	**SLD 129**	V129 MVX	**SLD 135**	V135 MVX
SLD 112	V112 MVX	**SLD 118**	V118 MVX	**SLD 124**	V124 MVX	**SLD 130**	V130 MVX	**SLD 136**	V136 MVX
SLD 113	V113 MVX	**SLD 119**	V119 MVX	**SLD 125**	V125 MVX	**SLD 131**	V131 MVX	**SLD 137**	V137 MVX
SLD 114	V114 MVX	**SLD 120**	V120 MVX	**SLD 126**	V126 MVX	**SLD 132**	V132 MVX	**SLD 138**	V138 MVX
SLD 115	V115 MVX	**SLD 121**	V174 MVX	**SLD 127**	V127 MVX	**SLD 133**	V133 MVX		
SLD 116	V116 MVX	**SLD 122**	V122 MVX	**SLD 128**	V128 MVX	**SLD 134**	V134 MVX		

SLD 139–172		Dennis Dart SLF SFD112BR1XGW1				Plaxton Pointer 2 9.3m		B27D	1999
SLD 139	V139 MVX	**SLD 146**	V146 MVX	**SLD 153**	V153 MVX	**SLD 160**	V160 MVX	**SLD 167**	V167 MVX
SLD 140	V140 MVX	**SLD 147**	V147 MVX	**SLD 154**	V154 MVX	**SLD 161**	V161 MVX	**SLD 168**	V168 MVX
SLD 141	V141 MVX	**SLD 148**	V148 MVX	**SLD 155**	V155 MVX	**SLD 162**	V162 MVX	**SLD 169**	V169 MVX
SLD 142	V142 MVX	**SLD 149**	V149 MVX	**SLD 156**	V156 MVX	**SLD 163**	V163 MVX	**SLD 170**	V170 MVX
SLD 143	V143 MVX	**SLD 150**	V150 MVX	**SLD 157**	V157 MVX	**SLD 164**	V164 MVX	**SLD 171**	V171 MVX
SLD 144	V144 MVX	**SLD 151**	V151 MVX	**SLD 158**	V158 MVX	**SLD 165**	V165 MVX	**SLD 172**	V172 MVX
SLD 145	V145 MVX	**SLD 152**	V152 MVX	**SLD 159**	V159 MVX	**SLD 166**	V166 MVX		

SLW 15–30		Scania N113CRL				Wright Pathfinder 320		B37D	1994
SLW 15	RDZ 6115	**SLW 19**	RDZ 6119	**SLW 23**	RDZ 6123	**SLW 27**	RDZ 6127		
SLW 16	RDZ 6116	**SLW 20**	RDZ 6120	**SLW 24**	RDZ 6124	**SLW 28**	RDZ 6128		
SLW 17	RDZ 6117	**SLW 21**	RDZ 6121	**SLW 25**	RDZ 6125	**SLW 29**	RDZ 6129		
SLW 18	RDZ 6118	**SLW 22**	RDZ 6122	**SLW 26**	RDZ 6126	**SLW 30**	RDZ 6130		

SR 1–106 — Mercedes-Benz 811D — Optare StarRider — B26F — 1988/9

SR 1	E155 CGJ	**SR 70**	F170 FWY	**SR 74**	F174 FWY	**SR 106**	G106 KUB
SR 2	E712 LYU	**SR 71**	F171 FWY	**SR 91**	G91 KUB		

T 1–66 — Leyland Titan TNTL11112RRsp — Park Royal — H44/24D — 1978/9

T 1	THX 401S	**T 11**	WYV 11T	**T 19**	WYV 19T	**T 28**	WYV 28T	**T 37**	WYV 37T
T 2	THX 402S	**T 12**	WYV 12T	**T 20**	WYV 20T	**T 30**	WYV 30T	**T 38**	WYV 38T
T 4	WYV 4T	**T 13**	WYV 13T	**T 21**	WYV 21T	**T 31**	WYV 31T	**T 39**	WYV 39T
T 6	WYV 6T	**T 14**	WYV 14T	**T 22**	WYV 22T	**T 32**	WYV 32T	**T 40**	WYV 40T
T 7	WYV 7T	**T 15**	WYV 15T	**T 23**	WYV 23T	**T 33**	WYV 33T	**T 66**	WYV 66T
T 8	WYV 8T	**T 16**	WYV 16T	**T 24**	WYV 24T	**T 34**	WYV 34T		
T 9	WYV 9T	**T 17**	WYV 17T	**T 25**	WYV 25T	**T 35**	WYV 35T		
T 10	WYV 10T	**T 18**	WYV 18T	**T 26**	WYV 26T	**T 36**	WYV 36T		

T 86–140 — Leyland Titan TNTL11112RRsp — Park Royal — H44/26D — 1979–80

T 86t	CUL 86V	**T 114**t	CUL 114V	**T 130**t	CUL 130V	**T 140**	CUL 140V
T 98t	CUL 98V	**T 120**t	CUL 120V	**T 137**t	CUL 137V		

T 142–230 — Leyland Titan TNTL11112RRsp — Park Royal — H44/26D — 1980

T 142t	CUL 142V	**T 175**	CUL 175V	**T 214**	CUL 214V	**T 223**	CUL 223V	**T 230**	EYE 230V
T 163	CUL 163V	**T 193**	CUL 193V	**T 222**	CUL 222V	**T 224**t	CUL 224V		

T 261w	GYE 261W	Leyland Titan TNTL112RR	Park Royal/Leyland	H44/26D	1981
T 262w	GYE 262W	Leyland Titan TNLXB2RR	Park Royal/Leyland	H44/26D	1981
T 263w	GYE 263W	Leyland Titan TNLXB2RR	Park Royal/Leyland	H44/26D	1981

T 264–868 — Leyland Titan TNLXB2RR — Leyland — H44/24D* — 1981–84

* T512 is O44/24D

T 264	GYE 264W	**T 437**	KYV 437X	**T 496**	KYV 496X	**T 540**	KYV 540X	**T 608**	NUW 608Y
T 266w	GYE 266W	**T 439**	KYV 439X	**T 497**	KYV 497X	**T 541**	KYV 541X	**T 609**	NUW 609Y
T 267w	GYE 267W	**T 441**w	KYV 441X	**T 498**	KYV 498X	**T 543**	KYV 543X	**T 610**w	NUW 610Y
T 268w	GYE 268W	**T 444**	KYV 444X	**T 500**	KYV 500X	**T 544**	KYV 544X	**T 613**d	NUW 613Y
T 272w	GYE 272W	**T 445**	KYV 445X	**T 501**	KYV 501X	**T 545**	KYV 545X	**T 614**	NUW 614Y
T 285	KYN 285X	**T 446**	KYV 446X	**T 502**	KYV 502X	**T 546**	KYV 546X	**T 616**	NUW 616Y
T 286	KYN 286X	**T 447**	KYV 447X	**T 503**	KYV 503X	**T 548**	KYV 548X	**T 617**	NUW 617Y
T 298	KYN 298X	**T 448**	KYV 448X	**T 504**	KYV 504X	**T 549**	KYV 549X	**T 624**	NUW 624Y
T 306	KYN 306X	**T 453**w	KYV 453X	**T 505**	KYV 505X	**T 550**	NUW 550Y	**T 625**	NUW 625Y
T 311w	KYV 311X	**T 454**	KYV 454X	**T 506**	KYV 506X	**T 551**	NUW 551Y	**T 627**	NUW 627Y
T 318	KYV 318X	**T 456**	KYV 456X	**T 508**	KYV 508X	**T 552**	NUW 552Y	**T 629**	NUW 629Y
T 320	KYV 320X	**T 458**	KYV 458X	**T 512**d	KYV 512X	**T 563**	NUW 563Y	**T 630**	NUW 630Y
T 326w	KYV 326X	**T 460**	KYV 460X	**T 513**	KYV 513X	**T 564**	NUW 564Y	**T 631**	NUW 631Y
T 331	KYV 331X	**T 461**	KYV 461X	**T 514**w	KYV 514X	**T 568**	NUW 568Y	**T 632**	NUW 632Y
T 334w	KYV 334X	**T 462**	KYV 462X	**T 515**	KYV 515X	**T 573**	NUW 573Y	**T 633**w	NUW 633Y
T 340w	KYV 340X	**T 465**	KYV 465X	**T 517**	KYV 517X	**T 578**	NUW 578Y	**T 637**w	NUW 637Y
T 360	KYV 360X	**T 466**w	KYV 466X	**T 521**	KYV 521X	**T 579**w	NUW 579Y	**T 640**	NUW 640Y
T 366w	KYV 366X	**T 467**w	KYV 467X	**T 522**	KYV 522X	**T 580**	NUW 580Y	**T 650**	NUW 650Y
T 368	KYV 368X	**T 469**	KYV 469X	**T 525**	KYV 525X	**T 581**	NUW 581Y	**T 652**	NUW 652Y
T 378	KYV 378X	**T 470**w	KYV 470X	**T 526**	KYV 526X	**T 583**	NUW 583Y	**T 653**	NUW 653Y
T 379	KYV 379X	**T 471**	KYV 471X	**T 527**	KYV 527X	**T 585**	NUW 585Y	**T 657**	NUW 657Y
T 380	KYV 380X	**T 473**	KYV 473X	**T 529**	KYV 529X	**T 589**	NUW 589Y	**T 658**	NUW 658Y
T 386	KYV 386X	**T 476**w	KYV 476X	**T 531**	KYV 531X	**T 592**w	NUW 592Y	**T 680**	OHV 680Y
T 387	KYV 387X	**T 480**	KYV 480X	**T 532**w	KYV 532X	**T 597**	NUW 597Y	**T 721**	OHV 721Y
T 394w	KYV 394X	**T 486**	KYV 486X	**T 533**	KYV 533X	**T 598**w	NUW 598Y	**T 740**	OHV 740Y
T 395	KYV 395X	**T 488**	KYV 488X	**T 535**	KYV 535X	**T 600**	NUW 600Y	**T 748**	OHV 748Y
T 406	KYV 406X	**T 490**	KYV 490X	**T 536**	KYV 536X	**T 602**w	NUW 602Y	**T 749**	OHV 749Y
T 428w	KYV 428X	**T 492**w	KYV 492X	**T 537**	KYV 537X	**T 603**	NUW 603Y	**T 770**	OHV 770Y
T 434	KYV 434X	**T 495**	KYV 495X	**T 539**	KYV 539X	**T 605**	NUW 605Y	**T 771**	OHV 771Y

T 772	OHV 772Y	**T 810**	OHV 810Y	**T 816**	RYK 816Y	**T 829**	A829 SUL	**T 847**w	A847 SUL
T 785u	OHV 785Y	**T 812**	OHV 812Y	**T 818**	RYK 818Y	**T 836**	A836 SUL	**T 848**	A848 SUL
T 797d	OHV 797Y	**T 813**	OHV 813Y	**T 821**	RYK 821Y	**T 837**	A837 SUL	**T 856**	A856 SUL
T 804	OHV 804Y	**T 814**	OHV 814Y	**T 822**	RYK 822Y	**T 841**	A841 SUL	**T 857**	A857 SUL
T 805	OHV 805Y	**T 815**	OHV 815Y	**T 828**	A828 SUL	**T 842**	A842 SUL	**T 868**	A868 SUL

T 877	A877 SUL	Leyland Titan TNTL112RR	Leyland	H44/26D	1984
T 880	A880 SUL	Leyland Titan TNTL112RR	Leyland	H44/26D	1984
T 881	A881 SUL	Leyland Titan TNL112RR	Leyland	H44/26D	1984
T 882	A882 SUL	Leyland Titan TNL112RR	Leyland	H44/26D	1984
T 883	A883 SUL	Leyland Titan TNL112RR	Leyland	H44/26D	1984
T 885	A885 SUL	Leyland Titan TNL112RR	Leyland	H44/26D	1984

T 925–1115 Leyland Titan TNLXB2RR Leyland H44/26D 1984

T 925	A925 SYE	**T 960**t	A960 SYE	**T 988**	A988 SYE	**T 1030**	A630 THV	**T 1101**	B101 WUV
T 926	A926 SYE	**T 961**	A961 SYE	**T 1003**	A603 THV	**T 1035**w	A635 THV	**T 1103**	B103 WUV
T 949t	A949 SYE	**T 965**t	A965 SYE	**T 1025**	A625 THV	**T 1036**	A636 THV	**T 1115**	B115 WUV
T 951	A951 SYE	**T 971**t	A971 SYE	**T 1028**	A628 THV	**T 1052**	A652 THV		
T 953t	A953 SYE	**T 978**	A978 SYE	**T 1029**u	A629 THV	**T 1065**	A65 THX		

TA 1–98 Dennis Trident SFD311BR1WGX2 Alexander ALX400 10.5m H51/22D 1999

TA 1	S801 BWC	**TA 21**	S821 BWC	**TA 41**	T641 KPU	**TA 61**	T661 KPU	**TA 82**	T682 KPU
TA 2	S802 BWC	**TA 22**	S822 BWC	**TA 42**	T642 KPU	**TA 62**	T662 KPU	**TA 83**	T683 KPU
TA 3	S803 BWC	**TA 23**	S823 BWC	**TA 43**	T643 KPU	**TA 63**	T663 KPU	**TA 84**	T684 KPU
TA 4	S804 BWC	**TA 24**	S824 BWC	**TA 44**	T644 KPU	**TA 64**	T664 KPU	**TA 85**	T685 KPU
TA 5	S805 BWC	**TA 25**	S825 BWC	**TA 45**	T645 KPU	**TA 65**	T665 KPU	**TA 86**	T686 KPU
TA 6	S806 BWC	**TA 26**	S826 BWC	**TA 46**	T646 KPU	**TA 66**	T699 KVX	**TA 87**	T687 KPU
TA 7	S807 BWC	**TA 27**	S827 BWC	**TA 47**	T647 KPU	**TA 67**	T667 KPU	**TA 88**	T688 KPU
TA 8	S808 BWC	**TA 28**	S828 BWC	**TA 48**	T648 KPU	**TA 68**	T668 KPU	**TA 89**	T689 KPU
TA 9	S809 BWC	**TA 29**	S829 BWC	**TA 49**	T649 KPU	**TA 69**	T669 KPU	**TA 90**	T690 KPU
TA 10	S810 BWC	**TA 30**	S830 BWC	**TA 50**	T650 KPU	**TA 70**	T670 KPU	**TA 91**	T691 KPU
TA 11	S811 BWC	**TA 31**	S831 BWC	**TA 51**	T651 KPU	**TA 71**	T671 KPU	**TA 92**	T692 KPU
TA 12	S812 BWC	**TA 32**	S832 BWC	**TA 52**	T652 KPU	**TA 72**	T672 KPU	**TA 93**	T693 KPU
TA 13	S813 BWC	**TA 33**	S833 BWC	**TA 53**	T653 KPU	**TA 73**	T673 KPU	**TA 94**	T694 KPU
TA 14	S814 BWC	**TA 34**	S834 BWC	**TA 54**	T654 KPU	**TA 75**	T675 KPU	**TA 95**	T695 KPU
TA 15	S815 BWC	**TA 35**	S835 BWC	**TA 55**	T655 KPU	**TA 76**	T676 KPU	**TA 96**	T696 KPU
TA 16	S816 BWC	**TA 36**	S836 BWC	**TA 56**	T656 KPU	**TA 77**	T677 KPU	**TA 97**	T697 KPU
TA 17	S817 BWC	**TA 37**	S837 BWC	**TA 57**	T657 KPU	**TA 78**	T678 KPU	**TA 98**	T698 KPU
TA 18	S818 BWC	**TA 38**	S838 BWC	**TA 58**	T658 KPU	**TA 79**	T679 KPU		
TA 19	S819 BWC	**TA 39**	S839 BWC	**TA 59**	T659 KPU	**TA 80**	T680 KPU		
TA 20	S820 BWC	**TA 40**	T640 KPU	**TA 60**	T660 KPU	**TA 81**	T681 KPU		

TA 99–222 Dennis Trident SFD311BR1XGX2 Alexander ALX400 10.5m H47/24D 1999

TA 99	VLT 14	**TA 115**	V115 MEV	**TA 131**	V131 MEV	**TA 147**	V147 MEV	**TA 163**	V163 MEV
TA 100	WLT 491	**TA 116**	V116 MEV	**TA 132**	V132 MEV	**TA 148**	V148 MEV	**TA 164**	V164 MEV
TA 101	V475 KJN	**TA 117**	V117 MEV	**TA 133**	V133 MEV	**TA 149**	V149 MEV	**TA 165**	V165 MEV
TA 102	V102 MEV	**TA 118**	V118 MEV	**TA 134**	V134 MEV	**TA 150**	V150 MEV	**TA 166**	V166 MEV
TA 103	V103 MEV	**TA 119**	V119 MEV	**TA 135**	V135 MEV	**TA 151**	V151 MEV	**TA 167**	V167 MEV
TA 104	V104 MEV	**TA 120**	V120 MEV	**TA 136**	V136 MEV	**TA 152**	V152 MEV	**TA 168**	V168 MEV
TA 105	V105 MEV	**TA 121**	V478 KJN	**TA 137**	V137 MEV	**TA 153**	V153 MEV	**TA 169**	V169 MEV
TA 106	V106 MEV	**TA 122**	V122 MEV	**TA 138**	V138 MEV	**TA 154**	V154 MEV	**TA 170**	V170 MEV
TA 107	V107 MEV	**TA 123**	V479 KJN	**TA 139**	V139 MEV	**TA 155**	V155 MEV	**TA 171**	V171 MEV
TA 108	V108 MEV	**TA 124**	V124 MEV	**TA 140**	V140 MEV	**TA 156**	V156 MEV	**TA 172**	V172 MEV
TA 109	V109 MEV	**TA 125**	V125 MEV	**TA 141**	V141 MEV	**TA 157**	V157 MEV	**TA 173**	V173 MEV
TA 110	V476 KJN	**TA 126**	V126 MEV	**TA 142**	V142 MEV	**TA 158**	V158 MEV	**TA 174**	V174 MEV
TA 111	V477 KJN	**TA 127**	V127 MEV	**TA 143**	V143 MEV	**TA 159**	V159 MEV	**TA 175**	V175 MEV
TA 112	V112 MEV	**TA 128**	V128 MEV	**TA 144**	V144 MEV	**TA 160**	V160 MEV	**TA 176**	V176 MEV
TA 113	V113 MEV	**TA 129**	V129 MEV	**TA 145**	V145 MEV	**TA 161**	V161 MEV	**TA 177**	V177 MEV
TA 114	V114 MEV	**TA 130**	V130 MEV	**TA 146**	V146 MEV	**TA 162**	V162 MEV	**TA 178**	V178 MEV

TA 179	V179 MEV	**TA 188**	V188 MEV	**TA 197**	V197 MEV	**TA 206**	V206 MEV	**TA 215**	V215 MEV
TA 180	V180 MEV	**TA 189**	V189 MEV	**TA 198**	V198 MEV	**TA 207**	V207 MEV	**TA 216**	V216 MEV
TA 181	V181 MEV	**TA 190**	V190 MEV	**TA 199**	V199 MEV	**TA 208**	V208 MEV	**TA 217**	V217 MEV
TA 182	V182 MEV	**TA 191**	V191 MEV	**TA 200**	V363 OWC	**TA 209**	V209 MEV	**TA 218**	V218 MEV
TA 183	V183 MEV	**TA 192**	V192 MEV	**TA 201**	V201 MEV	**TA 210**	V210 MEV	**TA 219**	V219 MEV
TA 184	V184 MEV	**TA 193**	V193 MEV	**TA 202**	V202 MEV	**TA 211**	V211 MEV	**TA 220**	V220 MEV
TA 185	V185 MEV	**TA 194**	V194 MEV	**TA 203**	V203 MEV	**TA 212**	V212 MEV	**TA 221**	V221 MEV
TA 186	V186 MEV	**TA 195**	V195 MEV	**TA 204**	V204 MEV	**TA 213**	V213 MEV	**TA 222**	V364 OWC
TA 187	V362 OWC	**TA 196**	V196 MEV	**TA 205**	V205 MEV	**TA 214**	V214 MEV		

V 301–352 Volvo Olympian YN2RC16V3 Northern Counties Palatine I H45/23D 1995

V 301	M301 DGP	**V 312**	M312 DGP	**V 323**	N323 HGK	**V 334**	N334 HGK	**V 345**	N345 HGK
V 302	M302 DGP	**V 313**	M313 DGP	**V 324**	N324 HGK	**V 335**	N335 HGK	**V 346**	N346 HGK
V 303	M303 DGP	**V 314**	M314 DGP	**V 325**	N325 HGK	**V 336**	N336 HGK	**V 347**	N347 HGK
V 304	M304 DGP	**V 315**	M315 DGP	**V 326**	N326 HGK	**V 337**	N337 HGK	**V 348**	N348 HGK
V 305	M305 DGP	**V 316**	M316 DGP	**V 327**	N327 HGK	**V 338**	N338 HGK	**V 349**	N349 HGK
V 306	M306 DGP	**V 317**	M317 DGP	**V 328**	N328 HGK	**V 339**	N339 HGK	**V 350**	N350 HGK
V 307	M307 DGP	**V 318**	M318 DGP	**V 329**	N329 HGK	**V 340**	N340 HGK	**V 351**	N351 HGK
V 308	M308 DGP	**V 319**	M319 DGP	**V 330**	N330 HGK	**V 341**	N341 HGK	**V 352**	N352 HGK
V 309	M309 DGP	**V 320**	M320 DGP	**V 331**	N331 HGK	**V 342**	N342 HGK		
V 310	M310 DGP	**V 321**	N321 HGK	**V 332**	N332 HGK	**V 343**	N343 HGK		
V 311	M311 DGP	**V 322**	N322 HGK	**V 333**	N353 HGK	**V 344**	N344 HGK		

VA 44–81, 122–148 Volvo Olympian OLY–5639 Alexander RL H51/28D 1997/98

VA 44	P644 SEV	**VA 57**	R157 VPU	**VA 70**	R170 VPU	**VA 123**	R123 EVX	**VA 136**	R136 EVX
VA 45	P645 SEV	**VA 58**	R158 VPU	**VA 71**	R171 VPU	**VA 124**	R124 EVX	**VA 137**	R137 EVX
VA 46	P646 SEV	**VA 59**	R159 VPU	**VA 72**	R172 VPU	**VA 125**	R125 EVX	**VA 138**	R138 EVX
VA 47	R747 XAR	**VA 60**	R160 VPU	**VA 73**	R173 VPU	**VA 126**	R126 EVX	**VA 139**	R139 EVX
VA 48	R148 VPU	**VA 61**	R161 VPU	**VA 74**	R174 VPU	**VA 127**	R127 EVX	**VA 140**	R140 EVX
VA 49	R149 VPU	**VA 62**	R162 VPU	**VA 75**	R175 VPU	**VA 128**	R128 EVX	**VA 141**	R141 EVX
VA 50	R150 VPU	**VA 63**	R163 VPU	**VA 76**	R176 VPU	**VA 129**	R129 EVX	**VA 142**	R142 EVX
VA 51	R151 VPU	**VA 64**	R164 VPU	**VA 77**	R177 VPU	**VA 130**	R130 EVX	**VA 143**	R143 EVX
VA 52	R152 VPU	**VA 65**	R165 VPU	**VA 78**	R178 VPU	**VA 131**	R131 EVX	**VA 144**	R144 EVX
VA 53	R153 VPU	**VA 66**	R166 VPU	**VA 79**	R179 VPU	**VA 132**	R132 EVX	**VA 145**	R145 EVX
VA 54	R154 VPU	**VA 67**	R167 VPU	**VA 80**	R180 VPU	**VA 133**	R133 EVX	**VA 146**	R146 EVX
VA 55	R155 VPU	**VA 68**	R168 VPU	**VA 81**	R181 VPU	**VA 134**	R134 EVX	**VA 147**	R147 EVX
VA 56	R156 VPU	**VA 69**	R169 VPU	**VA 122**	R122 EVX	**VA 135**	R135 EVX	**VA 148**	R148 EVX

VN 1–26 Volvo Olympian YN3RV16V3 Northern Counties Palatine I H49/31F 1996

VN 1	P801 GMU	**VN 5**	P805 GMU	**VN 15**	P815 GMU	**VN 19**	P819 GMU	**VN 25**	P825 GMU
VN 2	P802 GMU	**VN 6**	P806 GMU	**VN 16**	P816 GMU	**VN 20**	P820 GMU	**VN 26**	P826 GMU
VN 3	P803 GMU	**VN 7**	P807 GMU	**VN 17**	P817 GMU	**VN 23**	P823 GMU		
VN 4	P804 GMU	**VN 8**	P808 GMU	**VN 18**	P818 GMU	**VN 24**	P824 GMU		

VN 27–43 Volvo Olympian YN3RV16V3 Northern Counties Palatine I H49/25D 1996

VN 27	P527 HMP	**VN 31**	P531 HMP	**VN 35**	P535 HMP	**VN 39**	P539 HMP	**VN 43**	P543 HMP
VN 28	P528 HMP	**VN 32**	P532 HMP	**VN 36**	P536 HMP	**VN 40**	P540 HMP		
VN 29	P529 HMP	**VN 33**	P533 HMP	**VN 37**	P537 HMP	**VN 41**	P541 HMP		
VN 30	P530 HMP	**VN 34**	P534 HMP	**VN 38**	P538 HMP	**VN 42**	P542 HMP		

VN 82–110 Volvo Olympian OLY-4953 Northern Counties Palatine I H45/23D 1997/98

VN 82	R82 XNO	**VN 88**	R188 XNO	**VN 94**	R94 XNO	**VN 100**	R210 XNO	**VN 106**	R206 XNO
VN 83	R83 XNO	**VN 89**	R89 XNO	**VN 95**	R95 XNO	**VN 101**	R101 XNO	**VN 107**	R107 XNO
VN 84	R84 XNO	**VN 90**	R190 XNO	**VN 96**	R96 XNO	**VN 102**	R102 XNO	**VN 108**	R108 XNO
VN 85	R85 XNO	**VN 91**	R91 XNO	**VN 97**	R97 XNO	**VN 103**	R103 XNO	**VN 109**	R109 XNO
VN 86	R86 XNO	**VN 92**	R92 XNO	**VN 98**	R98 XNO	**VN 104**	R104 XNO	**VN 110**	S110 SHJ
VN 87	R87 XNO	**VN 93**	R93 XNO	**VN 99**	R207 XNO	**VN 105**	R105 XNO		

VN 111–121, 149–178		Volvo Olympian OLY-5639				Northern Counties Palatine I		H49/27D	1998
VN 111	R311 XNO	**VN 120**	R120 XNO	**VN 156**	R156 HHK	**VN 165**	R165 HHK	**VN 174**	R174 HHK
VN 112	R112 XNO	**VN 121**	R121 XNO	**VN 157**	R157 HHK	**VN 166**	R166 HHK	**VN 175**	R175 HHK
VN 113	R113 XNO	**VN 149**	R149 HHK	**VN 158**	R158 HHK	**VN 167**	R167 HHK	**VN 176**	R176 HHK
VN 114	R114 XNO	**VN 150**	R150 HHK	**VN 159**	R159 HHK	**VN 168**	R168 HHK	**VN 177**	R177 HHK
VN 115	R115 XNO	**VN 151**	R151 HHK	**VN 160**	R160 HHK	**VN 169**	R169 HHK	**VN 178**	R178 HHK
VN 116	R116 XNO	**VN 152**	R152 HHK	**VN 161**	R161 HHK	**VN 170**	R170 HHK		
VN 117	R117 XNO	**VN 153**	R153 HHK	**VN 162**	R162 HHK	**VN 171**	R171 HHK		
VN 118	R118 XNO	**VN 154**	R154 HHK	**VN 163**	R163 HHK	**VN 172**	R172 HHK		
VN 119	R119 XNO	**VN 155**	R155 HHK	**VN 164**	R164 HHK	**VN 173**	R173 HHK		

VP 4	630 DYE	Volvo B10M-60	Plaxton Paramount 3500 III	C49FT	1991
VP 5	WLT 890	Volvo B10M-60	Plaxton Paramount 3500 III	C49FT	1991
VP 7	H445 PPU	Volvo B10M-60	Plaxton Paramount 3500 III	C49FT	1991

616–640		Dennis Dart SFD412BR5TGD1				Alexander Dash 9.8m		B36F	1996
616u	P616 PGP	**621**	P621 PGP	**631**	P631 PGP	**636**	P636 PGP	**640**	P640 PGP
618	P618 PGP	**622**	P622 PGP	**632**	P632 PGP	**637**	P637 PGP		
619	P619 PGP	**623**	P623 PGP	**633**	P633 PGP	**638**	P638 PGP		
620u	P620 PGP	**624**	P624 PGP	**634**	P634 PGP	**639**	P639 PGP		

Previous registrations:–

472 YMF	J713 CYG	**WLT 491**	V474 KJN
630 DYE	H659 UWR, H654 UWR	**WLT 890**	H660 UWR, H655 UWR
E155 CGJ	E711 LYU, WLT 461	**WLT 898**	S210 WHK
H445 PPU	H655 UWR, H657 UWR, WLT 898	**XFF 813**	WLT 898
LFF 875	456 CLT	**XFF 814**	WLT 890
USK 625	WLT 980	**XSL 596A**	289 CLT
VLT 14	V473 KJN	**YLJ 332**	J715 CYG
WLT 461	L212 YAG	**YTS 820A**	599 CLT

Special liveries:–
The LCY buses carry blue livery and SLDs 32–34 green livery, both batches for London City Airport services.
DRL 121 carries blue livery and all-over advert for Tesco

On order:– 100 Dennis Trident/Alexander 10.5m
38 Dennis Trident/Alexander 9.9m
66 Dennis Dart/Plaxton

TELLINGS-GOLDEN MILLER Fleet numbers are not carried on the vehicles

2	K402 VPK	Mercedes-Benz 709D	Dormobile Routemaker	B25FL	1992
5	K405 VPK	Mercedes-Benz 709D	Dormobile Routemaker	B25FL	1992
7	M70 TGM	Mercedes-Benz 709D	Plaxton Beaver	B23F	1995
8	M80 TGM	Mercedes-Benz 709D	Plaxton Beaver	B23F	1995
9	M90 TGM	Mercedes-Benz 709D	Plaxton Beaver	B23F	1995
17	N70 TGM	Mercedes-Benz 709D	Plaxton Beaver	B23F	1996
21	M521 MPF	Dennis Dart 9SDL3053	East Lancs EL2000 9m	B30FL	1995
22	M522 MPF	Dennis Dart 9SDL3053	East Lancs EL2000 9m	B30FL	1995
23	M523 MPF	Dennis Dart 9SDL3053	East Lancs EL2000 9m	B30FL	1995
24	M524 MPF	Dennis Dart 9SDL3053	East Lancs EL2000 9m	B30FL	1995
27	P70 TGM	Mercedes-Benz 709D	Plaxton Beaver	B27F	1997
28	N528 SPA	Dennis Dart 9SDL3053	East Lancs EL2000 9m	B30FL	1995
29	N529 SPA	Dennis Dart 9SDL3053	East Lancs EL2000 9m	B30FL	1995
30	N530 SPA	Dennis Dart 9SDL3053	East Lancs EL2000 9m	B30FL	1995
33	L433 CPJ	Mercedes-Benz 811D	Plaxton Beaver	B31F	1994
34	F34 CWY	Mercedes-Benz 811D	Optare StarRider	B26F	1988
37	L437 CPJ	Mercedes-Benz 811D	Plaxton Beaver	B31F	1994
46	F46 CWY	Mercedes-Benz 811D	Optare StarRider	B26F	1988
55	P255 MLE	Mercedes-Benz 711D	Plaxton Beaver	B20FL	1997
56	P456 MLE	Mercedes-Benz 711D	Plaxton Beaver	B20FL	1997
60	E460 ANC	Mercedes-Benz 507D	Made to Measure	M16	1988
69	J969 JNL	Optare MetroRider MR03	Optare	B33F	1991
71	F71 SJX	Mercedes-Benz 709D	Onyx	DP24F	1989
73	P473 APJ	Mercedes-Benz 711D	Plaxton Beaver	B27F	1996
74	P474 APJ	Mercedes-Benz 811D	Plaxton Beaver	B18FL	1996
89w	G689 OHE	Mercedes-Benz 811D	Reeve Burgess Beaver	B18FL	1990
90w	G690 OHE	Mercedes-Benz 811D	Reeve Burgess Beaver	B18FL	1990
101t	E101 CGN	Renault-Dodge G10	Wadham Stringer	B31F	1987
120	H120 YGG	Mercedes-Benz 709D	Dormobile Routemaker	B27F	1990

124–129 DAF DE02RSDB250 — Optare Spectra 2 — H45/16D — 1999

124	T124 AUA	126	T126 AUA	128	T128 AUA
125	T125 AUA	127	T127 AUA	129	T129 AUA

130–139 DAF DE02RSDB250 — Plaxton President — H45/19D — 1999

130	T130 AUA	132	T132 AUA	134	T134 AUA	136	T136 AUA	138	T138 AUA
131	T131 AUA	133	T133 AUA	135	T135 AUA	137	T137 AUA	139	T139 AUA

141	D141 TMR	Mercedes-Benz L307D	Whittaker	M12	1987
204	L204 ULX	Mercedes-Benz 709D	Plaxton Beaver	B18FL	1993
205	L205 ULX	Mercedes-Benz 709D	Plaxton Beaver	B18FL	1993
206	L206 ULX	Mercedes-Benz 709D	Plaxton Beaver	B18FL	1993
216	BYX 216V	MCW Metrobus DR101/12	MCW	H43/28D	1979
231t	E231 FLD	Scania N112DRB	Van Hool Alizee L	B30D	1987

301–309 Dennis Dart SLF SFD612BR1XGW1 — Plaxton Pointer 2 8.8m — B26F — 2000

301	V301 MDP	303	V303 MDP	305	V305 MDP	307	V307 MDP	309	V309 MDP
302	V302 MDP	304	V304 MDP	306	V306 MDP	308	V308 MDP		

401–410 Dennis Dart — Plaxton Pointer 2 10.2m — . . . — 2000

401	403	405	407	409
402	404	406	408	410

501–514		Dennis Dart SLF SFD322BR1VGW1				Plaxton Pointer 10.6m		B39F	1998
501	R501 SJM	**504**	R504 SJM	**507**	R507 SJM	**510**	R510 SJM	**513**	R513 SJM
502	R502 SJM	**505**	R505 SJM	**508**	R508 SJM	**511**	R511 SJM	**514**	R514 SJM
503	R503 SJM	**506**	R506 SJM	**509**	R509 SJM	**512**	R512 SJM		

515–519		Dennis Dart SLF SFD322BR1WGW1				Plaxton Pointer 2 10.7m		B39F	1998
515	S515 JJH	**516**	S516 JJH	**517**	S517 JJH	**518**	S518 TCF	**519**	S519 TCF

590–596		Dennis Dart SLF SFD322BR1VGW1				Plaxton Pointer 10.6m		B39F	1997
590	P290 FPK	**592**	P292 FPK	**594**	P294 FPK	**596**	P296 FPK		
591	P291 FPK	**593**	P293 FPK	**595**	P295 FPK				

701–757		Mercedes-Benz O814 Vario				Plaxton Beaver 2 8.5m		B31F	1997–99
701	P701 LCF	**704**	P704 LCF	**707**	S707 JJH	**749**	S549 BNV		
702	P702 LCF	**705**	R705 MJH	**708**	S708 TCF	**754**	S554 BNV		
703	P703 LCF	**706**	R706 MJH	**748**	S548 BNV	**757**	S557 BNV		

801–811		Dennis Dart SFD				Plaxton Pointer 2 10.7m		. . .	2000
801		**804**		**807**		**810**			
802		**805**		**808**		**811**			
803		**806**		**809**					

837	H837 GLD	Mercedes-Benz 609D				North Western Coach Sales		C13F	1991

901–907		Volvo B10BLE				Alexander ALX300 12m		B..F	2000
901		**903**		**905**		**907**			
902		**904**		**906**					

985–993		Optare Excel L1000				Optare		B35F	1998
985	R985 EWU	**987**	R987 EWU	**989**	R989 EWU	**991**	R991 EWU	**993**	R993 EWU
986	R986 EWU	**988**	R988 EWU	**990**	R990 EWU	**992**	R992 EWU		

	DAF SB220LC550		Ikarus Citibus	DP42F*	1992–94
J801 KHD	J804 KHD	J807 KHD	J809 KHD	L511 EHD	
J803 KHD	J806 KHD	J808 KHD	J810 KHD	M806 RCP	

Special liveries:–
2, 5, 21–4, 28–30, 33, 37, 73, 74, 89, 90, 590–596 carry two-tone green.
55, 56, 204–204 carry white and green livery.
124–139, 216 carry red and black livery.
515–517 carry Kingston University branding.
707 carries an all-over advert for Thames Radio.
801–810 carry white and red livery.
811 and 812 are all white.
837 is white and yellow.
841, 844, 985–993 carry red white and blue livery.

THORPES

F134 UMD		Mercedes-Benz 709D	Reeve Burgess Beaver	B23F	1988
G901 UPP		Mercedes-Benz 709D	Reeve Burgess Beaver	B23F	1989
G894 XPX		Mercedes-Benz 811D	Wadham Stringer Wessex	B25F	1989
M191 TEV		Mercedes-Benz 709D	Wadham Stringer Wessex II	B20FL	1994

DLF 9	R309 NGM	Dennis Dart SLF SFD212BR1VGW1	Plaxton Pointer 10m	B33F	1997

DLF 29–40 Dennis Dart SLF SFD212BR1WGW1 Plaxton Pointer 2 10.1m B29D 1998

DLF 29	S529 JLM	**DLF 32**	S532 JLM	**DLF 35**	S535 JLM	**DLF 38**	S538 JLM
DLF 30	S530 JLM	**DLF 33**	S533 JLM	**DLF 36**	S536 JLM	**DLF 39**	S539 JLM
DLF 31	S531 JLM	**DLF 34**	S534 JLM	**DLF 37**	S537 JLM	**DLF 40**	S540 JLM

DLF 41	P41 MLE	Dennis Dart SLF SFD112BR1SGW1	Plaxton Pointer 9.2m	B27D	1996
LS 84	OJD 884R	Leyland National 10351A/2R	(Urban Bus)	B38F	1977
LS 96	OJD 896R	Leyland National 10351A/2R	(Urban Bus)	B38F	1977
LS 99	OJD 899R	Leyland National 10351A/2R	(Urban Bus)	B38F	1977
LS 195	THX 195S	Leyland National 10351A/2R (DAF)	(Urban Bus)	B36D	1978
LS 227	THX 227S	Leyland National 10351A/2R (DAF)	(Urban Bus)	DP34DL	1978
LS 268	YYE 268T	Leyland National 10351A/2R	(Urban Bus)	B38F	1978
LS 335	AYR 335T	Leyland National 10351A/2R	(Urban Bus)	B38F	1979
LS 337	AYR 337T	Leyland National 10351A/2R	(Urban Bus)	B38F	1979
LS 395	BYW 395V	Leyland National 10351A/2R	(Urban Bus)	B38F	1979
MB 2	K2 FET	Mercedes-Benz 709D	Alexander (Belfast) AM	B16FL	1993
MB 3	K3 FET	Mercedes-Benz 709D	Alexander (Belfast) AM	B16FL	1993
ML 514	J514 WTW	Mercedes-Benz 709D	Wadham Stringer Wessex	B19FL	1991
ML 520	J520 WTW	Mercedes-Benz 709D	Wadham Stringer Wessex	B20FL	1991
ML 529	J529 WTW	Mercedes-Benz 709D	Wadham Stringer Wessex	B23FL	1991
ML 530	J530 WTW	Mercedes-Benz 709D	Wadham Stringer Wessex	B15FL	1991
XL 100	N100 FET	Optare Excel L960	Optare	B27F	1996
XL 200	N200 FET	Optare Excel L960	Optare	B27F	1996
XL 300	N300 FET	Optare Excel L960	Optare	B27F	1996
XL 400	N400 FET	Optare Excel L960	Optare	B27F	1996

Special liveries:–
XL 100–400 carry dedicated Stationlink route branding. DLF class carry dedicated route branding for route 210.
ML 514–530 and M191 TEV are dedicated LT mobility buses.

TRAVEL LONDON

231–240 Optare Solo M850 Optare B25F 1999

231	S231 EWU	**233**	S233 EWU	**235**	S235 EWU	**237**	S237 EWU	**239**	S239 EWU
232	S232 EWU	**234**	S234 EWU	**236**	S236 EWU	**238**	S238 EWU	**240**	S240 EWU

401–422 Optare Excel L960 Optare B26D 1998

401	R401 HWU	**407**	R407 HWU	**412**	R412 HWU	**417**	R417 HWU	**422**	R422 HWU
402	R402 HWU	**408**	R408 HWU	**413**	R413 HWU	**418**	R418 HWU		
403	R403 HWU	**409**	R409 HWU	**414**	R414 HWU	**419**	R419 HWU		
404	R404 HWU	**410**	R410 HWU	**415**	R415 HWU	**420**	R420 HWU		
405	R405 HWU	**411**	R411 HWU	**416**	R416 HWU	**421**	R421 HWU		

WING'S BUSES

WB 1	V336 MBV	Dennis Dart SLF SFD212BR1XGW1	East Lancs Spryte 10.3m	B30D	1999
WB 2	V337 MBV	Dennis Dart SLF SFD212BR1XGW1	East Lancs Spryte 10.3m	B30D	1999
WB 3	V338 MBV	Dennis Dart SLF SFD212BR1XGW1	East Lancs Spryte 10.3m	B30D	1999